Contents

AMERICA
IN SO MANY
WORDS Words
That Have Shaped
America

ALLAN METCALF

DAVID K. BARNHART

HOUGHTON MIFFLIN COMPANY   Boston • New York

Library of Congress Cataloging-in-Publication Data

Barnhart, David K.
America in so many words : words that have shaped America / David K. Barnhart and Allan A. Metcalf.
p.   cm.
Includes bibliographical references and index.
ISBN 0-395-86020-2
1. English language—United States—Etymology. 2. English language—United States—History. 3. United States—History—Terminology. 4. Americanisms—History. I. Metcalf, Allan A. II. Title.
PE2831.B37   1997
422'.0973—DC21   97-14510

PICTURE CREDITS: 1611/tomahawk National Museum of the American Indian, Smithsonian Institution, neg. no. 29758 **1628/wigwam** National Museum of the American Indian, Smithsonian Institution, neg. no. 14418 **1633/buffalo** United States Department of Agriculture, Soil Conservation Service **1660/Pilgrim** *Men: A Pictorial Archive from Nineteenth-Century Sources* by Jim Harter. New York: Dover Publications, 1980. **1687 jimsonweed** Chris Costello **1733 barbecue** *Food & Drink* by Jim Harter. New York: Dover Publications, 1960. **1745/covered wagon** Kansas State Historical Society, Topeka, Kansas, ref. no. He.56, WAG.COV, .1908c, *1 **1760/gardenia** Courtesy Cooperativa Argentina de Floricultores Ltda. **1769/tar and feather** *The American Revolution: A Picture Sourcebook* by John Grafton. New York: Dover Publications, 1975. **1785/bug** *1800 Woodcuts By Thomas Bewick and His School* by Blanche Cirker. New York: Dover Publications, 1962. **1791/fishing pole** *1800 Woodcuts By Thomas Bewick and His School.* New York: Dover Publications, 1962. **1802/mammoth** Culver Pictures, Inc. **1814/keno** *Dictionary of Americanisms.* Chicago: University of Chicago Press, 1951. Art by Irvin Studney. **1825/blizzard** *New York in the Nineteenth Century* by John Grafton. New York: Dover Publications, 1980. **1837/Christmas tree** H. Armstrong Roberts, Inc. **1850/prohibition** Library of Congress, neg. no. LCUSZ62-15182 **1861/caboose** Courtesy of Rochester & Genesee Valley Railroad Museum/Rochester Chapter NHRS **1870/bathtub** Courtesy Kallista, Inc. **1883/skyscraper** Corbis/Bettmann - UPI **1892/sweatshop** Stock Montage, Inc. **1906/teddy bear** Courtesy of David K. Barnhart **1910/barbershop** H. Armstrong Roberts, Inc. **1918/D Day** National Archives and Records Administration/U.S. Signal Corps, neg. no. 111-SC-20903 **1934/whistlestop** H. Armstrong Roberts, Inc. **1939/juke box** H. Armstrong Roberts, Inc. **1951/rock and roll** H. Armstrong Roberts, Inc. **1960/sit-in** Corbis/Bettmann - UPI **1972/Watergate** H. Armstrong Roberts, Inc. **1979/stealth** H. Armstrong Roberts, Inc. - S. Feld **1995/newt** Wide World Photos - Joe Marquette

Manufactured in the United States of America
DOH 10 9 8 7 6 5 4 3 2

Introduction:

Representative

Words

America is built of words. Here are the best and the brightest of them, one for each year.

We Americans have added tens of thousands of words to the English language in the nearly four hundred years since speakers of English began living on this continent. A few of these words, like *sockdolager* (1827) and *tintinnabulation (1845)*, ring in our minds because of their oddity. But the most telling, and the most important, are ordinary building blocks of our everyday conversations: *apple pie* (1697), *mileage* (1753), *commuter* (1865), *gridlock* (1980), even *hello* (1885). They are so familiar it is hard to imagine they were once new.

This is a book that notices those words. Year by year, it shows words that have accumulated in our vocabulary to make us what we are today: *OK* (1839) and *nifty* (1863), *cool* (1949) and *groovy* (1937), *geek* (1978) and *soccer mom* (1996). Not all at once but bit by bit, the words we now take for granted have developed the American character.

For each year since the middle of the century of American independence, and for many earlier years from the time of the first English-speaking settlements, this book highlights one word or phrase of special significance that was added to the vocabulary in the particular year. Most of these words have retained or added to their importance in the years since. They designate the things we talk about, the attitudes we take. They are the names we call ourselves.

Our choicest American words, for the most part, are for practical use rather than grand pronouncements. We could say they are Representative words, not Senatorial words. In fact, when we make our most profound statements of principle, we employ language that is universal rather than identifiably American. "When in the course of human events . . ." employs no particularly American vocabulary, nor "Four score and seven years ago . . ." nor "I have a dream. . . ." These use philosophical, religious, and everyday terms that were already in the common stock of English. For distinctively American vocabulary we look instead to the journals of *planters* (1619) and *pioneers* (1817), tales of *cowboys* (1779) and *yuppies* (1984), marketing of *cure-alls* (1821) and *fast food* (1954), news of *filibusters* (1852) and *boondoggles* (1935). Some of these words had inauspicious beginnings but increased in importance over time. Some developed new senses and dropped their original ones. Some just burst upon the scene and found such comfortable niches in our language that it seemed as if they had been around forever.

History

We can sum up the development of our language *P.D.Q.* (1875), using one easy label for each century: "Nature" in the seventeenth century, "Independence" in the eighteenth, "Expansion" in the nineteenth, and "Science" in the twentieth.

The first great American contribution to the English language, in the 1600s, came from the need to name the amazing North American animals and plants. Some of the new names came from English words like *corn* (1608) and *catfish* (1612), adapted or combined to suit the new situation. Others like *raccoon* (1609) and *moose* (1613) were borrowed from the impressive languages spoken by the Indians, imitated as best as possible in English. We borrowed from the Indians' names for tools, like *tomahawk* (1611), and customs, like *caucus* (1763).

As the colonies developed a momentum of their own, so did their influence in the English language, with the innovation of *Thanksgiving* (1621), *public school* (1636), and *boss* (1635). The colonists conceived and changed the *frontier* (1676). The first *alumnus* (1696) graduated. The eighteenth century reflected the religious *awakening* (1736), mustered the *minuteman* (1774), and greeted the *cowboy* (1779) and *immigrant* (1789). In the nineteenth century the nation tapped its *mammoth* (1802) ambitions and *know-how* (1838) to create urban *skyscrapers* (1883) and *sweatshops* (1892). In the twentieth century we tested *IQ* (1916) and educated *rocket scientists* (1985).

Over the years, as the United States has gained international importance, we have increasingly exported our words to the rest of the world. Not just for spacious skies and amber waves of grain is America known, but for its words. All over the world people say *OK*. They wear *T-shirts* (1919), sleep in *motels* (1925), raise *teenagers* (1938), listen to *rock and roll* (1951) and develop *software* (1959), and in doing these things they often use our words for them.

The words of our past make clear that there was never a golden age from which we have degenerated into our current troubles. From the first days of the English language in North America, its speakers have been embroiled in difficulties, conflicts, failures, and calamities. Yet, as our vocabulary also shows, we have retained the optimism that coming times will be better and that we can, through sacrifice or ambition, not just pursue happiness but attain it.

Choices

Each year has seen dozens, sometimes hundreds of new American words. There have been two attempts to record them all: the four volumes—2528 pages—of the *Dictionary of American English* (1938–44) and two volumes—1911 pages—of the *Dictionary of Americanisms* (1951). Each averages well over ten entries to a page, so we begin with 20,000 or so words identified as American in origin. In the half century since the publication of those dictionaries, we have created many more

Americanisms and discovered earlier ones. This book makes no attempt to list them all. Instead, it seeks for each year the ones that have meant the most to us, either at the time of their creation or at the present day—or both.

Whatever the individual merits of the more than three hundred words and phrases chosen for this book, they all have the distinction of making a place for themselves in the American vocabulary. This is no mean achievement. Most terms that are invented, like most *gizmos* (1944), do not make it. To take a typical example, *OK* and the lesser-known *n.g.* are the only two survivors of the blizzard of humorous initialisms coined in Boston in 1839. On the other hand, some years in our history have seen an explosion of significant new words. In 1915, for example, arose *community center, flapper, handicapped, homeroom, parent-teacher-association, lowdown, goof, pink slip, runaround, schlock, skyhook, Tin Lizzie, cover girl, teammate,* and *black widow spider.* Of these, we chose *flapper* as most revealing of the attitudes of the time. Many of the words in this book are not necessarily distinguished; some are positively low. But they all are symptomatic of American thought and action.

Origins

Where did the words come from? Some are borrowed from other languages, like *raccoon* (1609) and *banjo* (1740). Others are familiar English words with new American meanings, like *corn* (1608) and *pioneer* (1817). Some are new combinations of familiar words, like *catfish* (1612), and other are corruptions or slang versions of words, like *wannabe* (1981). Some are abbreviations, like *AWOL* (1863) and *DJ* (1950). Some take people's names, like *gardenia* (1760) and *teddy bear* (1906), or place names, like *bunkum* (1819) and *Chautauqua* (1873). A few are imitative, like *katydid* (1752) and *duh* (1963). And a few—just a few like *sockdolager* (1827)—seem to have sprung from nowhere.

Not all of our entries are single words or abbreviations. Some are compounds made up of two or more words. But they are compounds that we treat as single words; only the accident of spelling makes *deadhead* (1841) look like one word and *hot dog* (1895) like two. *Drugstore* (1810) is spelled as one word, *skid row* (1931) as two, and *grass roots* (1901) sometimes as one, sometimes as two; but all are singular concepts. In such compounds, the whole is different from the sum of the parts. For example, the words *rock and roll* (1951) viewed individually do not have any obvious connection with music, and *couch potato* (1976) is not the name of a vegetable.

Each of our chosen words has been assigned to a year in which it was newly coined or newly prominent. For a few words, assigning the year was no problem at all. We know, for example, that *OK* was invented in 1839 and became popular almost immediately. And we know who Teddy Roosevelt was speaking to, on what day, when he launched the modern meaning of *muckraker* in 1906.

More typically, however, important Americanisms slip into our language without any formal announcement. They may have been widely known before the earliest available evidence. One day they just show up in writing and speech, seemingly already well established. This is the case especially with older words, but it is also true of many recent additions, like *dis* (1986) and *about* (1991). Scholars have sought their beginnings in old books, magazines, newspapers, diaries, letters, government records, and legal documents, but the search has only begun and many earlier sightings can be expected. For example, it was not until 1996 that researcher Barry Popik discovered a newspaper article that dates *hobo* as far back as 1848; previously it had been observed only from 1889. This book makes use of the best evidence available at present, and we look forward to further revelations that will improve our knowledge of a word's history. We have taken advantage of the necessary uncertainty about starting dates and made the choice for each year as significant a word as possible.

Every year there are many thousands of potential new words, some of them deliberately coined, others spontaneously created in response to new situations. They are like seeds in the ground, waiting for rain and favorable weather to sprout. Should we note the date when the seed was planted, when it sprouted, or when it became a full-sized plant?

Even for words that have well-documented beginnings, when they became known beyond a small circle and entered general use remains a question. Take the very recently prominent *Ebonics,* for example. We know that it was first coined in 1973 and used in a book in 1975. But not until mid-December 1996 did the word emerge from obscurity into national discussion, and not until early 1997 did *–onics* or *–bonics* become a well-established suffix used to create new words. Any of these years could have been the year for *Ebonics.* We chose 1997.

At whatever date these words can be said to have entered our language, they have all given shape to the ongoing project that is America. They have helped us determine who we are, where we have been, and where we are going.

Note on Sources

For the information in this book we are indebted above all to two great dictionaries published by the University of Chicago Press: *A Dictionary of American English on Historical Principles,* edited by William A. Craigie and James R. Hulbert (4 volumes, 1938–44) and *A Dictionary of Americanisms on Historical Principles,* edited by Mitford M. Mathews (2 volumes, 1951). Also essential at every point was the monumental *Oxford English Dictionary,* 2nd edition (Oxford University Press, 1989).

Two new dictionaries in progress have provided invaluable aid and inspiration: the *Dictionary of American Regional English*, edited by Frederic G. Cassidy and Joan Houston Hall (3 volumes, A–O; Belknap Press of Harvard University Press, 1985–96) and the *Random House Historical Dictionary of American Slang,* edited by J. E. Lighter (1 volume, A–G; Random House, 1994).

For new words, we have drawn especially on the *Third Barnhart Dictionary of New English,* edited by Robert K. Barnhart, Sol Steinmetz and Clarence L. Barnhart (H.W. Wilson, 1990); *Fifty Years Among the New Words: A Dictionary of Neologisms, 1941–1991,* edited by John Algeo and Adele S. Algeo (Cambridge University Press, 1991), and *The Oxford Dictionary of New Words* compiled by Sara Tulloch (Oxford University Press, 1992). An essential guide has been *The Barnhart New-Words Concordance,* compiled by David K. Barnhart (Cold Spring, NY: Lexik House, 1994, supplement 1995).

We have relied extensively on three periodicals: *The Barnhart Dictionary Companion* (1981–), a quarterly to update general dictionaries; *American Speech* (1926–), publishing numerous articles on American words; and *Comments on Etymology* (1971–), with significant new material on the origins of American slang. Valuable information on slang also comes from Barry Popik's postings on ADS-L, the American Dialect Society E-mail discussion list.

An essential source on the origins of political terms is *Safire's New Political Dictionary* by William Safire (Random House, 1993). On New York City, *The City in Slang: New York Life and Popular Speech* by Irving Lewis Allen (Oxford University Press, 1993).

We have also consulted numerous books about American English. Two of the most important are *The American Language* by H. L. Mencken, edited and abridged by Raven I. McDavid, Jr. (Knopf, 1963) and *I Hear America Talking: An Illustrated Treasury of American Words and Phrases* by Stuart Berg Flexner (Van Nostrand Reinhold, 1976).

Sources often consulted on the early colonial years include *The European Discovery of America: The Northern Voyages A.D. 500–1600* by Samuel Eliot Morison (Oxford University Press, 1971) and *The Complete Works of Captain John Smith (1580–1631) in Three Volumes*, edited by Philip L. Barbour (University of North Carolina Press, 1986).

Helpful older works include *Dictionary of Americanisms* by John Russell Bartlett, 4th edition (Little, Brown, 1877); *Americanisms Old & New* by John S. Farmer (Thomas Poulter, London 1889); *An American Glossary* by Richard H. Thornton (J. B. Lippincott, 1912); *American Dialect Dictionary* by Harold Wentworth (Thomas Y. Crowell, 1944).

We have also been helped by *The American Heritage Dictionary of the English Language, Third Edition* (Houghton Mifflin, 1992), and *Merriam-Webster's Collegiate Dictionary, Tenth Edition*, electronic edition (Merriam-Webster, 1995).

Some other sources of particular value for individual entries are listed below. This is by no means a complete list, but we are especially grateful for the following: 1640 *pull up stakes*, 1675 *scalp*, 1696 *alumnus, alma mater*, 1721 *classmate*: *The Diary of Samuel Sewall 1674–1729*, edited by M. Halsey Thomas (2 volumes; Farrar, Straus and Giroux, 1973). 1762 *armonica*: *The Papers of Benjamin Franklin, Volume 10 (January 1, 1762, through December 31, 1763)*, edited by Leonard W. Labaree (Yale University Press, 1966). 1783 *passenger pigeon*: *The Passenger Pigeon: Its Natural History and Extinction* by

A.W. Schorger (University of Wisconsin Press, 1955). 1839 *OK*: Four articles by Allen Walker Read in *American Speech,* Volume 38 (1963): 5–27, 83–102; Volume 39 (1964): 5–25, 243–67. 1876 *moxie*: Frederic G. Cassidy, "The Etymology of *Moxie,*" *Dictionaries* 16 (1995): 208–11. 1921 *media*: Stuart Y. Silverstein, "The First Word on the Algonquin Round Table," *OED News* Series 2 No. 5 (January 1997): 4–5. 1974 *streak*: Randy Roberts of the Western Historical Manuscript Collection at the University of Missouri, Columbia, for materials from the Peter Tamony collection.

Acknowledgments

I express here my deep appreciation for research assistance in this project of my wife, Hollis, my brother, Robert, and the staffs of the Vassar College Library and the Desmond-Fish Library (Garrison, N.Y.). I am greatly appreciative, too, of the resources placed at my disposal by David and Cathy Lilbourne at Antipodean Books, Maps & Prints and of the assistance of Mark Lacko, Tracy Strong, and Geraldine Baldwin.

—David K. Barnhart   *Lexik House, Cold Spring, New York*

*A*t MacMurray College, I am grateful to librarians Ronald Daniels, Penelope Mitchell, and Mary Ellen Blackston and their student assistants, who have opened the doors and resources of Henry Pfeiffer Library for me. I have also been helped countless times, in ways they often do not know, by my students and colleagues here, and by American Dialect Society colleagues on the Internet.

In Julian Hall, my adopted home for most of the writing, I have greatly appreciated the hospitality of Nadine Szczepanski and the support of William DeSilva. Across town, at Illinois College, James Davis gave valuable advice. And every day I appreciate the concern of my wife, Donna Metcalf, in making this work worthwhile.

At Houghton Mifflin, this book would not have been possible, let alone on time, without the encouragement, sound advice, and watchfulness of Executive Editor Joseph Pickett. It has also benefited greatly from the work of Senior Editor David Pritchard, Associate Editor Beth Anderson, Editorial Assistant Maura Hadro, and Senior Art and Production Coordinator Margaret Anne Miles.

—Allan A. Metcalf   *MacMurray College, Jacksonville, Illinois*

THE

ENGLISH

IN AMERICA:

1497–1750

*T*he story of the English language in North America begins almost exactly five hundred years ago, on July 24, 1497. At about 5 A.M. that midsummer day, Captain John Cabot, along with some of the eighteen-member crew of his ship *Mathew,* set foot on the eastern coast of what we now call Canada and spoke the first words of English ever heard on this side of the Atlantic.

Modern historians do not know where Cabot landed that first time. Most likely it was present-day Newfoundland; Cabot's own happy notion was that they had reached Asia. For our story, his mistake doesn't matter. What does matter is that they had come from the port of Bristol in England and thus spoke English. (Cabot himself was Italian, but like Columbus he had taken up residence in another country to further his maritime projects.)

As it happens, the voyage of the *Mathew* had no influence whatsoever on the later development of American English. Cabot and his men saw signs of human habitation: traps, fish nets, and a painted stick. But they met nobody, so they did not learn any native words to import into English. Nor did they stay to start an English-speaking settlement. They soon got back on board their ship, looked at a few more islands from a safe distance, and then returned in high spirits to Bristol on August 6, confident that they had found a short way to Asia.

That set the pattern for the next century. The English found North America a nice place to visit, but they didn't want to live there.

Later English explorers did meet some of the native peoples of the Atlantic seaboard. They began the process of enriching the English language with local names for the strange flora and fauna of the continent. Translations of tales by travelers from other nations also brought American words into English, including the first word we list in this book, *canoe* (1555).

But the real impetus for adding American stock to the English language came when the English finally decided to put down roots in North America. It was in territory that, at the suggestion of Sir Walter Raleigh, they called *Virginia* in 1585 by gracious permission of their "virgin queen" Elizabeth I. Raleigh sponsored the first of their attempts, a colony on Roanoke Island off the coast of what is now North Carolina in 1585. Those English settlers gave up in 1586, then returned to Roanoke in 1587, only to vanish mysteriously before the next English ship could visit in 1590. They left behind as a message to the visitors only the letters "CROATOAN," neatly carved on a tree. The word was borrowed from American Indian speakers in the vicinity and referred to an island some fifty miles to the south. *Croatoan* is thus the first word known to be recorded by the English on the North American continent, and the first forwarding address. Unfortunately, by the time English explorers went looking for the ex-Roanoke colonists some thirty years later, the forwarding notice had expired.

In the early 1600s, the English language finally came to North America for good. The first successful Virginia colony, made famous by Captain John Smith's accounts, began at what the English called *Jamestown* (after King James I) on May 14, 1607. By accident, a second English-speaking colony began far to the north of Virginia in December 1620. The *Mayflower* set out for Virginia but landed on Cape Cod instead. (No one knows for certain why their destination changed.) The ship's passengers found a suitable harbor north of the Cape and established the Plymouth Plantation there, soon to be joined by others in what was called *New England* (1616), the land of the Massachusetts and other tribes.

At the time of these visits and settlements, the inhabitants of what is today the United States were speaking other languages. In fact, they were speaking hundreds of different languages, all as sophisticated as the languages of Europe, and most with more complicated grammar than English.

Along the Atlantic coast, the English first encountered languages of the Algonquian family, including Delaware in the south and Massachusett, Narragansett, Abenaki, and Penobscot in the north. As they variously aided, traded, and debated with the English newcomers, speakers of Algonquian languages gave us *skunk* (1588), *muskrat* (1607), *raccoon* (1609), *opossum* (1610), and *moose* (1613) on land, and in the water *terrapin* (1613) and *quahog* (1643), a clam; *chinquapin* (1612), a kind of chestnut, and *hickory* (1670); *puccoon* (1612), a plant producing red dye, and *atamasco* (1629), a lily; *persimmon* (1612), *tuckahoe* (1612), an edible root, and *cushaw* (1698), a kind of squash; *hominy* (1629), *pone* (1634), and *samp* (1643), cornmeal mush; *kinnikinnick* (1729), a mixture of leaves for smoking, *moccasins* (1612), *tomahawk* (1611), *pocosin* (1634), or "dismal swamp," *squaw* (1634), *papoose* (1634), *wigwam* (1628), *wampumpeag* (1627), *powwow* (1624), and *netop* (1643), a friend.

Sometimes, rather than borrowing from the Indians, the newcomers made use of familiar English words to name the unfamiliar. For example, in America they created new meanings for *turkey* (1607), *corn* (1608), *clapboard* (1632), and *bluff* (1666). They created new combinations of old English words in *bluefish* (1623), *johnnycake* (1739), and *groundhog* (1742).

And the English colonists also borrowed from other Old World languages, as speakers of those languages intermingled with the English in the new. From Spanish, for example, the settlers got *tamale* (1691) as well as words like *canoe* and *barbecue* (1733) that ultimately came from Indian languages;

from Dutch, *boss* (1649) and *cookie* (1703); and from Bantu languages of West Africa, *tote* (1677).

After the initial burst of new names in the early 1600s, over the next century the American colonies contributed at a relatively slow rate to the development of the English language. The colonies were, after all, lightly populated, and they were greatly dependent on England not just for manufactured goods but for matters of culture and learning. Significant contributions to American English as we know it now were relatively rare.

Only as the eighteenth century developed would we begin thinking of ourselves and our language as distinctively American. But already we were developing our own concepts and practices, and words to name them: *frontier* (1676), *public school* (1636), and *alumnus* (1696), *alma mater*, (1696) and *classmate* (1713). We experienced *religious awakenings* (1736). We invented *schooners* (1716), sold goods at *stores* (1721), and began to build *covered wagons* (1745). And we were the first to have speeches and books that were *lengthy* (1689).

1555 canoe

Long before any English-speaking person paddled one in American waters, *canoe* was an English word for an American Indian invention. If by "discover" we mean "tell the Europeans," then Columbus discovered the canoe while he was busy discovering America. He observed natives of the West Indies traveling across the water in boats made of a single large tree, hollowed out with a sharp stone, and propelled with paddles. Columbus called the vessel by the name the Cariban Indians of Haiti gave it: *canoa*. The author of a 1555 book that explained the canoa for English readers said it is "very longe and narowe," with room for as many as forty paddlers.

In 1608, shortly after the founding of the first English colony in Virginia, Captain John Smith reported that the settlers were following the Indian example and getting around in "canowes." So it happened also on later frontiers as European settlers pressed westward. These canoes were not all of the hollow-log variety, which was especially suited for uninterrupted travel on the water. Within the North American continent, where frequent portages were necessary between rivers and lakes, the lightweight birch-bark canoe was preferred. And to navigate the birchless plains farther west, canoes were made of buffalo hide.

In recent times, Americans have tinkered with the materials of canoes, making them of wood, fiberglass, plastic, and aluminum. Especially with these new materials, there still is no other human-powered vessel so portable, maneuverable, speedy, and sturdy for travel in shallow and narrow waters. In all likelihood, there are far more canoes plying American waters today than there ever were before Columbus landed.

1588 skunk

Thomas Hariot went as scientific observer with the English expedition that established the short-lived Roanoke colony. His *Briefe and True Report of the New Found Land of Virginia,* published in 1588, includes the first list of Algonquian Indian words translated into English. Most of his translations didn't make it into the English vocabulary, but we can recognize the beginnings of modern *skunk* in *Saquenúckot.* He describes it as one of "two kindes of small beastes greater than conies [rabbits] which are very good meat." Hariot does not mention the distinctive defensive odor of the skunk, perhaps because his book was intended to advertise the advantages of life in Virginia. A book of 1634 about New England was more candid, naming "Squunckes, Ferrets, Foxes" among "the beasts of offence."

1602 Indian

Columbus started it. When he found land after sailing westward across the Atlantic, he thought he had succeeded in his "Enterprise of the Indies," arriving at the distant part of the world that included Japan, China, and India. So naturally he called the inhabitants *indios,* or in English, *Indians.*

Who was to say any different? It took quite a while before Europeans could think the unthinkable, that an enormous continent stood between them and the Indies. Meanwhile, *Indian* became established as the name for the people of the continent.

A century later, it was established among English explorers too. We find an example as early as 1602, when speakers of English set foot for the first time on what would later be known as NEW ENGLAND (1616). In the summer of that year, a ship with two dozen "gentlemen" and eight crew members visited and named Cape Cod and Martha's Vineyard and settled briefly on another island before returning to England with a precious cargo of sassafrass. In their report, published that fall, they follow the lead of Columbus in referring to the native inhabitants as *Indians,* as for example, "We saw manie Indians, which are tall big boned men."

But by then Columbus's geographical mistake had been recognized and corrected. The land was known as America, not India. Why were the inhabitants still called *Indians*?

Perhaps because it was still the best available choice. While *Indian* was a mistake, it was respectful, almost worshipful, to the Europeans who imagined the exotic Indies. A name could be chosen from the hundreds of original languages spoken on this continent, but to choose a word from one Indian language would be to exclude the others. And *American* would not do because it was used for everyone born on this continent, regardless of ancestry.

Of course *Native American* has gained a large following in recent years, but it has the same problem as *American:* a literal meaning that can apply to everyone born here. And *First Nations,* a term now widely used in Canada, gives no sense of place. Despite periodic objections from those who prefer *Native American,* both *Indian* and *American Indian* remain accepted and popular, especially in view of their continued use by Indians themselves. This is one mistake that seems to have been inspired.

1607 turkey

Whoever named the bird *turkey*—a word that English speakers began mentioning as long ago as 1541—made a big mistake. Although that bird came from Guinea in Africa, the English apparently first imported it from Turkish merchants. So, naturally, they called it a *turkey*. When English speakers established their first colony in Jamestown, Virginia, in 1607, they thought they saw turkeys there too. "We found an Ilet, on which were many Turkeys," wrote one. These birds were not from Turkey and were not related to the guinea fowl of Africa. But *turkeys* they were called, and *turkeys* they remain.

Much of what we know about the Jamestown colony was written by Captain John Smith, whose efforts preserved the colony from collapse and who in turn was preserved by the Indian "princess" Pocahontas. Smith's accounts of the colony frequently mention turkeys as food, gifts, and objects of trade. In 1607, Smith writes, to celebrate the first peace after the first armed clash, the Indians brought "Venison, Turkies, wild foule, bread, and what they had, singing and dauncing in signe of friendship till they departed." Elsewhere Smith noted that the Indians made warm and beautiful cloaks from turkey feathers. Further north, as the Plymouth colony neared the end of its first year in 1621, Governor William Bradford likewise observed "great store of wild Turkies, of which they tooke many." Undoubtedly turkeys were among the "fowl" served at the first THANKSGIVING (1621) dinner.

Despite those significant beginnings and Ben Franklin's lobbying, the turkey lost to the bald eagle in the contest for American bird. And it is a loser in modern American slang, too. Since the 1920s, *turkey* has been a term for a play or movie that is a failure, and since the 1950s for a person who is incompetent. But though the turkey never succeeded in becoming the American symbol, it did become the American feast. Thanksgiving is *Turkey Day,* and the turkey has gobbled its way into our language more than any other bird. Though we never "talk eagle," we talk turkey when we speak frankly. *Cold turkey* also means plain talk and can refer to the shock effect of "quitting cold" from an addiction.

1608 corn

To English speakers at the time of the first colonies, *corn* meant grain—the staff of life. The main grain was known simply as *corn;* all lesser grains had particular names. So in England, where wheat was chiefly cultivated, *corn* meant wheat; in Scotland and Ireland, *corn* meant oats. Crossing over to America, English adventurers found a different staff of life cultivated by the Indians. The native American grain, with big juicy kernels in rows around a central core, immediately became the essential crop of the new settlers as well, so it preempted the designation *corn.* Even today, though the United States grows vast quantities of wheat, oats, sorghum, barley, and rice, corn remains in first place as the chief grain crop of North America.

To distinguish our *corn* from the European grains, and in recognition of those who first cultivated it, the English later called this grand new grain by the fuller name *Indian corn.* That term is attested in a London document of 1617. Meanwhile, the only way wheat could be called *corn* in America was in the designation *English corn,* used in the Plymouth colony of New England as early as 1629.

But from the start, the native American grain was dominant enough that *corn* alone would do for it. In 1608, telling of the difficulties of the first permanent English colony in the summer of 1607, Captain John Smith wrote, "Shortly after, it pleased God (in our extremity) to move the Indians to bring us Corne, ere it was half ripe, to refresh us, when we rather expected when they would destroy us."

1609 raccoon

In December 1607, Captain John Smith was brought before Powhatan, the "emperor" of the Indians, who was lying on a high bed "covered with a great Covering of the *Rahaughcums.*" Smith reported this in his *True Relation* of the Jamestown colony, published in 1608. Later in the *True Relation* he mentions Powhatan sending him "many presents of Deare, bread, *Raugroughcuns.*" We enter this Algonquian Indian word for 1609, a year after Smith's publication, because unlike CORN (1608) it must have taken a little while for the English language to digest.

Not until Smith's *Map of Virginia,* published in 1612, does he offer a description of the creature we now know as the *raccoon:* "There is a beast they call *Aroughcun*, much like a badger but useth to live on trees as Squirrels doe."

1610 opossum

In 1610, to encourage their supporters back home, members of the Virginia Company caused to be printed in London a pamphlet called *A True Declaration of the Estate of the Colony in Virginia.* This gives the first mention in print of creatures they called "Apossouns, in shape like to pigges." Like RACCOON (1609), *opossum* is a borrowing from an Algonquian Indian language.

1611 tomahawk

Two different lists of Algonquian Indian words compiled in 1612 include *toma-hawk,* so we can safely assume it was in the vocabulary of the Jamestown colonists by 1611. One list, by William Strachey, gives it as "a hatchet, *tacca hacan, tama-haac.*" In a glossary attached to his 1612

Map of Virginia, Captain John Smith hacked it as "*Tomahacks. Axes. Tockahacks.* Pickaxes."

Smith's earlier *True Relation* of 1608 gave the first English explanation of the function of this implement. He did not use the word *tomahawk,* but he wrote about Indians having "Swords like Pollaxes." And indeed the tomahawk was the Indian equivalent of both sword and ax, being the chief weapon in hand-to-hand combat as well as a tool for digging and chopping.

1612 catfish

Another miracle of North American nature: a fish that looks like a cat! In a list of two dozen "fish we were best acquainted with" accompanying *A Map of Virginia,* published in 1612, Captain John Smith includes "Catfish." He gives no further explanation, perhaps assuming that his newly formed word is description enough.

1613 moose

This creature first came to the notice of the English in a book written in 1613 about a voyage to what would be called NEW ENGLAND (1616): "Captaine Thomas Hanham sayled to the Riuer of Sagadahoc 1606. He relateth of their beasts . . . redde Deare, and a beast bigger, called the Mus." The name comes from the Eastern Abenaki Indian language and means "he trims or cuts off," referring to the way the moose eats bark and twigs off trees.

In his 1616 *Description of New England,* Captain John Smith was sufficiently impressed to list first among animals there, "Moos, a beast bigger then a Stagge."

1614 Manhattan

As early as 1614, the name *Manhattes* appears on an English map, naming the Indian tribe that lived on the island where

New York City now has its center. In 1626 the Dutch came and gave the Manhattes twenty-four dollars in goods to vacate the land. The Indians left, but their name stayed to designate the island. Less than forty years later the English took over without paying the Dutch a cent.

In the late nineteenth century, new meaning was distilled from the old word with the invention of the Manhattan cocktail, made of sweet vermouth, whiskey, and bitters. In the early twentieth century it became additional food for thought as the name of tomato-based Manhattan clam chowder.

1615 cunner

In his *Description of New England,* written after a voyage there in 1614 and published in 1616, Captain John Smith catalogs the abundance of herbs, woods, birds, fishes, and beasts in that yet uncolonized land. The fishes are "Whales, Grampus, Porkpisces [porpoises], Turbut, Sturgion, Cod, Hake, Haddock, Cole [pollock], Cusk, or small Ling, Shark, Mackerell, Herring, Mullet, Base, Pinacks, Cunners, Pearch, Eels, Crabs, Lobsters, Muskles, Wilkes [whelks], Oysters, and diverse others etc." Most of these were familiar to the English, but the cunner is distinctive to the New England coast.

"In the harbors we frequented," Smith adds, "a little boye might take of Cunners, and Pinacks, and such delicate fish, at the ships sterne, more then sixe or tenne can eate in a daie; but with a casting-net, thousands when wee pleased." Today among other names it is also called *bait-stealer* because the small perchlike fish eats bait intended for others.

1616 New England

In the year Shakespeare died, *New England* was born. This was in fact four years before any English speakers permanently settled in that northern location. But in 1616 it was already the subject of the book *A Description of New England,* by that busy explorer and promoter Captain John Smith, who had visited the land two years before.

According to Smith, New England owes its name to Sir Francis Drake. Not that Drake ever saw or talked about New England, but in sailing around the world he stopped in 1579 at a place on the Pacific coast of North America and claimed it as *Nova Albion,* the Latin for "New England." Following Drake's lead, Smith designated the region at a similar latitude on the Atlantic coast by the same name, translated into plain English.

The very words *New England* show the direction of Smith's thinking. This was to be an extension of Old England, not a new kind of community. The map in his book gives only English names for the places of New England, and he provides an accompanying list showing thirty American Indian names replaced by English ones: *Accomack* by *Plimouth, Massachusets River* by *Charles River, Kinebeck* by *Edenborough,* to list a few. Some of those changes succeeded. But what eventually happened after the Plymouth colonists landed four years later has turned out differently than Smith had imagined, for Indian names as well as English ones still cover the New England landscape.

1617 mother country

To find a representative American word for the year 1617, when the struggling Jamestown colony was the only English-speaking habitation in North America, we need to travel to Leyden, Holland. There the religious separatists who had left England in 1607 were making plans for the voyage that would establish the Plymouth colony in New England three years later. Two of them, John Robinson and William Brewster, wrote in a letter of December 1617, "We are well weaned from the delicate milke of our mother countrie, and enured to the difficulties of a strange and hard land, which yet in a great parte we have by patience overcome."

England was, of course, the mother of all countries for the English-speaking colonists, and these Americans-to-be were the first to call England the *mother country.* And the history of the next two centuries would show that the colonists' relationship with the mother country was as touch-and-go as that between any human mother and child.

1618 punk

Something like *punk* has been smoldering in American English for hundreds of years, undergoing drastic changes of meaning from century to century. It began as a bizarre kind of overcooked corn, explained in a 1618 account of certain Indians in Virginia: "Some of them, more thriftye then cleanly, doe burne the coare of the eare to powder, which they call pungnough, mingling that in their meale, but yt never tasted well in bread or broath." Around that time, also, *punk* was a word for "ashes" in the Delaware Indian language.

A couple of centuries later, *punk* had become a word for the slow-burning sticks used in kindling fireworks. By 1889 it was a slang term for a cigarette, and by the end of the century *punk* had a sense "worthless" as in a story by George Ade: "And this crowd up there was purty-y-y punk."

Today's first meaning of *punk*, a small-time hoodlum, developed in the period between the World Wars. And in the late 1970s *punk* came to designate bizarre clothing and body decorations associated with loud and aggressive rock music. To the general public, it still has an unpleasant taste.

1619 planter

In its earliest sense, *planter* meant a person who helped "plant" or found a colony, often called a *plantation*. Thus, the founders of Plymouth Plantation called themselves "adventurers and planters" in a document drawn up on the eve of their departure for New England in 1620.

But by then the modern meaning of *planter* had already begun to develop in Virginia. Ten years of precarious existence seem to have taught the English adventurers there one lesson: The way to get rich was tobacco. It was the one export crop that earned big money, and those who were planters of this crop began to become a wealthy elite. In 1619 the Virginia House of Burgesses used *planters* in this sense: "Provided first that the Cape Marchant do accept of the Tobacco of all and everie the Planters here in Virginia."

As they sold more tobacco and bought more land, these planters needed more laborers, so they imported African slaves in ever-increasing numbers. *Planter* thus became the name for an owner of a large estate worked by slave labor. At first it referred to tobacco growers in Virginia and Maryland, but by the end of the seventeenth century it was applied to owners of PLANTATIONS (1645) in general, regardless of the crop, and anywhere in the South—in fact anywhere in the tropical and subtropical English-speaking world.

There was another more modest early meaning for *planter:* any individual farmer, regardless of size or type of holdings. An article in the *South Carolina Gazette* of 1732 refers to "the poorer sort of Planters." But they were overshadowed, in terminology as well as trade, by wealthy owners.

In the nineteenth century, as human labor began to be replaced by mechanical, *planter* was the name given to a device for planting seeds.

Although labor-intensive plantations of the old sort are long gone, people still evoke the fortunate lifestyle of the plantation owner when they make planter's punch, a rum-based cocktail that is a twentieth-century invention.

1620 seat

The English speakers who came to North America intended to be seated. Scouting the land five months before the first colonists arrived in New England, a certain Mr. Dermer wrote in June 1620 regarding Plymouth, "I would that the first plantation might hear be seated, if ther come to the number of 50. persons, or upward." In the next century, George Washington continued this use of the verb *seat:* "It would give me pleasure

to see these lands seated by particular societies," he wrote in 1784. But by the nineteenth century, *seat* was unseated and Americans would settle instead.

<u>1621 Thanksgiving</u>

The religious duty, and pleasure, of thanksgiving to God was well established in England before any English speakers came to America, but it was the American colonials who made a feast of it. After the successful harvest of 1621 in the first year of pious Plymouth colony, Governor William Bradford called for a celebration. But rather than spending the day in prayer, the colonists set the pattern for future American Thanksgivings by inviting the neighbors to a big family dinner, with roast fowl as the main dish. It is described in a book published the next year:

> Our harvest being gotten in, our Governour sent foure men on fowling, that so we might after a more speciall manner reioice together, after we had gathered the fruit of our labours; they foure in one day killed as much fowle, as with a little helpe beside, served the Company almost a weeke, at which time amongst other Recreations, we exercised our Armes, many of the Indians coming amongst vs, and amongst the rest their greatest King Massasoit, with some nintie men, whom for three days we entertained and feasted and they went out and killed fiue Deere, which they brought to the Plantation and bestowed on our Governour, and upon the Captaine, and others.

Two years later, after another abundant harvest, Governor Bradford again "set apart a day of thanksgiving." It was quite some time, however, before we Americans got the idea of doing it every year. The early Thanksgivings were special events, commemorating triumph over adversity. George Washington called for the first national *Thanksgiving Day* on November 26, 1789, after the independence of the United States was assured. But it took the Civil War to put Thanksgiving on the calendar for good, beginning with President Lincoln's proclamation in 1863 of a *Thanksgiving Day* at the end of November.

Of the customs established by the pious New England colonists, all that we still celebrate in modern America is Thanksgiving. Thankfully, the many cultures that make up the modern American crazy quilt still share a day to count their blessings and eat.

1622 parched corn

As a word for the result of roasting, *parched* is attested in English as far back as the 1400s. However, *parched corn* is an American term and food.

When CORN (1608) is raw, it does not keep well. Parch it, however, and it can be carried in a pouch and eaten as one travels along or stored for later use. An account of the Plymouth colony, published in 1622, reports that on a visit to an Indian village the previous summer a group of colonists "bought about a handfull of Meale of their parched Corne." At that time of year, they added, the corn was "very precious."

For travelers in the woods, parched corn was as useful then as trail mix is now. Roger Williams, writing about the Indians of New England, reported that they found "parch'd meal . . . a readie very wholesome food, which they eate with a little water, hot or cold." A century and a half later, Lewis and Clark took parched meal with them on their great expedition to the Northwest and the Pacific Ocean. Parched corn sustained soldiers in the Civil War, and in the recollections of George Armstrong Custer's widow it also sustained the postwar army on the western frontier. "Officers and men subsisted on parched corn and horse-flesh," she wrote in 1890.

1623 bluefish

In 1622, John Pory, secretary of the Virginia colony, traveled to England on a ship that explored the Atlantic coast all the way north to Plymouth. "As concerning the blew fish," he noted, "in delicacie it excelleth all kinde of fish that ever I tasted."

From that day to this, the bluefish has been such a dish that it has spawned a dozen other names. Its coloring gave it the names *bluefish* and *blue,* as well as *greenfish* and *whitefish.* According to the *Dictionary of American Regional English,* its other aliases include *chopper, fatback, horse mackerel, jumbo, skipjack, snapper, snapping mackerel,* and *tailor.*

1624 swamp

England had marshes, bogs, and fens, but only America had swamps. And, according to that tireless promoter Captain John Smith, what a difference! The Virginia rivers, he wrote in his 1624 *Generall Historie,* are "free from any inundations, or large Fenny unwholsome Marshes." He continues, "For salt Marshes or Quagmires, in this tract of James Towne River I know very few; some small Marshes and Swamps there are, but more profitable than hurtfull." Smith does not explain what a swamp is, or how it could be "profitable," but the American swamp clearly is to be preferred over the English muck. A swamp would be fertile, and it would not lack for water.

The lay of the land and its suitability to farming were paramount concerns to the English colonists. In the 1600s they noted *swamp lots* (1637), *swamp land* (1663), and *swamp meadows* (1697). They gave *swamp* names to plants like the swamp wood tree (1666) and the swamp oak (1681) and animals like the swamp robin (1769) and swamp quail (1778).

And then there were the swamp angels. The term was used facetiously as early as 1857 to refer to people who live in the swamps or BACKWOODS (1709). During the Civil War, at the siege of Charleston, South Carolina, the large Union Army gun that fired shells from the swamp into the city was soon nicknamed the *Swamp Angel.*

1625 powwow

The Indians taught the English settlers not only about the natural features of their new home, but also about politics, business, and diplomacy. A powwow was a shaman or worker of magic. A report from New England, published in 1625, refers to "a *Powah*, one of special note amongst them." A pow-wow was also a council meeting or conference, often involving a certain amount of noisy ceremony. When in the course of succeeding centuries American politicians or tradespeople got together to celebrate and plan, there was no better name for it than *powwow*, a meeting with a "wow."

In the twentieth century, American Indians have developed their own modern sense for *powwow*. It is now the name for a gathering at which traditional Indian dances and songs are performed.

1626 breeze

We have to drift perhaps a little off course to find wind for our sails in 1626. It is in a book published by Captain John Smith, who had spent the past twenty years writing about North America. Thus we can hope for some sort of American connection to his book of terms used by sailors, *An Accidence for Young Sea-men: Or, Their Path-way to Experience.* For the winds, he lists, in order of severity, "A calme, a brese, a fresh gaile, a pleasant gayle, a stiffe gayle, it overblowes, a gust, a storme, a spoute, a loume gaile, an eddy wind, a flake of wind, a Turnado, a monthsoune [monsoon], a Herycano [hurricane]."

This apparently is the first use of *breeze* (an older word, from the Spanish *briza*) to refer to a gentle wind. The next year, in his *Sea Grammar*, Smith explains: "When there is not a breath of wind stirring, it is a calme or a starke calme. A Breze is a wind blowes out of the Sea, and commonly in faire weather beginneth about nine in the morning, and lasteth till neere night."

1627 wampumpeag

A legal document of July 1627 regarding the trade by members of the Plymouth colony "for beaver and other furrs and comodities" refers to "the whole stock of furrs, fells, beads, corne, wampampeak, hatchets, knives, etc. that is now in the storre." In the Massachusett Indian language, *wampumpeag* meant "string of white beads," beads made of shells that served as money. They made money, too, for the traders of Plymouth. As Governor Bradford explains in his history, "But that which turned most to their profite, in time, was an entrance into the trade of Wampampeake." By 1636, while they were lengthening their profits, they had shortened the name to *wampum*.

At first the manufacture of wampumpeag was a monopoly of the Narragansett and Pequot tribes in New England. Two varieties of shell were used: white from the whelk (a sea snail with a spiral shell) and purple from the quahog (a clam with purple and white shell). The shells were strung as beads or woven into belts not only as a medium of exchange but also to record diplomatic relationships among the Indian tribes and to show kinship.

One particularly significant example of wampum was the "Great Chain," which represented the Iroquois Confederacy through thirteen figures, each holding one end of a wampum belt in a chain. Such "documents" were entrusted to a wampum keeper who, when disputes arose, would produce the treaty belt and expound the terms of the agreement.

In later centuries, traders and explorers traveling westward from the Allegheny Mountains to the plains carried wampum with them as a medium of exchange. Exploring the lands acquired in the Louisiana Purchase of 1803, Meriwether Lewis and William Clark carried with them five pounds of white wampum along with glass beads in many colors.

1628 wigwam

Two documents from New England in 1628 record *wigwam*, the Eastern Abenaki Indian name for an Indian house or tent, or indeed any kind of similarly constructed shelter. "We built us our wigwam, or house, in one hour's space," says one. According to the other, the Indians say that when someone dies "Tanto carries them to his *wigwam*, that is his house."

One type of wigwam was that of the Ojibwa, an Algonquian tribe. They made a dome-shaped arrangement of poles covered with bark, animal skins, or reed mats, with a firepit in the middle. Following Indian examples, the English colonists soon learned to use similar materials to make what they called *English wigwams* (1631), arched but long with flat ends and often with a stone fireplace and chimney at one end.

In the nineteenth century, another kind of wigwam took on political significance. It was the name given to a large temporary building constructed for a national political convention. One of the most famous of these, called simply the "Wigwam", housed the Republicans in Chicago in 1860. Thanks to that circumstance, Abraham Lincoln could have advertised his humble origins by saying, not only was he born in a LOG CABIN (1770), he was nominated in a Wigwam.

1629 hominy

Like England, the Virginia colony had its gentlefolk and commoners, masters and servants. After twenty years of hardship, all were beginning to enjoy some prosperity, such that even the servants ate well, according to reports received back in England by Captain John Smith. He gave particulars of their diet, including hominy, in his *Continuation of the Generall Historie of Virginia*, written in 1629. "Their servants," Smith wrote, "commonly feed upon Milke Homini, which is bruized

Indian corne pounded, and boiled thicke, and milke for the sauce; but boiled with milke, the best of all will oft feed on it."

The Indians gave them the idea for both the word and the food. Hominy is an English adaptation of an Algonquin dish Smith described in his 1612 *Map of Virginia:* "the branne they boile 3 or 4 houres with water, which is an ordinary food they call Ustatahamen."

Adapted to the colonists' tastes, hominy remained a staple in the South for centuries to come, where it is now better known as *hominy grits* or just plain *grits.*

1630 rattlesnake

It is an American creature as well as an American word. Writing about his experiences in Salem, Massachusetts, in an account published in 1630, Francis Higginson observed that "There are some Serpents called Rattle Snakes, that haue Rattles in their Tayles." That year in England, Captain John Smith commented that some would-be settlers of Massachusetts Bay returned complaining "of the danger of the rattell Snake."

Before he ever mentioned the word *rattlesnake,* Smith knew of the creature from his earlier adventures in Virginia. His 1612 *Map of Virginia* explains that some of the Indians "on their heads weare the wing of a bird, or some large feather with a Rattell. Those Rattels," he adds, "they take from the taile of a snake."

With an image of the snake and the legend "Don't Tread on Me," the rattlesnake flag became an emblem of the rebellious colonies a century and a half later. It was the first American flag, flown by John Paul Jones on the ship *Alfred* on December 3, 1775.

1631 patent

Since the Middle Ages, the English had announced official grants of privileges by means of letters patent, that is, "open letters." So when the English government claimed authority over North America, it issued letters patent granting lands to colonies and individuals. But the down-to-earth colonists in America were the first to refer to the land itself as a *patent*. We read in the *Massachusetts Bay Record* for 1631, "Noe person w[ha]tsoeuer shall trauell out of this pattent, eithr. by sea or land, without leaue from the Governr, Deputy Governr, or some other Assistant." In 1632, also in New England, a certain Stephen Batchelor was "required to for-bear exercising his gifts as a pastor or teacher publicly in our patent."

In that century we also find such spinoff terms as *patentee* (one to whom a grant of land has been given, 1640), *patent line* (the boundary of a land grant, 1675), and *patent* as a verb (to obtain a patent of land, 1675). Nor did the practice of granting lands by patent cease following the American Revolution and the independence of the United States in the next century. *A Guide for Emigrants,* written in 1831, notes that the Military Bounty Tract "was set apart by Congress and patented for soldiers who served in the last war."

The usual meaning of *patent* today, however, has to do with Article 1, section 8 of the United States Constitution, which authorizes Congress "to promote the Progress of Science and useful Arts, by securing for limited Times to Authors and Inventors the exclusive Right to their respective Writings and Discoveries." In 1836, an act of Congress established the Patent Office, headed by a Commissioner of Patents, to issue this kind of patent to inventors.

1632 clapboard

American ingenuity made something new of clapboard. In England clapboard was used for barrels; the English who became Americans learned to apply it to houses.

The clapboard oak staves used to make English barrels were imported from the Baltic. But North America abounded with oak too, and the first cargo shipped from Jamestown back to England at the start of the settlement in 1607 included clapboard for this purpose.

In New England, also, the colonists made clapboards of oak. But after a few winters there, the English adventurers discovered another use for them. English houses were "half-timbered," with plaster filling the space between framing timbers. Half-timbering did not give enough protection from the fierce winters of New England, so for extra insulation the colonists clapped clapboard on the outside walls. We have a 1632 report of "a small house near the wear at Watertown, made all of clapboards."

The colonists soon learned to overlap clapboards and make them specifically for houses, with one edge thinner than the others. This style was so successful that it has remained in use to the present for all kinds of American housing, even where winter insulation is not needed.

1633 buffalo

By about 1633, English-speaking settlers on the mid-Atlantic coast had caught glimpses of one of North America's most awesome creatures. In thinking of a name for it, the settlers remembered *buffalo,* a word borrowed in the previous century, probably from the Portuguese, that referred to an exotic ox of the Far East. (It ultimately goes back to a similar word in Greek.) So we read in a description of Maryland, published in London in 1635, "In the upper parts of the countrey there are Bufeloes, Elkes, Lions, Beares, Wolves, and Deare there are in great Store."

In later centuries, as settlement moved westward, *buffalo* (or *buffaloes*; there are two ways to form the plural) loomed ever larger in the American landscape and vocabulary. They loomed largest in the open spaces of the Great Plains, in herds by the millions. Buffalo gave their name to Buffalo, New York, and to more than twenty other towns and cities, as well as to countless buffalo trails and roads, fords and crossings, creeks and ridges, springs and wallows. There are buffalo birds, fish, beetles; even buffalo gnats. Plants have been named *buffalo bean, berry, burr, clover, grass, pea,* and *weed.* Plains Indians not only subsisted on buffalo but invoked their spirits with a buffalo dance. After the Civil War, regiments of black soldiers stationed on the plains were termed *buffalo soldiers* by the

Indians in tribute to their looks and determination, and the name *buffalo soldier* honorably referred to military African Americans in the twentieth century as well.

Even as the buffalo dwindled in number to fewer than one thousand at the end of the nineteenth century, they expanded their range in the American vocabulary with the verb *to buffalo,* meaning "to intimidate, outsmart, confuse." Its image appeared by the millions on the buffalo nickel, coined from 1913 to 1938. And the buffalo buffaloed extinction to the point where they now number in the hundreds of thousands.

1634 squaw

Of the words borrowed from the Indians, *squaw* has not fared so well, although it began without prejudice. In various Algonquian Indian languages it could be translated as "woman," "young woman," "queen," or "lady." In the English of New England, as early as 1622, *squaw* was used as a modifier in the phrase *Squa Sachim,* meaning an Indian ruler who was a woman. By 1634, English speakers were using *squaw* to refer to any Indian woman, and even in humor to an English woman too. We find it that year in a book by William Wood called *New England's Prospect:* "If her husband come to seeke for his Squaw and beginne to bluster the English woman betakes her to her armes which are the warlike Ladle, and the scalding liquors."

But even this early use shows *squaw* carrying undignified connotations. The English language already had *woman, wife,* and *lady* for respectful reference. As used by English speakers, *squaw* did not have a specialized meaning, which would have given it some dignity, like POWWOW (1625) or WIGWAM (1628). Instead, *squaw* appears in contexts of humor or disparagement, as in this comment of 1642: "When they [Indians] see any of our English women sewing with their needles, or working coifes, or such things, they will cry out, Lazie *squaes!*"

Squaw did have literary usefulness for writers like James Fenimore Cooper who attempted to give their work the flavor of Indian language. "The wicked Chippewas cheated my squaw," says an Indian character in Cooper's *The Last of the Mohicans* (1826).

In the 1800s, speakers of American English coined a number of terms supposedly associated with squaws. These include plant names like *squaw root* (1815), used as medicine, and *squaw corn* (1824), a soft multicolored variety. They also include *squaw winter* (1874), a name for an early cold spell associated with INDIAN SUMMER (1777). *Squaw* itself has such negative associations nowadays that there have been efforts to remove it from place names like *Squaw Mountain* and *Squaw Lake.*

1635 boss

As far as we know, the first boss arrived in English-speaking North America on November 28, 1635. This is the entry for that date in the journal of John Winthrop of Massachusetts Bay: "Here arrived a small Norsey bark, of twenty-five tons, sent by the Lords Say, etc., with one Gardiner, an expert engineer or work base, and provisions of all sorts, to begin a fort at the mouth of Connecticut."

That *base* was the Dutch word we now know as *boss.* Ironically, boss Gardiner was building a fort to keep out the Dutch, who had settled New Amsterdam (later New York) to the south. But the English language readily admitted the Dutch word. And *boss* grew in popularity over the years, gradually taking the place of *master* as the latter became associated with slavery. "As I would not be a slave, so I would not be a master," in Lincoln's later words. *Boss* was plain and emphatic, too, making it a useful informal substitute for words like *employer, supervisor,* and *foreman.*

In the nineteenth century, only *boss* would do to describe a new kind of political leader who came to dominate local politics through patronage and corruption. The most notorious was the ruler of New York City in the mid-nineteenth century, "Boss" William Tweed. From that kind of boss it was a short jump in meaning to refer to a leader of organized criminal activity as *boss.* Indeed, political and criminal bosses often cooperated, and it could be hard to tell which was which.

But those bosses did not tarnish the basic meaning of the word. *Boss* remains a respectful way of addressing a person to acknowledge that person's leadership or authority. And in modern slang use, *boss* as an adjective means "excellent, outstanding, superior," if sometimes said humorously instead of with awe. It's a boss word.

1636 public school

Speaking of schools, when the English say *public,* we say *private.* The famous public schools of England are run by private governing bodies, charge tuition, take students from throughout the nation, and admit only a chosen few. In America, they would be private schools. But the English speak of them as *public* because they serve the public welfare, educating the elite of the nation, and because they had their beginnings as endowed public charities, educating children who were too poor to have private tutors.

The earliest record of *public school* in North America shows a different sense of *public* developing here. In 1636 the Court of the Massachusetts Bay Colony "voted for the erecting a publick Schooll or Colledge in Cambridge." That was none other than the school we now know as Harvard University. Like the English public schools, it charged tuition, drew students from the entire land, and was selective in admissions; but unlike the English, at the time of its founding and for some time after it was supported by public money.

After that, our current American meaning of *public school* was not long in coming. In 1647 the first public elementary school was established in Massachusetts using public moneys. In 1669 we find mention of "the Publick Schoole in Roxbury," and in 1710 in Boston a committee proposed "to Erect a Brick Building . . . to be let out for the Support of a Publick writing School in the Town." Massachusetts eventually required the establishment of a public elementary school in any community of at least fifty families. Communities of one hundred or more families were obliged to have a secondary school as well.

Following the American Revolution, education achieved considerable attention as a unifying factor for the nation, one consequence of which was the concept of state public school systems. In government lands opened for settlement, the Continental Congress of 1785 ordained that "There shall be reserved the lot N 16, of every township, for the maintenance of public schools, within the said township."

1640 pull up stakes

One of the earliest customs the colonials developed in America was pulling up stakes. Originally these were actual wooden stakes, driven into the ground to mark the boundaries of land allotments. Private property was a concept unknown to the American Indians but industriously pursued by the colonial governments, which later established LAND OFFICES (1681) to handle the transactions.

To move entailed retrieving these markers, that is to pull up or pluck up stakes that had marked the previous residence. When we first encounter this phrase in a 1640 letter, it has already acquired a figurative use: "I am loth to hear of a stay [in New England], but am plucking up stakes with as much speed as I may." The author of the letter, Thomas Lechford, was an attorney who resided three or four years in Boston before returning to England.

In 1703, Samuel Sewall of Boston in his journal demonstrated the literal use of the phrase and also for the first time in the opposite expression, to *set stakes:* "I hear Mr. Sherman had run a Line within mine at Kibbee's ... Went to my Bounds, asserted them ... then ordered Kibbee to pull up the Stakes. Told Mr. Lynde's Tenants what my bounds were, and that within them was my Land; forwarn'd them of coming there to set any Stakes, or cut any Wood."

Perhaps it is symbolic of American restlessness that this first attestation of *setting* stakes comes so much later than *plucking* or *pulling* them up. Similarly, SETTLER (1695) came much later than *adventurer* as a name for the restless inhabitants of the original English-speaking colonies.

1645 plantation

It was not new to call a colonial settlement a *plantation*. That was the term used for the earliest English colonies, both in Virginia and in New England. But as the PLANTERS (1619) prospered, *plantation* took on a new American meaning, "an individual homestead or farm." This is mentioned in a Connecticut notice of 1645 regulating the purchase of "any plantation or land." For the most part, however, northerners preferred to speak of *farms*.

Not so in the South, where individually owned plantations of tobacco, sugar cane, rice, and cotton grew grand and opulent through slave labor. Starting in the eighteenth century, *plantation* came to mean just such a place, the focus of Southern wealth, culture, and mythology until the time of the Civil War, as opposed to the cities of the industrial and mercantile North. Thus, leading Southern political figures like George Washington and Thomas Jefferson had plantations, while northerners Ben Franklin and John Adams did not.

1647 cranberry

The Indians would have referred to the berries as *sassamanesh* if they were served at the first THANKSGIVING in 1621. The English would have known them as *marsh-whorts, fen-whorts, fen-berries, marsh-berries,* or *moss-berries.* But strangely enough, in 1647 we find a sermon by Massachusetts minister John Eliot, "Apostle to the Indians," asking this about the wonders of nature: "Why are Strawberries sweet and Cranberries sowre?"

We will leave Eliot's question to the theologians and botanists and instead pursue the solution to a linguistic mystery: Why did the English-speaking residents of New England adopt this name *cranberry*?

Perhaps the Dutch of New Amsterdam taught them to savor it. *Cranberry* is related to German *kranbeere* and Low German or Dutch *kronbere* or *kranebere.* In those languages, as in English, the word means "crane-berry," referring to the bird known as the crane. What does the crane have to do with the berry? Some say the stem on which the berry grows has the shape of a crane; others say the European bogs harbored cranes whose diet included these crane-berries.

Then as now, cranberries were a favored food. John Josselyn, visiting from England in 1663, reported that "The Indians and English use them much, boyling them with Sugar for Sauce to eat with their Meat, and it is a delicate sauce."

The term *cranberry sauce* shows up a century later in the diary of John Adams in the entry for April 8, 1767. After mentioning that he "found a fine Wild Goose on the Spit and Cramberries stewing in the Skillet for Dinner" at a certain Dr. Tuft's, he adds that Tufts invited him "to dine upon wild Goose and Cramberry Sause."

Indians also taught the colonists to make pemmican. This combination of dried meat, melted animal fat, and cranberries was a nutritious food with a long shelf life.

1654 pumpkin pie

It is as American as APPLE PIE (1697), if not more so. True, the English had the name *pompion,* from which *pumpkin* derives, before they had any American colonies, but the first pumpkin pie was apparently served on our side of the Atlantic. Even the first attested use of *pumpkin* is in writing about America, *The Simple Cobbler of Aggawam in America* (1647). But it is in Edward Johnson's 1654 *History of New England . . . until . . .1652, or the Wonder-Working Providence of Sions Saviour* that we find both *pumpkin* and *pumpkin pie* given their just desserts: "And let no man make a jest at Pumpkins, for with this fruit the Lord was pleased to feed his people to their good content, till Corne and Cattell were increased." He also mentions *pumpkin pies,* but regrettably without a recipe: "This poor wilderness hath . . . plenty of wine and sugar . . . quince tarts instead of their former Pumpkin Pies."

If any holiday can be called American it must be THANKS-GIVING (1621), and there are no more American foods for that day than TURKEY (1607) and pumpkin pie. Later our menu expanded to include pumpkin pudding (1805), pumpkin bread (1819), pumpkin soup (1884), and pumpkin butter (1893).

But even in Johnson's affirmation we find the pumpkin treated with less than full respect. To call a person a *pumpkin* or *pumpkin head* does not show admiration, as in a 1768 satire: "Come shake your dull noddles, ye Pumpkins, and bawl." *Pumpkin head* also refers to the earliest of American hair styles. The barber supposedly put a pumpkin shell over the head of a New England colonist and cut along the shell's edges to trim the hair into the proper Puritan shape.

1660 Pilgrim

The religious dissenters who left England for Holland in 1608 and then left Holland for Plymouth, Massachusetts, in 1620, where they founded the first successful English colony in New England, considered themselves pilgrims. This was not at all a

new word. What was new was that later in the century these and other early English settlers would come to be known not just as *pilgrims* but as *the Pilgrims*, with a capital *P*.

The inspiration for their pilgrimage came from the New Testament, specifically Paul's letter to the Hebrews, where he writes of the faithful of earlier times: "These all died in faith, not having received the promises, but having seen them afar off, and were persuaded of them, and embraced them, and confessed that they were strangers and pilgrims on the earth. . . . And truly, if they had been mindful of that country from whence they came out, they might have had opportunity to have returned. But now they desire a better country, that is, an heavenly . . ." (Heb. 11:13–16).

That was the frame of mind of the English religious separatists who departed for New England in the summer of 1620, according to the history written a decade later by their governor, William Bradford: "So they lefte that goodly and pleasante citie [Leyden], which had been ther resting place near 12. years; but they knew they were pilgrimes, and looked not much on those things, but lift up their eyes to the heavens, their dearest cuntrie, and quieted their spirits."

In later times, as the pilgrim spirit of these and other early settlers of New England continued to be emphasized, they began to be spoken of as *the Pilgrims*. Early evidence for this comes in 1660 with mention of the Pilgrims Harbour in New Haven Colony. In another century or two, schoolchildren were learning about the landing of the original Pilgrims on Plymouth Rock on December 11, 1620.

1666 bluff

Bluff was a nautical term that underwent a sea change when it crossed the ocean to North America. English sailors had used *bluff* to refer to the front of a ship that was vertical instead of leaning out. They also used *bluff* for a coastline with a similar look, one that was "bold and almost perpendicular." Americans took the word ashore in Savannah, Georgia, and by 1666 were speaking there of *bluff land*, high land that rises steeply from its surroundings. Before long the second part of the phrase was dropped, and Americans in Georgia and South Carolina referred to high or steeply sloping river banks simply as *bluffs*. Eventually there were bluffs throughout English-speaking North America, sometimes even when there was no river.

Because bluffs were often covered with trees, both in the Southeast and the northern plains some Americans used *bluff* to mean an isolated clump of trees rather than the land. But from the more familiar meaning of *bluff,* that towering river bank, came a more significant American innovation. Since a bluff puts up a high imposing front, we said that someone or something that put on a show of intimidation was *bluffing*, a use attested as early as 1839. And we particularly applied that verb to the game of poker, where bluffing about the worth of one's hand is a fine art. Bluffing is so important to the poker player that the game itself was sometimes called *bluff,* also in the 1830s. For that matter, the word *poker* first entered the English language in the United States, borrowed from the French as long ago as 1834.

1669 scow

The CANOE (1555), the *scow,* and the SCHOONER (1716) were the American boats of the sixteenth, seventeenth, and eighteenth centuries respectively. Unlike the other two, there was nothing romantic about the scow, a large flatbottom riverboat, but in the days before good roads it did America's heavy hauling.

We borrowed the word as well as the boat from the Dutch. Our first reference to it comes from colonial New York, a center of Dutch influence on English in the New World. In the 1669 *Annals of Albany,* a city that was named Fort Orange under the Dutch, we read, "The Governor hath given me Orders ... to provyde a scow to help ye souldiers in their provision of fire wood."

Scows were the naval vessels of choice for a famous victory of the American Revolution. On Christmas Eve 1776, when George Washington captured 918 surprised Hessians at Trenton, New Jersey, without a struggle, his troops were ferried across the river by a fleet of scows.

In the twentieth century, the scow finally acquired a touch of glamour. We have used *scow* since the 1920s to refer to a racing yacht that is flatbottom like a conventional scow but outfitted for competition with bilge boards.

1670 huckleberry

A 1670 description of Long Island said, "The Fruits natural to the Island, are Mulberries, Posimons, Grapes great and small, Huckelberries." The huckleberry, named after the similar English hurtleberry, is small and dark, something like a blueberry. The resemblance is such that in some places *huckleberry* is used as the name for the blueberry.

Both in agriculture and in the American vocabulary, the huckleberry has been humble. In the 1800s, *huckleberry* meant "a small thing," as in an 1844 account from West Virginia: "Why, this thing laying here ain't a circumstance—hardly a huckleberry to him." A small bet was "a huckleberry to a persimmon." By virtue of its lowly status, however, *huckleberry* was chosen for the title role in one of the most renowned of American novels, Mark Twain's *The Adventures of Huckleberry Finn* (1884), starring a character introduced in a supporting role in *The Adventures of Tom Sawyer* (1876). "No, one doesn't name his characters haphazard," Twain told an interviewer in 1895. "Finn was the real name of the other boy, but I tacked on the 'Huckleberry.' You see, there was something about the name 'Finn' that suited, and 'Huck Finn' was all that was needed to somehow describe another kind of a boy than 'Tom Sawyer,' a boy of lower extraction or degree."

1671 mush

Porridge made of rice or oatmeal was an English innovation of the 1600s. The American settlers improved on it by making it with our Indian corn and then giving it the homespun name *mush,* derived from the "mash" used in brewing and as food for horses and cattle. Mush is celebrated in a 1671 poem which explains that the corn "being groun'd and boyl'd, Mush they make / Their hungry Servants for to slake." Five years later another poem declared, "Merchants car'd not a rush / For other fare than Jonakin and Mush." The name *Jonakin* later became JOHNNYCAKE (1739).

In much of the country, mush is still made of cornmeal today, but in the states along the Pacific coast, mush can be any hot cereal.

1675 scalp

In warfare, the Indians had lessons for the colonists just as the colonists had for the Indians. True, the Indians lacked firearms, but they fought with skill, tactics, and courage, and made expert use of natural cover, impressing even their fiercest military counterparts from across the sea. They also had a method of confirming and commemorating kills in battle that particularly impressed the Europeans.

As evidence that an Indian had killed his enemy, he would cut off the man's scalp with the hair on it and carry it home, there to be honored as a trophy. The verb *scalp* must have been in use to describe this practice by 1675, because it appears in a book of 1676: "Laying him for dead, they flead (or skulp'd) his head of skin and hair."

The newcomers did not shrink from learning the technique. In 1697 Samuel Sewall of Boston noted in his diary the story of a young man taken captive by Indians: "The single man [an Indian] shewed the night before, to Samuel Lennarson, how he used to knock Englishmen on the head and take off their Scalps; little thinking that the Captives would make some of their first experiment upon himself. Samuel Lennarson kill'd him."

Fortunately, that kind of scalping exists only in history, but present-day scalpers (1869) still actively scalp tickets to shows and sporting events, making a killing by buying the tickets at list or cut-rate prices and then turning around and selling them to the highest bidder.

1676 frontier

If there is a single word that shaped the American experience, it is *frontier*. So, at least, it was argued at the turn of the last century, when the frontier as we had known it for nearly three hundred years came to an end. On that occasion, historian Frederick Jackson Turner said, "The peculiarity of American institutions is, the fact that they have been compelled to adapt themselves to the changes of an expanding people—to the changes involved in crossing a continent, in winning a wilderness, and in developing, at each area of this progress, out of the primitive economic and political conditions of the frontier into the complexity of city life."

Frontier was not a new word to the English-speaking settlers of the Atlantic colonies, but they applied it in a new way. The beginnings can be seen in a 1676 account of "Calling downe our Forces from the defence of the Frontiers, and most weake Exposed Places." As Turner wrote two centuries later, "The American frontier is sharply distinguished from the European frontier—a fortified boundary line running through dense populations. The most significant thing about the American frontier is, that it lies at the hither edge of free land." American Indians, with un-European ideas about nations and property, did not erect barricades to the flow of settlers west. So the settlers thought of the frontier not as a marked border but as the place where civilization dwindled away and wilderness began.

All this came to an end when the country was settled from coast to coast. What would Americans do without the frontier? Turner wondered. We didn't. We kept right on, preserving the frontier by extending the meaning of the word. We invented "new frontiers," in space or science or medicine or politics, the most famous being the new frontier adopted as a theme of John Kennedy's presidential campaign in 1960: "We stand today on the edge of a new frontier, . . . a frontier of unknown opportunities and paths, a frontier of unfulfilled hopes and threats. . . . The new frontier . . . is not a set of promises, it is a set of challenges. It sums up not what I intend to offer the American people, but what I intend to ask of them."

1677 tote

North and South already showed dialect differences half a century after the first speakers of English had arrived. Where northerners said *carry,* southerners said *tote.* In 1677, the soldiers of the Governor of Virginia were commanded "to goe to work, fall trees and mawle and toat rails, which many . . . refusing to doe, he presently disarm'd them."

Those soldiers were white, but much of the toting in the South was done by African slaves. So it is not surprising that *tota* and *tuta,* meaning "to pick up" or "to carry" in Bantu languages of west central Africa, have been proposed as precursors of this word whose origin is undetermined.

It has remained a regional or or slang word for most of its long life. But today *tote* is known throughout the English-speaking world thanks to the tote bag, an invention of about 1900.

1681 land office

The European colonists in America brought with them an idea alien to the first North Americans, that of ownership of the land. From the Europeans' point of view, the land ultimately belonged to the sovereign, who granted it to a colony, which in turn could grant it to individuals. And the supply of new land to the west seemed inexhaustible, to be obtained by treaty or war with the Indians. So in the colonies, transactions dealing with land became much more of a business than they had been in the MOTHER COUNTRY (1617), where land titles were already established.

To take care of this business, the colonies provided land offices. We have a record of one in a Maryland law of 1681, "An Act relating to the Land Office." But the real growth of the land offices occurred in the nineteenth century, when the whole continent was parceled out. The function of the land office was defined by America's first lexicographer, Noah Webster, in his 1828 dictionary: "In the United States an office in which the sales of new land are registered, and warrants issued for the location of land, and other business respecting unsettled land is transacted."

As the westward spread of settlers became a wave and then a tidal wave, the eagerness to register land claims and the push to purchase land created crowds at land offices. So picturesque is the image that *land-office business* became a descriptive for brisk business. "A practical printer," said the New Orleans *Picayune* in 1839, "could do a land-office business here." In 1875 the *Chicago Tribune* remarked, "The tap-rooms adjoining the polls were all open and doing a 'land-office' business." In Louisville in 1887, the *Courier-Journal* reported, "The doughty burglar . . . has been doing a land-office business the past few days."

Land offices in the old sense are gone, but *land-office business* continues doing a land-office business in our language today.

1684 backlog

When the time comes to set a fire in the fireplace, one of the essential ingredients is the backlog, a large log so called because it is set at the back. Increase Mather mentions it in a dramatic scene from his 1684 book *Illustrious Providences:* "The spit was carried up the chimney, and came down with the point forward, and stuck in the backlog."

Describing a farmhouse in a snowstorm in the 1770s, Hector St. John de Crèvecoeur mentions "an enormous back-log, without which a fire is supposed to be imperfectly made and to be devoid of heat." A thorough description of a fire properly laid is found in *Knickerbocker Magazine* for February 1852: "The 'log' has been placed; the 'back-log' has surmounted it; the 'top-stick' crowns the apex; the 'forestick' rests against the 'and-irons'; and the intermediate 'cob-house' of timber, fired by the faithful 'kindling-wood,' is all ablaze, and roaring up the chimney."

As fireplaces and backlogs yielded to central heating towards the end of the nineteenth century, *backlog* began to blaze in figurative use. At first this new *backlog* just meant "an accumulation," as in an 1883 Boston article about bicycling: "The roads seemed to improve, and, the back-log of raw eggs and milk beginning to take effect, the pace was improved." Later it acquired its modern meaning "accumulation of work unfinished." From the mid-twentieth century, we have a 1947 *Chicago Daily News* example: "This is hardly attributable to new-car production, which still counts order back-logs in the millions."

1687 jimsonweed

Jamestown, the first English-speaking colony in North America, gave us the name of our first English-speaking hallucinogen. Commemorating what might be considered a colonial Woodstock is the name *Jamestown weed,* as described in a 1687 *Letter from Mr. John Clayton . . . Giving an Account of Several Observables in Virginia.* When certain soldiers "went to gather a Sallad," Mr. Clayton explains, "lighting in great Quantities on an Herb called *James-town-weed,* they gathered it; and by eating thereof in plenty, were rendered apish and foolish, as if they had been drunk, or were become idiots."

That this "James-town-weed" had unusual pharmacological properties was confirmed in a 1709 description: "The Seed it bears is very like that of an Onion; it is excellent for curing Burns, and asswaging Inflammations."

By the 1800s, the once prominent city of Jamestown was reduced to a few ruins, and *Jamestown weed* was likewise reduced to its present form, *jimsonweed*. A 1977 book of useful plants says jimsonweed "is extremely poisonous," but adds, "In Appalachia, poultices made of the leaves have been used to treat wounds and kill pains while in the Southwest it has been used as an hallucinogenic."

1688 bald eagle

Bald is beautiful in America today, thanks to a name chosen three centuries ago and explained in a 1688 scientific account: "The Second is the Bald Eagle, for the Body and part of the Neck being of a dark brown, the upper part of the Neck and Head is covered with a white sort of Down, whereby it looks very bald, whence it is so named."

In 1782, after six years of debate in Congress and the efforts of three different committees, the bald eagle was chosen to adorn the Great Seal of the United States. There it holds the arrows of war in one talon and the olive branch of peace in the other, with a ribbon in its mouth bearing our motto, *E pluribus unum,* "one from many." Above these emblems shines its unadorned bald head.

Since then the bald eagle has signified the United States on everything from the presidential flag to the back of the dollar bill. It is still found in the wild, too, in all parts of the country, feeding on rodents and dead fish.

1689 lengthy

Was it because we Americans were in a hurry? We not only invented *lengthy,* but used it to complain about the length of actions and writings. As early as 1689 in a Massachusetts document we find, "I very much fear a dreadfull, lengthy, wasting Indian war."

In his diary for January of 1759, young John Adams used *lengthy* to complain about his own writing. He had written a sermon addressed to himself: "Which, dear Youth, will you prefer? a Life of Effeminacy, Indolence and obscurity, or a Life of Industry, Temperance, and Honour?" After several hundred such words, Adams ended, "(I grow too minute and lengthy.)" Ben Franklin, also, as well as Thomas Jefferson, George Washington, and Alexander Hamilton, made good use of *lengthy.* The British criticized it in the eighteenth century but picked it up themselves in the nineteenth.

The first collection of Americanisms, written by John Pickering in 1816, remarks that we used the word for "writings or discourses. Thus we say, a *lengthy* pamphlet, a *lengthy* sermon, &c." Nowadays it needs no lengthy discussion to acknowledge the continuing usefulness of the word.

1691 tamale

Yes, a *tamale* or a *hot tamale* is a contemporary Mexican dish, popular in the Southwest, and its name comes via Spanish from the Nahautl language of the Aztecs of Mexico. But it happens that Americans who spoke English learned of it before the seventeenth century was over. Something like a tamale was a staple of the Indians of Virginia. Although he does not use the name, Captain John Smith wrote about it as early as 1612: "Their corne they rost in the eare greene, and bruising it in a morter of wood with a Polt [pestle], lappe it in rowles in the leaves of their corne, and so boyle it for a daintie."

The name itself is given in the account of another writer in 1691: "There are five or six kinds of beans—all of them very good, also calabashes, watermelons and sunflowers. The seed of all of these, mixed with corn make very fine *tamales*."

Tamales is the plural. From it English speakers derived *tamale* in the nineteenth century, not noticing that the Spanish singular is *tamal*. Today the definitive ingredients are meat, cornmeal, and red pepper, the latter giving us the expression *hot tamale*, which has been used to mean "a clever fellow" or "a sexy woman." That expression can heat up our language in other ways too, as in this 1996 editorial from the *Herald-Sun* of Durham, North Carolina: "So instead of the convenience of a sensible rating system, parents will have to divine what lies behind a six-tier rating system that begins with TV-G (suitable for all ages) and ends with TV-M (don't let the kiddies near this hot tamale)."

1695 settler

In the early 1600s, people who came from England to live in a new colony or plantation were called PLANTERS (1619), *adventurers, the company,* or simply *inhabitants.* Nobody thought of calling them *settlers,* perhaps because their situation was too unsettled. Only after nearly a century of colonization do we find evidence that *settler* was beginning to be used. A notice of a Massachusetts boundary, published in 1696, makes *settler* an alternative to *goer:* "the lines or highway which divides the land of the first goers or first settlers of Woodstock and the stayers, or other inhabitants of Roxbury."

In the next century, *settler* settled for good in our American vocabulary, as in a 1739 Georgia reference to "a Builder of Boats and a Settler there." Before the end of the eighteenth century, *settler* was the usual word, as in this example from Benjamin Franklin's "Rules by Which A Great Empire May Be Reduced to a Small One" of 1773: "Those remote provinces have perhaps been acquired, purchased, or conquered, at the sole expence of the settlers, or their ancestors, without the aid of the mother country."

1696 alumnus *and* alma mater

Colleges and universities had existed in England for centuries, but the founding of Harvard College in 1636 opened the way for American innovations in higher education. We Americans were apparently the first to speak of *alumnus* of an *alma mater*. Both of these terms were used affectionately by Samuel Sewall, Harvard Class of 1671, in his diary for October 12, 1696. Concerning a meeting at the college that day, he wrote, "Lt. Govr. complemented the President &c., for all the respect to him, acknowldg'd his obligation and promis'd his Interposition for them as become such an Alumnus to such an Alma Mater: directed and desired the Presdt. and fellows to go on; directed and enjoined the students to obedience." The lieutenant governor, William Stoughton, was a member of the Harvard Class of 1650, and on the occasion reported by Sewall he was helping the college renew its charter.

In a later century, Americans were among the first to open higher education to women and were the first to use the feminine *alumna,* plural *alumnae* (contrasting with masculine *alumni*), for women graduates. An 1882 book on women's education refers to "the Alumnae and Alumni of Oberlin," the first college that was coeducational (1881, another American word).

1697 apple pie

Samuel Sewall, distinguished ALUMNUS (1696) of Harvard College and citizen of Boston, went on a picnic expedition to Hog Island on October 1, 1697. There he dined on apple pie. He wrote in his diary, "Had first Butter, Honey, Curds and Cream. For Dinner, very good Rost Lamb, Turkey, Fowls, Applepy."

That is the first, but hardly the last, American mention of a dish whose patriotic symbolism is expressed in a 1984 book by Susan Purdy, *As Easy as Pie:* "This is IT!—what our country and flag are as American as. Since the earliest colonial days, apple pies have been enjoyed in America for breakfast, for an entrée, and for dessert. Colonists wrote home about them and foreign visitors noted apple pie as one of our first culinary specialties."

We cannot claim to have invented the apple pie, just to have perfected it. As long ago as 1590, the English poet Robert Greene wrote in his *Arcadia,* "Thy breath is like the steame of apple-pyes." But Noah Webster's American dictionary of 1828 suggests a difference between British and American versions, the American having more crust: "a pie made of apples stewed or baked, inclosed in paste, or covered with paste, as in England." In England nowadays the term is more commonly *apple tart.*

American versions of apple pie are almost as many as the varieties of apples. There is, for example, apple cobbler (1859) with thick dough, the deep-dish apple dowdy or pandowdy (1880), apple crisp (1932) with a crumbly crust, and apple slump (1831), which, according to an 1848 writer, is "made by placing raised bread or dough around the sides of an iron pot, which is then filled with apples and sweetened with molasses."

Apple pie figures in our figurative language, too, as in the expressions *simple as apple pie* (since everyone supposedly knows how to make apple pie) and, though not an Americanism, *apple-pie order* (1780). But it was only in the twentieth century, apparently in the 1960s, that we began to be "as American as apple pie."

1698 portage

Not only did we paddle our own CANOE (1555), we carried it too. The French, the first Europeans to explore by canoe in North America, gave us a word for it: *portage.* It is explained in Louis Hennepin's *New Discovery of a Vast Country in America* of 1698: "We ... brought up our Bark to the great Rock of Niagara, ... where we were oblig'd to make our Portage; that is, to carry over-land our Canow's and Provisions, and other Things, above the great Fall of the River, which interrupts the Navigation. ... The Portage was two leagues long."

Captain Meriweather Lewis found need for the term in his 1805 journal of the Lewis and Clark exploration of the

Missouri River and the Northwest: "I . . . ordered him to keep sufficiently near the river to observe its situation in order that he might be enabled to give Capt. Clark an idea of the point at which it would be best to halt to make our portage."

With little change, the term has survived in recreational canoeing today. "When you canoe a river like the Wisconsin," says a 1997 report, for example, "you need as much information as possible to help you plan a safe, successful journey. You'll portage around numerous dams, and you need to plan your camping according to what islands are available."

1701 colonist

English-speaking colonies had been located in North America for nearly a century before their inhabitants were spoken of as *colonists.* We find the earliest record of the word in a document from Pennsylvania in 1701. "If good colonists were brought into them," it declares, "there might be raised some thousands of pounds." Before this the inhabitants of a colony had been called PLANTERS (1619), *adventurers, the company,* or more recently SETTLERS (1695).

Use of the new word *colonist* went along with the growing importance and prosperity of the individual as opposed to the earlier emphasis on the concerns of the colony as a whole.

1703 cookie

You won't hear *cookie* in England. But you will in the United States, thanks to our Dutch forebears. *Cookie* is a Dutch term meaning "little cake." It was brought to the New World by the Dutch settlers of New Amsterdam. Though they lost the colony to the English, who promptly renamed it New York in 1674, the Hollanders maintained their hearty practices. In 1703, it was reported, certain New York residents of Dutch ancestry laid out for a funeral "rum, beer, gloves, rings," one and a half gross of pipes, and eight hundred "cockies." Cookies were also a Dutch treat for New Year's Day, along with pound cake, wine, and a drink called *cherry bounce* (made of cider, whiskey and cherries).

During the 1700s the sweet, flat little cakes became the favorites of New Yorkers of all backgrounds. In 1786, for example, a New York newspaper complained about "idle boys, who infest our markets and streets, with baskets of *cookies*." From New York, cookies made themselves at home throughout the country by means of travelers, recipes, and hungry children. In the late twentieth century, when a children's television show wanted to associate a leading character with a culinary passion, who else could they imagine but a monster who loved cookies?

1709 backwoods

The English-speaking populace in the period of settlement before the American Revolution clung to the Atlantic seaboard. Places not close to the centers of habitation were somewhere else, in what was called the *backwoods*. The word is noted in 1709 by the author of *A New Voyage to Carolina* in regard to the pheasant: "He haunts the back Woods, and is seldom found near the Inhabitants."

Later in the eighteenth century we first find the name for a person who lives in the backwoods, in a 1774 letter to the Colonial Office in London: "Stired up the old inveteracy of those who are called the back-woods-men, who are Hunters like the Indians and equally ungovernable."

These backwoodsmen were self-reliant as well as independent. A certain J. F. D. Smyth, in his 1784 book *A Tour in the United States of America,* reported that he was "Accompanied . . . by my faithful back-wood's man, whom at first I considered as little better than a savage. . . . These American back-wood's men can perform a little . . . almost in every handicraft of necessary mechanical trade."

Usually the term was not a compliment. John Pickering, that early collector of Americanisms, explained in 1818 that *backwoodsman* was "a name given by the people of the commercial towns in the United States, to those who inhabit the territory westward of the Allegany mountains. . . . This word is commonly used as a term of reproach (and that only, in familiar style) to designate those people, who, being at a distance from the sea and entirely agricultural, are considered as either hostile or indifferent to the interests of the commercial states."

America had backwoods women too, though it took us until the nineteenth century to recognize them. *Knickerbocker* magazine in 1840 commented on "all the endless drudgery belonging to the life of a backwoods-woman." And in 1884 Ella Rhodes Higginson wrote about one in *Harper's Magazine:* "Mrs. Jackson—a plain, estimable backwoods-woman, . . . sat smoking her corn-cob pipe."

1711 jackknife

Americans may not have been the first to think of making a knife safe and portable by giving it a blade that folds into the handle, but we were the first to call it a *jackknife.* Our earliest notice is in the official records of Springfield, Massachusetts, for 1711: "One Dozen of Jack Knives, at six pence the knife" on one occasion, and "Eleven iron handled Jack knives" on another.

Jackknives were a traditional accouterment for boys who were growing up in America. Without them the playing of mumble-te-peg (an English game which antedates *jackknife* by eighty years at least) and the whittling of sticks (which probably antedates English and perhaps even the Bronze Age) can only be practiced by the possessors of the larger and more formidable sheath knife (1837). The practical advantage to the jackknife lies in its relatively safe transportability in one's pocket.

Where did we get the term? Perhaps it came from the Scottish word for a similar knife, *jockteleg knife* or *Jock the Leg Knife,* attested as early as 1672. Or perhaps it was from *Jack* meaning "sailor," since the knife was used by sailors.

In modern times, the figure of a jackknife opening and closing has found application beyond the tool itself. Its name has been given not only to a style of diving (1922), but to a highway accident where a tractor-trailer truck folds in on itself.

1712 catnip

Since the Middle Ages, the English had called it *cat mint,* because it belongs to the mint family, and because cats, domestic and wild, go wild for it. Since the late Middle Ages, the English had also called it *nep.* A recipe of about 1420 calls for seasoning "with persoley, sauge, ysope, savery, A little nep."

In America, in the eighteenth century, we nipped the *nep* and added the *cat* to make it *catnip.* The first evidence is from Massachusetts in 1712: "He boiled tansy, sage, hysop, and catnip in some of ye best wort." In this country, *Nepeta cataria* has been known as *catnip* ever since. Perhaps *nip* represents an attempt to make sense of the word; we can think of a cat nipping the plant, or being nipped by it.

1713 classmate

From the early days of Harvard College, Americans had been innovative in identifying students by the year of their graduating class. The man who pioneered the use of ALUMNUS (1696) and ALMA MATER (1696), Samuel Sewall, one of eleven members of the Harvard Class of 1671, also recorded the earliest example of *classmate* in his diary for June 5, 1713: "Charlestown Lecture being over, Col. Phillips came p.m. and found the Nomination over. He had spoken for my Classmate Capt. Saml. Phips to the Governor, that would Nominat him for a Justice."

Near the end of his life, on December 22, 1727, Sewall returned from a funeral to reflect, "I have now been at the Interment of 4 of my Class-mates," adding, "Now I can go to no more Funerals of my Class-mates; nor none be at mine; for the survivers . . . are extremly enfeebled."

In addition to *classmate,* two other *mate* words associated with American college life (though first used in other contexts) had their beginnings on this side of the Atlantic. Later in the eighteenth century came *roommate* in a line in William Dunlap's play *The Father, or American Shandyism* (1789): "We were room-mates at Halifax."

And in 1915 we find *teammate* in an American book on tennis. M. E. McLoughlin wrote in *Tennis as I Play It:* "Service and the net position go together, the initial stroke giving the server the opportunity to reach the net where his team-mate is already stationed."

One other American *mate* is prominent in politics: *running mate*. We used it first (1868) in horse racing, to designate a horse that helps the leader by setting the pace for it. Around 1900 *running mate* began to be applied to another kind of horse race, the political contest.

1716 schooner

With timber abundant, shipbuilding was a major industry in New England. Early in the eighteenth century a builder of Gloucester, Massachusetts, announced a new model, which he called a *schooner*. According to maritime historians, the schooner was actually not much different from previous models of "fore-and-aft rigged ships with two masts, the smaller sail on the foremast, and the mainsails gaff-rigged," but the name *schooner* caught on the way *sports car* did in the twentieth century. It could be sailed with a smaller crew than could a square-rigged ship, sometimes in an emergency by a crew of just one.

There is a story that the name derived from a bystander's remark when the first such ship was being launched: "How she scoons upon the water." At that, the captain replied, "A scooner let her be!" The only problem with this story, first reported in 1790, is that *scoon,* meaning "to skim along the surface," is an obscure Scottish word, otherwise not attested in North America.

A hint at the origin of the schooner is in a 1721 letter by Moses Prince of Gloucester: "Went to see Capt. [Andrew] Robinson's lady. This gentleman was the first contriver of schooners, and built the first of the sort about eight years ago." The earliest mention of the word *schooner* on record is from Boston in 1716: "James Manson ye Skooner Mayflower from North Carolina."

Quickly the ship design and the term gained great popularity in North American waters. It also spread throughout Europe, so that *schooner* is found in Dutch, German, Swedish, French, Danish, and Russian. The spelling most commonly encountered in English is *schooner,* probably taking on the *sch–* from Dutch names like *Schuylkill* and such words as *school* and *scheme.*

In the nineteenth century, COVERED WAGONS (1745) were nicknamed *prairie schooners* (1841) because of their resemblance to the familiar craft. By 1877 *schooner* had also come to mean a tall beer glass, perhaps in recollection of the ship's mast.

1721 store

As "a collection of things," *store* was known in English centuries before English speakers came to North America. But as "a collection of things to be sold"—that was an American invention.

We used *store* rather than the British *shop* because of the way business was conducted in the colonies. Distances were great, travel was difficult, cities and even towns were few. It was necessary for the colonists, like the American Indians, to be largely self-sufficient. They laid in their own stores, both home grown and imported. When they had excess or need, they would trade from each other's stores. So in a Philadelphia weekly newspaper of 1721 we read, "At a Store under George Mifflins House . . . are several Sorts of English Goods to be sold." In time, such stores became the equivalent of English shops.

Or perhaps not quite. *Store* suggests abundance, and Americans have always been interested in life, liberty, and the pursuit of abundance. Rather than being content with little shops, we continue to conglomerate big stores, mega and super, where we can find abundance of everything under one roof.

1730 two bits

Originally, a bit was a piece of real money. More precisely, it was the name used in English-speaking North America for a Spanish silver *real*. Eight of these bits made a Spanish dollar, known as a *peso* in Spanish, in English a *piece of eight*.

Long before the United States had its own existence, then, let alone its own money, the bit was established as one-eighth of a dollar. As early as 1683, *Spanish Bitts* are mentioned in colonial records of Pennsylvania. And *two bits* was the term for a quarter of a Spanish dollar. That amount is recorded in 1730 in the diary of John Comer of Rhode Island: "I saw peach trees in ye blossom and many delightful varieties. Cost me two bitts."

Those were the days when money was money. Coins made of precious metal had the value of the metal, and were accepted for that value, regardless of their country of origin. The "bit" bit the dust at the end of the eighteenth century, when coinage of the new United States of America was established on the decimal system and the dime became the smallest silver coin. But in our language *bit* lived on, especially in the phrase *two bits*. The vanishing of actual bits changed *two bits* into a slang way of saying "twenty-five cents" or "a quarter." As slang, it also can just mean "cheap," as in *two-bit saloon* (1875) and *two-bit politicians* (1945 and many other years).

1732 logger

The disappearance of America's virgin forests coincides with the appearance of the word *logger* and the attitude it implies: A tree is just a log waiting to be born. From the very first, the loggers who cut down trees had their critics. The first instance of *logger*, from 1732, is such a case: "Mr. Byfield's proceedings, of which he complained, have so animated the loggers that more waste has been committed this last winter than for many years past." A century later, a character in James Fenimore Cooper's novel *The Prairie* (1827) complains, "It will not be long before an accursed band of choppers and loggers will be following."

A more charitable view of loggers is offered in a 1734 record from New Hampshire: "Many Towns raising a generall Contribution among the Logers for him."

Logs served many purposes in colonial America. They were the building material of choice for housing (LOG CABIN 1770), fencing (*log fence* 1651, *rail fence* 1649), transportation (*log canoe* 1752), and general building (*logwork* 1721). And the importance of clearing logs for new settlement prompted LOGROLLING (1792).

One word that surprisingly has nothing to do with the American *logger* is the older English *loggerhead,* meaning "a slow-witted person," used by Shakespeare among others. In a thick-headed argument, people are said to be *to loggerheads* (1680) or *at loggerheads* (1831).

1733 barbecue

Many years before the United States was founded, before English speakers occupied the Southwest, and before tract houses with backyard grills spread across the suburban plains, Americans had already invented barbecues. The first barbecues, in fact, were the invention of the Taino Indians of Haiti, who dried their meat on raised frames of sticks over the fire. Spanish explorers translated the Taino word as *barbacoa,* and in due course English settlers along the Atlantic coast had their own *barbecues.*

One summer day in 1733, Benjamin Lynde, a substantial citizen of Salem, Massachusetts, wrote in his diary, "Fair and hot; Browne, Barbacue; hack overset." That is, on this hot day he went to the Brownes to attend a barbecue, and his carriage (or maybe his horse) tipped over. His experience may have been upsetting, but it indicates that the social occasion

of the barbecue was established by that time. Large animals would be roasted whole on frames over hot fires, and neighbors would be invited to dine.

In later centuries, as settlement pressed westward, the barbecue went along with it, reaching an especially grand size in Texas, where a pit for fuel might be dug ten feet deep. Present-day barbecue grills are likely to be small and portable, fueled by charcoal or propane or electricity, and capable of cooking only parts of an animal at a time, but they still operate out of doors and provide a reason for inviting the neighbors over.

1736 awakening

In the winter of 1734–35, the mild-mannered Reverend Jonathan Edwards, minister of the church in Northampton, Massachusetts, was astounded. People actually were listening to his sermons and following his advice. We are all sinners, he had said; our works will not justify us; God alone is the source of salvation. These words ended the "carnal security" of his congregation. Their talk turned to nothing but religion, and they began living godly lives. Even "the vainest and loosest"! Even young people! And this behavior was spreading from

Northampton to other towns up and down the Connecticut River Valley.

In a famous letter published in 1736, Edwards called this a "general awakening." He used the term *awakening* because it involves awakening the conscience to the individual's state of sin and need for God's grace. There was, for example, "a young woman that had been one of the greatest company-keepers in the whole town, in whom there appeared evident a glorious work of God's infinite power and sovereign grace; a new and truly broken, sanctified heart." Edwards observed, "God made it, I suppose, the greatest occasion of awakening to others, of anything that ever came to pass in the town."

As it turned out, this awakening of Connecticut Valley communities was just a prelude to what would be called the *Great Awakening,* which began in 1740. Stimulated by itinerant preachers, the Great Awakening swept back and forth through the colonies from New England to the South for many years. These awakenings set a pattern for American religious experience that continues to the present day, but the word we now use is REVIVAL (1799). In modern times, *awakening* usually refers to secular experiences, as in the book titles *The Awakening,* Kate Chopin's 1899 novel about a woman's growing self-awareness, and *Awakenings,* Oliver Sacks's 1973 account of victims of Parkinsonism who are energized by a miracle drug.

1738 ten-foot pole

William Byrd, perhaps the wealthiest man in the American colonies as well as one of the best American writers of his time, joined an expedition in 1728 to survey the boundary between North Carolina and Virginia. In his *History of the Dividing Line,* published in 1738, we find our earliest reference to a ten-foot pole: "We found the ground moist . . . insomuch that it was an easy matter to run a ten-foot pole up to the head in it."

A century later, the ten-foot pole was less of a surveying instrument than a metaphorical measure of social, political, or legal distance. "Can't touch him with a ten-foot pole" was in an 1848 list of "Nantucketisms." Though few people ever handle an actual ten-foot pole, such expressions have gone the distance in our language through the present day.

1739 johnnycake

Among the many uses to which hungry Americans put CORN (1608), one of the most popular was known in the North as *johnnycake*. It was another name for what we would now call *cornbread,* and was cooked in a variety of ways: on a board facing the fire, on a griddle, or in a frying pan. The name may be related to the earlier *jonakin* (see MUSH 1671). Later the johnnycake was also known as a *journeycake,* presumably because it was thought of as a cake you could take on a journey.

Here is a twentieth-century version of johnnycake from New Bedford, Massachusetts: Combine a cup of white cornmeal with a teaspoon salt, two tablespoons flour, and a tablespoon sugar. Scald with boiling water until every grain swells. Gradually add half a cup of milk until the batter is thick. Allow more cooking time than for ordinary pancakes.

1740 banjo

African Americans brought the banjo to our shores. It could be heard in this hemisphere before the middle of the eighteenth century, according to a 1740 history of Jamaica that says Africans who were brought there had "other Musical Instruments, as a *Banjil,* not much unlike our Lute in any thing but the Musick." Since then it has struck such a chord with Americans that *lute* would need explaining, not *banjo.*

The banjo was well established in the North American colonies when a Virginian noted it as entertainment at a party in 1774: "A great number of young people met together with a Fiddle and Banjo played by two Negroes, with plenty of Toddy." In that same year Philip Fithian of Princeton, New Jersey, attended a social event where "several negroes & Ben &

Harry are playing on a banjo & dancing." And a few years later Thomas Jefferson declared in his *Notes on the State of Virginia* that "the instrument proper to them [Negroes] is the Banjor, which they brought hither from Africa."

The ultimate origin of the banjo is unknown. It may be an adaptation of a Portuguese guitar, the *banza*, brought to West Africa in the 1600s. But whatever its beginnings, in the hands of Africans who brought it to North America, it became the basis for distinctively energetic and distinctively American music, instrumental in the later development of forms as diverse as JAZZ (1913) and BLUEGRASS (1750).

The equally distinctive shape of the instrument, with its circular body and long narrow neck, has inspired the names *banjo clock*, for a clock shaped like a banjo, invented in 1802; *banjo shovel*, for a shovel with a round scoop; and *banjo eyes*, for wide-open eyes.

1742 groundhog

Among the strange new American animals that added so much to the vocabulary of American English, the groundhog does not loom large. The SKUNK (1588) and the OPOSSUM (1610) are more colorful, the BUFFALO (1633) and the grizzly bear more awe-inspiring. But of all the animals on the continent, only the lowly, unremarkable groundhog has its own day.

The groundhog also has an older, more curious name. Settlers as long ago as 1674 referred to it as a *woodchuck*, borrowing the name from one of the Algonquian Indian languages but spelling it as a combination of two English words. This attempt to make sense of the borrowing resulted in such nonsense as the tongue twister, "How much wood could a woodchuck chuck if a woodchuck could chuck wood?"

Meanwhile, in the middle colonies, the wood-chucking creature acquired another name, *groundhog*, that goes back at least as far as 1742. In that year the Pennsylvania botanist John Bartram wrote, "The *Monac*, or groundhog . . . will be as tame as a cat." *Groundhog* may have been a translation from the Dutch *aardvarken*, meaning "earth pig," or it may just have been inspired by the observation that this pudgy rodent burrows in the ground. In any case, it was as a *groundhog* that it got its day, February 2. The ceremony has remained as it was in this 1871 explanation: "On that day the ground-hog comes annually out of his hole, after a long winter nap, to look for his shadow. If he perceives it, he retires again to his burrow, which he does not leave for six weeks—weeks necessarily of stormy weather. But if he does not see his shadow, he stays out of his hole till he can, and the weather is sure to become mild and pleasant." In Punxsutawney, Pennsylvania, "Punxsutawney Phil" now does the Groundhog Day forecasting for the whole nation.

1744 ice cream

Italy apparently invented the delicious practice of adding sweetener and flavoring to cream and freezing it, and England heard of this iced cream before the colonies did, but we Americans can at least claim to have invented the modern name for it—dropping the *d* to make *ice cream*. In Philadelphia as long ago as 1744 there was mention of "some fine Ice Cream" served with strawberries and milk. For centuries after that, *Philadelphia ice cream* was the name for ice cream of a distinctive type, made without eggs. Philadelphia was also the birthplace of the ice cream soda. That first combination of America's favorite treat with America's favorite beverage took place in 1874 at the Franklin Institute in Philadelphia.

The rest of the country, too, participated in the enthusiasm for ice cream. When we did not make it by hand at home, we went in colonial days to ice cream houses, then in the early 1800s to ice cream gardens and ice cream saloons, and finally, toward the end of that century, to ice cream stands and ice cream parlors. And the process of making it was improved by Nancy Johnson's invention of the ice cream freezer in 1846.

A major invention of the late nineteenth century was the ice cream sundae. Its odd name comes from *Sunday*, but why is still anyone's guess. Some say it was first sold only on that day of the week. In 1904 St. Louis was the birthplace of what became known as the *ice cream cone*. It was invented at the world's fair there, the Louisiana Purchase Exposition, supposedly when a vendor of ice cream ran out of cups and had edible ones made by a pastry shop next door. The twentieth century has also seen the American invention of the ice cream bar, which is on a stick with a coating; the ice cream sandwich; soft ice cream, which is dispensed from a spout; premium ice cream with the richest of ingredients; and imitation ice milk with the poorest.

1745 covered wagon

The English defined it as a wagon with a tilt, *tilt* being "a canvas awning or cover." We Americans just covered our wagons and gave them the plain descriptive name *covered wagon*. In 1745, New Englanders who sailed north to Cape Breton Island and negotiated the surrender of the French Canadian fortress of Louisbourg mentioned covered wagons in their conditions: "That the commander in chief now in Garrison shall have liberty to send off covered waggons to be inspected only by one officer of ours."

In the nineteenth century, covered wagons earned renown as they carried pioneers across the Great Plains and the Rockies to settle in Oregon and California. They were also known as *Conestoga wagons* (1750) because they were first manufactured in the Pennsylvania town of Conestoga and *prairie schooners* (1841) because they looked like ships sailing through the tall grass.

And in the twentieth century, *The Covered Wagon,* an epic silent film of 1923 made from Emerson Hough's best-selling novel of the previous year, not only established the genre of the movie Western but also ensured that *covered wagon* would remain a familiar term to modern Americans. When the first aircraft carriers were constructed in that decade by putting tops on warships, they too were honored with the nickname *covered wagon.*

1748 buck

The Indians taught the European settlers the value of a buck. In the eighteenth century, that meant a deerskin, used for trading in its own right and as a unit of value for trading anything else. So in 1748, while in Indian territory on a visit to the Ohio, Conrad Weiser wrote in his journal, "He has been robbed of the value of 300 Bucks"; and later, "Every cask of Whiskey shall be sold . . . for 5 Bucks in your town."

In the next century, with deerskins less often serving as a medium of exchange, the buck passed to the dollar. A Sacramento, California, newspaper reported this court judgment in 1856: "Bernard, assault and battery upon Wm. Croft, mulcted in the sum of twenty bucks."

Inflation has hit *buck* in the later twentieth century, so that in big-bucks transactions *buck* can mean one hundred or even one hundred thousand dollars. But sometimes a *buck* is still just a buck.

Passing the buck is a different matter. In the late nineteenth century, poker players designated the dealer with a marker they called the *buck,* apparently so named because it was often a knife with a handle made of buckhorn. When responsibility for dealing changed to the next player, they passed the buck.

1750 bluegrass

In New England in the mid-eighteenth century, bluegrass was considered a nuisance. In his book *Field-Husbandry,* published in 1751, Jared Eliot insisted that "The Land that you would improve this way, must be intirely free from Blue Grass, called by some Dutch Grass, or Wire Grass."

To the west, however, it looked better. "All the Way from the Shannoah Town to this Place," wrote Christopher Gist of Pennsylvania in that same year, is "full of beautiful natural Meadows, covered with wild Rye, blue Grass and Clover."

It remained for Kentucky to bring *bluegrass* to full flower, however. The place where bluegrass grows best has been known since the nineteenth century as the *Bluegrass State.* In the mid-twentieth century, *bluegrass* became even more famous as the name for a kind of music invented and cultivated in that part of the country.

THESE

UNITED STATES:

1751–1800

*I*n a mere fifty years during the second half of the eighteenth century, we Americans underwent the most drastic transformation in our history. In 1751, we belonged to separate English colonies; by 1800, we had our own United States of America. We remained *Yankees* (1765) and *southerners,* and we maintained allegiance to our own respective states. But we began thinking as a nation, as *Americans,* a word whose meaning changed significantly on July 4, 1776. And we established a national government that would remain basically the same more than two centuries later, making it at the start of the twenty-first century the oldest continuous form of government in the world.

For over one hundred years, English-speaking settlements on the Atlantic coast had developed from outposts of the *mother country* (1617) to communities with their own American customs and perspectives, exemplified in the entries for those early years. By the mid-eighteenth century, as these communities prospered and communicated, they gradually began to have more in common. This is reflected in our language as early as 1754 with the use of *union* to refer to the colonies as a whole.

During this time, we continued to name the distinctive natural features of our continent, from the *prairie* (1773) to the *bayou* (1767), from the beautiful *gardenia* (1760) to the deadly *Venus's flytrap* (1771), from the *lightning bug* (1778) to *Indian summer* (1777). One of the newly named, the abundant *passenger pigeon* (1783), fell victim to our relentless expansion a century later.

But we were increasingly occupied with matters other than just living on the land. In fighting for independence, we came up with the first consciously coined American word: *minuteman* (1774). We met the first *cowboys* (1779). When the fighting was over, we concerned ourselves with *veterans* (1798). We discussed government, inventing *lynch law* (1780) and *blue laws* (1781) as well as the great Constitution of 1787. We paid *mileage* (1753), voted for a *ticket* (1756), held *caucuses* (1763, from the Algonquian), objected to *squatters* (1788) and welcomed *immigrants* (1789). We even began, belatedly, to discuss the *abolition* (1787) of slavery.

It has been said that a language is merely a dialect with an army and navy. For example, the language spoken in northern Germany is considered just a dialect of German, while a very similar language in neighboring Holland is considered a separate language, Dutch. The English spoken on both sides of the Atlantic was never so different that anyone thought of it as two completely different languages. But it is no coincidence that the independence of these United States coincided with the first remarks about a separate American language, or at least about "Americanisms."

The Reverend John Witherspoon, a Scotsman, signer of the Declaration of Independence and former president of Princeton University, proudly coined this word for a series of articles published in the *Pennsylvania Journal and Weekly Advertiser* in 1781. He was bothered that educated persons displayed "errors in grammar, improprieties and vulgarisms which hardly any person of the same class in point of rank and literature would have fallen into in Great Britain." But at the same time, in a spirit of patriotic independence, he declared,

"It does not follow in every case that the terms or phrases used are worse in themselves, but merely that they are of American and not of English growth. The word *Americanism,* which I have coined for the purpose, is exactly similar in its formation and significance to the word *Scotticism.*"

With that Witherspoon launched an enterprise that has not abated since, of identifying Americanisms that distinguish our version of English from that on the other side of the Atlantic. The significant change at the founding of our nation is the idea of an American standard in language separate from the English. Whether to praise or condemn it is another matter, but the existence of a distinctly American way of speaking has not been doubted since.

1751 chowder

It begins with the cooking pot, called in French a *chaudière.* Perhaps New Englanders got it from trade or military expeditions to French Canadian outposts up north like Louisbourg (see COVERED WAGON 1745). The idea is to toss in whatever you have on hand, particularly seafood, salt pork, vegetables, and often crackers and milk, to make a thick hot stew or soup.

In 1751 we find that chowder is already the subject of poetry. On September 2 of that year, rhymed "Directions for making a chouder" appeared in the *Boston Evening Post:* "First lay some Onions to keep the Pork from burning, Because in Chouder there can be no turning."

A century later, the great New England orator and statesman Daniel Webster (1782–1852) had his own recipe for chowder. According to a 1931 cookbook, it supposedly went like this: "Take a cod of ten pounds, well cleaned, leaving on the skin. Cut into pieces one and a half pounds thick, preserving the head whole. Take one and a half pounds of clear, fat, salt pork, cut in thin slices. Do the same with twelve potatoes. Take the largest pot you have. Try out the pork first; then take out the pieces of pork, leaving in the drippings. Add to that three parts of water, a layer of fish, so as to cover the bottom of the pot; next a layer of potatoes, then two tablespoons of salt,

1 teaspoon of pepper, then the pork, another layer of fish, and the remainder of the potatoes."

Fill with water to cover the ingredients and boil for twenty-five minutes. Then add a quart of boiling milk and ten hard crackers, split and dipped in cold water. After five more minutes of boiling, "the chowder is then ready and will be first rate if you have followed the directions."

1752 katydid

In the summer of 1743, Pennsylvania botanist John Bartram accompanied ambassador Conrad Weiser to peace negotiations with the Iroquois Indians in what is now New York State. Eight years later the journal of his trip was published in London as *Observations on the Inhabitants, Climate, Soil, Rivers, Productions, Chemicals, and other matters worthy of Notice made by Mr. John Bartram in his travels from Pennsylvania to Onondaga, Oswego, and the Lake Ontario in Canada.* That was in 1751. By 1752, therefore, copies were circulating in the American colonies, where the call of the a certain insect could be noted on page 70: "The great green grass-hopper began to sing (*Catedidist*) these were the first I observed this year."

Or was it *chittediddle*? That was Meriwether Lewis's spelling in his 1804 record of the Lewis and Clark expedition. The name has also been spelled *kittledee, kittydid,* and *cataded,* among others, in attempts to imitate the sound.

All those names have faded out, however, in favor of *katydid* for the simple reason that *katydid* is made up of familiar English words. As early as 1784, a travel writer remarked about "a very singular insect" on Long Island: "They are named by the inhabitants here *Katy did's.*" Perhaps the grasshoppers were just having a monotonous conversation in English.

But if, in their conversation, all the katydids agree that "Katy did," it would seem unnecessary for them to discuss it at length. And all katydids don't sound alike, either. So that led to a tongue-in-cheek explanation: Some of the insects say "Katy did," others "Katy didn't." Neither side wins the argument, but it gives them an excuse to argue all night in the song we still hear all over the North American continent.

1753 mileage

It was part of Ben Franklin's contribution to the idea of a UNION (1754) of the colonies. How could members of a united colonial council be persuaded to travel vast distances for meetings? How could they be fairly compensated for traveling different distances? Franklin's down-to-earth solution was mileage, payment of a certain amount per mile of travel. The idea must have been in his head for at least a year when in 1754 Franklin wrote a list of "Short hints towards a scheme for uniting the Northern Colonies" and included "Members Pay: —— Shillings sterling per Diem during their sitting and milage for Travelling expences."

More than twenty years later, when we declared our independence, we had not forgotten the mileage, as in a 1776 report that "the militia were promised their mileage and billeting-money."

Subsequently, in the new United States, Congress was happy to award itself mileage. In 1797 there was "a bill for allowing full mileage to members of the Senate and House of Representatives."

At first mileage seems to have been limited to legislatures and the military, but it soon became a practice in private business as well. Transportation has changed from those ship-and-horseback days, but we still measure our distances in miles and compensate ourselves with mileage.

1754 Union

Two decades before the Declaration of Independence was written, the English colonies already felt the need for closer connections. In Albany, New York, in June 1754, a Congress of commissioners from seven of the colonies concerned themselves with "some method of effecting the Union between the colonies" and gave the opinion that "a Union of all the Colonies is . . . at present absolutely necessary for their security and defence." On July 10, 1754, the commissioners issued a "Plan of a Proposed Union of the Several Colonies of Masachusets-bay, New Hampshire, Coneticut, Rhode Island, New York, New Jerseys, Pensilvania, Maryland, Virginia, North Carolina, and South Carolina, For their Mutual Defence and Security, and for Extending the British Settlements in North America."

No such union took place at that time, but the way was prepared for a decisive break and a firmer union later in the eighteenth century. At the time of the Declaration of Independence, Thomas Jefferson was among those who referred to the United States as the *Union*. And the Constitution of 1787 directed that the president "shall from time to time give to the Congress information of the State of the Union."

During the Civil War, Abraham Lincoln declared, "My paramount object is to save the Union." That kind of reference gave *Union* a Northern flavor, as opposed to the *secession* of the South. Once the war was over, *Union* again referred to the whole United States. A new state was said to be admitted to the Union. And every January the president still informs the Congress of the State of the Union.

1755 warpath

A pathway regularly followed by Indians when going to war was called in English simply a *warpath,* as on a map published in 1755: "Canoes may come up to the Crossing of the War Path." One path in particular, from the Ohio country to western North Carolina, was named *Warriors' Path.*

It was not long before any path could be called a *warpath* if it was being used to bring people to war, whether Indians or not. Those who were preparing for battle were *on the warpath,* as may be said even today of anyone who is looking for a fight. We have, for example, a line from Mark Twain's *Tramp Abroad* in 1880: "She was on the war-path all the evening."

1756 ticket

Americans have long been devoted to voting and to the secret ballot. So as far back as 1755 we find Ben Franklin explaining that in Pennsylvania "every one votes . . . as privately as he pleases, the Election being by written Tickets folded up and put into a Box." By 1764, political parties had already found it useful to suggest that voters choose their particular ticket, or printed list of candidates. Today, voting remains the ticket to democracy, and voting a *straight ticket* is a party's hope, though there are more nowadays who will vote a *split ticket*— both of which are terms from the nineteenth century.

1757 breechclout

The earliest *clout* recorded in our language was not the Chicago political variety but America's first practical summer clothing: the *breechclout*, that is, "a clout or piece of cloth to cover one's breech," that is, buttocks. While European settlers sweated in heavy wool and leather during the steamy North American summers, American Indian males would strip down to a waistband holding one decorative flap in front and one behind. Occasionally the settlers would try it too, as in Rufus Putnam's *Memoirs* of 1757, which also pointed out a disadvantage of the skimpy clothing: "Nothing to cover us from the Natts & Musketoes but a Shirt and Breech-Clout."

Why *clout* instead of *cloth*? Well, *clout* is more specific; it means "a piece or patch of cloth," suggesting the small size of a breechclout. But since *clout* with this meaning has become obsolete, later writers did use *breechcloth* instead, starting as early as 1793.

American comfort ultimately won out over European habit. Today American males of any ancestry can sometimes be seen out of doors in the summer with little more covering than that the breechclout afforded long ago.

1758 Indian file

Among other things, American Indians even taught the new-comers from Europe how to walk: in the woods, in a group—best to go one behind the other, in single file. This was termed *Indian file* as early as 1758 in Massachusetts: "Set out for Fort Edward in an Indian file, Major Putnam in the front." And *Indian file* it has been ever since. The term can also be used metaphorically, as it was in an 1890 article: "On these gray cloud-tattered skies, an Indian file of crows, clamoring as they go, gives a wild kind of charm."

1759 valedictorian

In addition to ALUMNUS (1696), ALMA MATER (1696), and CLASS-MATE (1713), our first college seems also to have given us our first valedictorian. In his diary for 1759, the Reverend Edward Holyoke, president of Harvard College, noted that "Officers of the Sophisters chose Valedictorian." Made up of suitably sol-emn words from Latin, *valedictorian* simply means "farewell sayer."

Twenty years later, there is a record of a valedictory ora-tion at the College of New Jersey in Princeton by one of the six graduating students. The practice spread to colleges and schools throughout the land, so that now it is customary everywhere to appoint the student with the highest academic standing as valedictorian to speak at commencement.

While we were at it, we invented a title for the runner-up: *salutatorian,* from Latin "greeter," first noted in the 1847 edi-tion of Noah Webster's *American Dictionary.*

1760 gardenia

Not its eminence in the garden, but the eminence of its gar-dener gave the gardenia its name. The gardener was aptly

named: Dr. Alexander Garden, a noted botanist of South Carolina. In Dr. Garden's honor, a whole genus of tropical trees and shrubs was named *Gardenia* in 1760 by none other than the classifying botanist Dr. Carolus Linnaeus himself, at the request of an American friend who had sent a specimen to Linnaeus in Sweden. His specimen, with glossy dark green leaves and fragrant white flowers, was the Cape jasmine, the plant we call the *gardenia* today.

1761 peace pipe

Nowadays the Surgeon General reminds us of the health hazards of tobacco, but in earlier times on the North American continent it saved lives. That was when leaders of American Indian nations smoked it in a long-stemmed ceremonial pipe after negotiating treaties of peace. Smoking the pipe and passing it signified their commitment to the treaty as surely as a signature.

The French had a name for the pipe before the English did. They called it a *calumet,* their word for the reed from which its stem was made. In an English translation from the French, *calumet* is given as early as 1698. But the characteristic that gave the calumet its importance also gave it a descriptive English name. We can pass *peace pipe* into American English in 1761, a year after a certain George Croghan wrote that term in his journal of "Tours in the Western Country," published four years later: "Brother to Confirm what we have said to you I give you this Peace Pipe." The name was well established in 1779 when George Rogers Clark noted its importance among the Illinois: "I told them I would defer smoking the Peace Pipe until I heard that they had called in all their Warriors."

For making pledges to end disputes, we still say *smoking the peace pipe,* though nowadays negotiations may take place without tobacco in a no-smoking conference room.

1762 armonica

In the eighteenth century, Ben Franklin was America's one-man band, and his instrument was the armonica. It was his own invention, an improvement on the water-filled musical glasses he had heard during a visit to London. "Being charmed with the sweetness of its tone, and the music . . . produced from it, I wished only to see the glasses disposed in a more convenient form, and brought together in a narrower compass, so as to admit of a greater number of tones," Franklin explained. He turned the glasses into shallow hemispheres and nested them on a horizontal wooden rod that could be rotated with a pedal. The glasses were thus precisely tuned and close together, enabling virtuoso performances.

Franklin's explanation was in a letter of July 13, 1762, to Giambatista Beccaria, professor of physics at Turin, Italy. "In honour of your musical language," he wrote, "I have borrowed from it the name of this instrument, calling it the Armonica."

No, not the harmonica, although the laugh would be on him within a few years when people would insist on beginning it with a *ha.* But *armonica* or *harmonica,* Franklin's instrument enjoyed success well into the nineteenth century. A twentieth-century musician described it as having "the effect of coming from nowhere and the slow dying away into silence, which is a quite magical effect." The armonica was popular enough in Europe to attract the attention of Wolfgang Amadeus Mozart, who composed an Adagio and Rondo for armonica, flute, oboe, viola, and cello, K. 617. Franklin himself played the armonica and had one in his home.

The armonica has no connection with what we call a *harmonica* today. Invented by an Austrian, the Mundharmonik was introduced to America by Matthias Hohner during the time of the Civil War. This harmonica is constructed of reeds with individual holes through which a player blows or draws in air to set the reeds vibrating. The armonica was a large box on a stand; the modern harmonica is usually small enough to fit into a pocket.

1763 caucus

One of the most important features of American politics, the caucus, seems to have an American Indian origin. It may go back to a word Captain John Smith reported in his 1624 *Generall Historie of Virginia:* "In all these places is a severall [separate] commander, which they [the Indians] call Werowance, except the Chickahamanians, who are governed by the Priests and their Assistants, or their Elders called *Caw-cawwas-soughes.*"

A century later, when the politically active elders of Boston met to choose candidates for public office, they called their meeting a *caucus.* We find the word in young John Adams's diary for February 1763: "This day learned that the Caucas Clubb meets at certain times in the Garret of Tom Daws, the Adjutant of the Boston Regiment. . . . There they smoke tobacco till you cannot see from one End of the Garrett to the other. . . . they choose a Moderator, who puts Questions to the Vote regularly, and select Men, Assessors, Collectors, Wardens, Fire Wards, and Representatives are Regularly chosen before they are chosen in the Town. . . . They send Committees to wait on the Merchants Clubb and to propose, and join, in the Choice of Men and Measures."

Although primary elections now take the place of some caucuses, and smoke-filled rooms are an exception rather than the rule, the caucus remains a distinctively American way for like-minded politicians to arrive behind closed doors at a common cause or candidacy that they can then separately support in public.

1764 bust

It busted out in a Massachusetts advertisement of 1764: "Stray'd or stolen . . . a Bay mare, with a cut main, and a Bust on the near Side of the Hind Flank." At that point it was just a New England way of saying *burst,* in the same *r*-dropping way that CUSS (1815) developed from *curse.* By the next century, however, *bust* occupied a place of its own in American speech. One morning in 1806 Meriwether Lewis, of the Lewis and Clark expedition, noted that "Windsor busted his rifle near the muzzle." In 1832, after the Whig Henry Clay lost the presidential election to Andrew Jackson, the joke was, "Why is the Whig party like a sculptor? Because it takes Clay and makes a bust."

By the mid-nineteenth century, banks busted or went bust when they went bankrupt; people would go on a bust of drinking; a failure was a bust, and so was a celebration.

We now have *boom and bust* (1943) and several *bust* phrases that mean strain or laugh: *bust a hamstring* (1903), *bust a gut* (1912), and *bust my buttons* (1921). *Bust* runs the gamut from slang to standard. When it is used to mean "to explode or fall apart or be arrested," *bust* is generally slang. In the sense of failing (especially financially) it is informal, as *busting the bank* in gambling lingo, while in the specialized sense of taming a horse it is standard, the only way to say *busting a bronco.*

The related word *buster* is an often unfriendly term of address, as well as something large or remarkable. There are, too, some downright humorous derivatives of *bust* in *busticated* (broken, 1916) and *bustified* (pot-bellied, 1939). And the rhyming of the words *bust* and *trust* gave us an important term in American history, *trustbuster* (1903).

1765 Yankee

From the beginning, *Yankee* has been a fighting word. We first come across it in the names of pirates: one *Captain Yankey,* also known as *Yankey Duch* (presumably meaning "Dutch"), mentioned in 1683 and 1684, and a Captain John Williams, known as *Yankey* or *Yanky,* in 1687 and 1688.

By 1765, it had been applied specifically to inhabitants of New England, and not as a compliment. A poem published that year called *Oppression, a Poem by an American,* has as its hero "a Portsmouth Yankey," with the note, "our hero being a New-Englander by birth, has a right to the epithet of Yankey; a name of derision, I have been informed, given by the Southern people on the Continent, to those of New-England."

The British liked *Yankee,* too, when they wanted a derisive epithet for the New England provincials. They set it to music in the song "Yankee Doodle," said to have been composed by a British army surgeon "in derision of the provincial troops."

Then came the American Revolution, and the word as well as the world turned upside down. What had been an insult became a boast. Yankees used that name proudly for themselves as they fought the British, and "Yankee Doodle" became the marching song of the revolution.

But if *Yankee* was now a term of endearment, how could southerners express their derision toward the people of the North? Simple enough. Add a prefix, and you have fighting words once again: *damned Yankee* or plain *damyankee.* They appear as early as 1812, in this threat: "Take the middle of the road or I'll hew you down, you d'—d Yankee rascal."

Even in the twentieth century, when *Yankees* has often just seemed to signify the name of a baseball team, southerners still call northerners *Yankees* when they are annoyed with them. And during the World Wars, when we told our allies "the Yanks are coming," we meant fighting men.

1766 levee

It is time for a detour to the Gulf of Mexico. In 1766, Captain Harry Gordon made a journey from Pittsburgh down the Ohio and Mississippi rivers to New Orleans, Mobile, and Pensacola. That was territory that had taken on new interest for English speakers because the defeat of the French in the Seven Years War had pushed the boundary of British control far to the west and south. From his travels Gordon brought back a couple of new words, *levee* and BAYOU (1767), which are contained in a journal that was published many years later.

He found levees in New Orleans. As a French visitor had observed there in 1719, "Devant la ville il y a une levée et par derrière un fossé." That is, in front of the city is a *levée* and behind it a *fossé*. Both were necessary to prevent the Mississippi River from running wild through the city.

We had plenty of words to translate *fossé: ditch* or *trench* would do nicely, perhaps better than old-fashioned *moat*. But the available translations for *levée—embankment, sea-wall, dike*—didn't quite convey the picture of what was needed to hold off the mighty Mississippi. So *levée*, which simply means "raised," became the English word for the earthworks raised along that river and others in North America.

Gordon's journal mentions "Levée's of Earth to keep off the Floods." Another account, published in 1770, shows the author attempting to explain the structure in English but ending with the French word, saying that New Orleans "is secured from the inundations of the river by a raised bank, generally called the Levée." The accent mark has been lost in the intervening centuries, but New Orleans still has levees today.

1767 bayou

After visiting the city of LEVEES (1766), Captain Harry Gordon wrote, "We left New Orleans . . . and lay that night at the Bayoue." *Bayou* was the second of two Louisiana French words in his journal that were to become part of the American English vocabulary, just as Louisiana itself would become part of the United States in 1803.

Unlike *levee,* however, *bayou* is not originally a French word. We owe it to the Choctaw Indians, who showed the French around when they began to arrive in what they called *Louisiana* early in the eighteenth century. The French were familiar with the Mississippi River, of course, but not with the sluggish little streams flowing into it in the flatlands near the Gulf of Mexico. This, said the Choctaw, is a *bayuk*. Bien entendu, said the French, *bayou*.

In American English, it took some experiments in spelling before we settled on *bayou.* We also wrote *bayoo, byo,* and *bay-you* in attempts to reflect the pronunciation.

To this day in Louisiana, *bayou* retains its original meaning of "a small slow stream." In other parts of the United States, the word has been adapted to the terrain. In the West, a bayou can be simply a ravine or dry streambed. In the North and West, a bayou can be a small lake or lagoon, especially one next to a river or lake.

1768 bee

Because they were sociable and busy as bees, when people got together to work or play in early America that is what they called it. The *Boston Gazette and Country Journal* in October 1769 reported that "Last Thursday about Twenty young Ladies met at the House of Ms. Nehemiah Liscome, here, on purpose for a Spinning Match: (or what is call'd in the Country a Bee)." There were bees for neighborly work like sewing, quilting, knitting, and paring; plowing, chopping wood, husking corn, raising barns, painting, and roofing. For entertainment there were singing bees and even kissing bees.

"Everyone has heard of the 'frolic' or 'bee,' " explained one author in 1837, "by means of which the clearing of lots, the raising of houses, the harvesting of crops is achieved." In 1846 another wrote, "They came cheerfully to the 'bee,' and after the usual amount of eating, drinking, swearing, and joking, the house . . . was raised and covered in."

Thanks to the orthographical oddities of English, one kind of bee has persisted to the present day and become a formal national competition: the spelling bee.

1769 tar and feather

The practice of smearing a body with tar and then sprinkling the tar with feathers was not original to America. As long ago as 1189, during the reign of Richard the Lionhearted, it was prescribed in the British navy as punishment for theft. But English colonials brought it ashore in North America and made such use of it that it now is thought of as American. It was described as the "present popular punishment for modern delinquents" in 1769.

The term *tar and feather* is ours, too, and dates from that time. Richard Thornton's 1912 *American Glossary* has more than a dozen examples of *tar and feather* for the years 1769 through 1775, starting with a newspaper account from October 30, 1769. "A person," reported the *Boston Chronicle,* "was stripped naked, put into a cart, where he was first tarred, then feathered." The *Newport Mercury* for December 20, 1773, carries a "Notice to the Committee on Tarring and Feathering": "What think you, Captain, of a halter round your neck—ten gallons of liquid tar decanted on your pate—with the feathers of a dozen wild geese laid over that to enliven your appearance?"

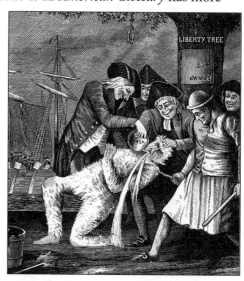

During the American Revolution, rebels made examples of British loyalists by tarring and feathering. A memoir of 1774 refers to "the Liberty Boys, the tarring-and-feathering gentlemen." That year a notable victim was "Mr. John Malcomb, an officer of the customs at Boston, who was tarred and feathered, and led to the gallows with a rope about his neck."

The prohibition in the 1791 Bill of Rights against "cruel and unusual punishments" may have helped discourage the practice of tarring and feathering, which seems to have vanished by the end of the nineteenth century. *Tar and feather* remains in our language today, but only as a figure of speech for public humiliation.

1770 log cabin

That magic ingredient of American politics, the log cabin, was not native either to North America or to England. No, it was born in Sweden and brought to these shores by Swedish immigrants who settled in the Delaware Bay area. For a century it was known simply as a *log house,* as in this 1663 ordinance from Maryland: "Be itt Enacted . . . that a Logg howse be built Twenty foot Square . . . for a Prison."

Then someone had the idea to substitute *cabin* for *house.* We find *log cabin* in a Virginia document of 1770 with specifications for "a log cabbin twenty four feet long and twenty wide for a Court House." With that change of wording, a utilitarian building could become a humble abode. The westward movement of the frontier in subsequent years was marked by the construction of log cabins in the wilderness. Thus the log cabin became the symbol of pioneer America: plain and unpretentious, yet solid and sturdy.

What an opportunity for the aspiring politician! That opportunity was finally recognized by political strategists in the presidential campaign of 1840. Supporters of Martin Van Buren, "Old Kinderhook," proclaimed "O.K." (1839) across the land to boost their candidate. They denounced his opponent, William Henry Harrison, for living in a log cabin in the BACK-WOODS (1709) and subsisting on corn dodger and hard cider (American items, one attested from 1834 and the other from 1789). Harrison actually lived in a mansion, not a log cabin, but the chance was too good to miss. He "campaigned from a log cabin built on a wagon bed that had a seemingly bottomless cider barrel attached," explains political historian William Safire. "The crowds loved it." And they elected Harrison.

From then on, candidates fortunate enough to have been born in a log cabin made the most of it. One of them, as we all still know, was Abraham Lincoln.

1771 Venus's flytrap

In 1770, in London, merchant and botanist John Ellis published the first description of "a new sensitive plant, called *Dionaea muscipula:* or, Venus's fly-trap." Beauty and the beast: *Dionaea,* referring to the mythical goddess of love and beauty (Venus, daughter of Dione), because it is a little flowering plant; *muscipula,* Latin for "mousetrap," because its leaf snaps shut in about half a second when an insect is lured to its bright red surface. Spikes protruding from the edges of the leaf form a narrow cage for the insect. The leaf swells to close the gap and secretes a fluid that digests the insect in about ten days. Then the leaf grows a little and opens up, ready for the next visitor.

Ellis's description would have reached the Venus's flytrap's native land, the swampy coastland of North and South Carolina, by 1771. Of course, the little herbaceous carnivore was already known there. It had been described a decade earlier by Arthur Dobbs, governor of North Carolina, who called it *Fly Trap Sensitive.* Though its more imaginative name came from an Englishman, we can safely include the Venus's flytrap among the American wonders of nature.

One other American plant has been identified with Venus. *Venus's pride* (1784) is one of the many names for the *bluet, Houstonia caerulea*—a.k.a. *baby tear, diamond flower, innocence, Quaker ladies, skybloom, star violet,* and *wild forget-me-not.* But only *Venus's flytrap* (or *Venus flytrap,* as we sometimes now spell it) is a femme fatale.

(No insects were harmed in the making of this entry.)

1772 totem

Using an animal as a symbol to designate a family or individual was a custom native to both Europe and North America. To Europeans, the animal (or plant) painted on a special background was known as a *coat of arms.* To American Indians, it was a *totem.*

The word *totem*, from the Ojibwa language, was noted in a traveler's report of the early 1770s, along with its similarity to English coats of arms: "To these are added his badge, called, in the Algonquin tongue, a totem, and which is in the nature of an armorial bearing."

But there were significant differences too. The totem was more democratic than the coat of arms in that it applied to every member of the clan or tribal group, not just those belonging to the aristocracy. And it was not just a symbol but a way of life. A writer of the 1790s explains the difference: Each Indian has "his *totam,* or favourite spirit, which he believes watches over him. This *totam* they conceive assumes the shape of some beast or other, and therefore they never kill, hunt, or eat the animal whose form they think this *totam* bears."

Totem proved such a distinctive word that we now use it to characterize any object held sacred by a group because of the bond the group feels with it. At the end of the twentieth century, this could be used to refer to any object that provides or symbolizes group identity—such as a team mascot, like the Michigan Wolverine, or even a chunk of Wisconsin cheese sculpted in foam and worn on the head by fans of the Green Bay Packers.

1773 prairie

The French got there before the English, and they had a word for it: *prairie,* their name for a meadow. But what they encountered, in what is now Indiana, Illinois, Iowa, and points north and west, was more than your everyday meadow. It was a seemingly endless sea of grass as high as a person's head, teeming with flowers and bugs and other critters. And not a tree in sight.

There was nothing like this in England, and no English word for it. Besides, the French, who were the first Europeans in that part of the country, had already taken to calling it *prairie,* so *prairie* it became. In English, it is attested as early as 1773 in the journal of a traveler on the Illinois River: "The lands are much the same as before described, only the Prairies (Meadows) extend further from the river."

By the early 1800s, as more and more travelers and settlers ventured into prairie land, the parenthetical definition was no longer needed. *Prairie* became a descriptive term for the distinctive flora and fauna of these lands. It was applied to animals that took the prairie as their habitat: the prairie dog, not a dog but a rodent (1774); the prairie hen (1804) or chicken (1839), a kind of grouse, and numerous other birds, including the prairie bobolink, crane, falcon, finch, hawk, lark, owl, and warbler. Many plants also took the name *prairie*, including the prairie bean, clover, daisy, gourd, grass, onion, plum, potato, rose, sage, thistle, tomato, turnip, and willow. Settlers heading west across the prairies traveled in large COVERED WAGONS (1745) called *prairie schooners* because they looked like small ships sailing through the tall grass.

As governments were established in the prairie lands, Illinois became known as the *Prairie State*—and so did North Dakota. But the prairie celebrated in those nicknames was soon gone, converted to prime farmland by burning and draining. Only a few small remnants of the original tallgrass prairie escaped domestication. Fortunately, some of these are now being protected and restored.

1774 minuteman

Just a minute! That's how long it was supposed to take for an American patriot to leave his work, grab his firearm, and muster for duty. With the war for independence in the offing, in 1774 the Massachusetts legislature reformed its militia, removing officers sympathetic to the British and establishing seven regiments, each to be one-third "minute men" who were "to be ready at a minute's warning with a fortnight's provision, and ammunition and arms." Such were the men who were warned by Paul Revere on April 18, 1775, that the British were coming and who routed the British at the battles of Lexington and Concord the next day.

A few other colonial legislatures followed Massachusetts's example, but more important, it proclaimed to all the colonies an ideal of a citizen who was ready to drop everything and fight for independence at a moment's notice. Statues of minutemen and Minuteman National Historical Park in Lexington recall the inspirational value of the ideal.

Minuteman may be the first consciously coined Americanism. In addition to our sense of the patriotic, it appeals to our need to hurry, manifested in later American inventions like the steamboat and airplane, telegraph and television, instant replay and instant credit, microprocessors and microwave ovens, express checkout lanes and FAST FOOD (1954) drive-throughs.

The twentieth century revived the military use of *minuteman* as the name for an intercontinental ballistic missile developed by the U.S. Air Force and first tested in 1961. During a quarter century of the COLD WAR (1946), a thousand *Minuteman* missiles stood in silos in the United States, ready to fire at the Soviet Union with a moment's notice. Fortunately, unlike their American Revolution predecessors, they never were called to actual combat.

1775 on picket

In a year when we Americans were first noticed drinking eggnog and firing buckshot, we also contributed to the English language by being on picket. That activity is referred to in a letter to Nathan Hale, who later regretted that he had but one life to give for his country. At the time of the letter, during the siege of Boston, Hale had nothing more to regret than being on military duty out in the countryside, keeping watch over movements of the British army quartered in the city. The letter to Hale, dated December 10, 1775, declares, "Your being on Picquet is a sufficient excuse that you wrote no more."

As that spelling indicates, *picquet* comes from the French. Earlier in the century the British used it as a designation for sharp-ended tree trunks and posts driven into the ground to form a defensive stockade. Then *picquet* began to designate soldiers who kept watch, perhaps because they stood like picquets. Our American contribution was the phrase *on picquet,* used to mean "standing guard." We also helped change the spelling to the modern *picket* around the time of the Civil War. And in the modern world we keep the original meaning of the word alive by building picket fences.

1776 American

When our representatives in General Congress, Assembled, on July 4, 1776, declared "That these United Colonies are, and of Right ought to be, Free and Independent States," the question immediately arose: What do you call the citizens of the newly named *United States of America*? Our answer was to shorten that mouthful to its last word and add *n,* a choice that has vexed our neighbors in Canada and Mexico ever since.

For are not they too Americans? But consider the alternatives. We could be called *United Statesians*, as Canadian and English writers have suggested. Our own citizens have proposed *Usonians, Usans, Usarians, Ustatians, Unisians, Unitans, Fredonians,* and *Columbians. Columbia,* in fact, was a serious possibility for the name of our country; it was already in use in 1775 by the poet Phyllis Wheatley, and it has been a favorite of poetic patriots ever since, as in the song "Columbia, the Gem of the Ocean." That name was taken so seriously that our nation's capital is located in the District of Columbia. But to this day nobody has improved on the flatly descriptive *United States of America*, and so its people have remained *Americans.*

The name *America* had been current ever since a German cartographer, Martin Waldseemüller, named the continent after explorer and navigator Amerigo Vespucci in 1507. Colonists from England, a century later, at first reserved the designation *Americans* for the original native inhabitants. Soon, however, the descendants of English settlers felt native enough to call themselves *Americans,* thereby to distinguish themselves from English visitors or immigrants. By 1700, writers on both sides of the Atlantic were discussing what it means to be an American—referring this time to the descendants of those who came from Europe. It remained for the Declaration of Independence to change all Americans from colonists of England to citizens of their own country.

1777 Indian summer

We first encounter *Indian summer* in the essay, "A Snow Storm as it affects the American Farmer," written sometime in the 1770s by a Frenchman turned American farmer, J. Hector St. John de Crèvecoeur. Here he describes the approach of winter in the Hudson valley:

> Great rains at last replenish the springs, the brooks, the swamps, and impregnate the earth. Then a severe frost succeeds which prepares it to receive the voluminous coat of snow which is soon to follow; though it is often preceded by a short interval of smoke and mildness, called the Indian Summer. This is in general the invariable rule: winter is not said properly to begin until these few moderate days and the rising of the waters have announced it to Man.

Why the respite from the impending advance of winter was called *Indian summer* is anybody's guess—and everybody has guessed. Some of the explanations offered early in the nineteenth century after the term was well established were that it got its name because Indians predicted it, or explained it, to European settlers; that it was at a time of year when Indians moved to winter hunting grounds; even that Indians caused it by setting smoky fires to drive game out of hiding.

Whatever its origin, Indian summer became a fixture of American weather and language. In the nineteenth century it acquired literary and figurative uses as well. In 1843, for example, John Greenleaf Whittier wrote of "The Indian Summer of the heart!" while in 1867 Oliver Wendell Holmes could mention "an Indian summer of serene widowhood."

1778 lightning bug

In his *Travels through the Interior Parts of North America,* published in 1778, Jonathan Carver explains that "The Lightning Bug or Fire Fly is about the size of a bee." What a bright idea! Whichever American first thought of *lightning bug* deserves credit for a bold stroke of invention, combining the brilliance of lightning with a down-to-earth word—BUG (1785)—that the English were learning to disdain.

Firefly is the older, British, and more literary term, but it has lost its glow to the homegrown *lightning bug* in nearly every corner of the present-day United States, except the Pacific Coast and the far north.

1779 cowboy

Before it had any special application to America, *cowboy* was used in England with the obvious meaning: "a boy who took care of cows." Or he could have been a man, for *boy* implied not only youth and boyish attitudes but also low status.

Although the descriptive but uncomplimentary word *cowboy* was already around, Americans did invent two new meanings for it. The first, now forgotten meaning came during the American Revolution. It was the revolutionary patriots' term for pro-British raiders who operated in the boundary between American and British forces in Westchester County, New York. They harassed and plundered the rural districts; a later writer said, "they went around in the bushes armed with guns and tinkling a cow-bell so as to beguile the patriots into the brush hunting for cows." On the other side there were equally troublesome pro-independence raiders called *skinners.*

A quite different kind of cowboy came to national and worldwide attention after the Civil War, when for two decades thousands of cowboys drove millions of longhorn cattle from Texas to the new transcontinental railroads in Kansas and Colorado. The English speakers who first settled the Southwest had learned the skills of controlling cattle from Spanish-speaking *vaqueros,* a name translated crudely as *buckaroos.* But those who hired the minimum-wage, equal-opportunity horsemen for the big cattle drives of 1866–86 simply called them *cowboys*, a term attested as early as 1849, and that was the name that stuck. And though they were poorly paid and worked under the harshest conditions, or perhaps just because of those circumstances, the cowboy became the most enduring legend of the American West. Building on this legend, *cowboy* today still is used to mean someone who is reckless, impulsive, and dangerous. It can also be modified to mean someone who merely puts on airs of being tough or sophisticated: a *drugstore cowboy*.

1780 lynch law

If we Americans think "the courts are slow, uncertain, and unduly sympathetic with the rights of the accused," as one author wrote in 1905, what do we do about it? Nowadays we petition our legislators for stricter laws and our courts and police for stricter law enforcement. Until recently, however, our nation was notorious for quite a different solution to the problem, one that avoided the law entirely.

Lynch's law, lynch law, or just plain *lynching,* as it is now known, had its birth on the Virginia frontier in the 1780s during the American Revolution. It was named either after Captain William Lynch of Pittsylvania County or after Colonel Charles Lynch of Bedford County. It could well have been named for both, because both men independently organized their neighbors to defend their property against outlaws and disgruntled pro-British Tories. Both Lynch organizations not only captured suspicious characters but gave them fair trials and punished them if convicted. The punishment at Charles's court was usually thirty-nine lashes.

As the frontier moved westward over the course of the next century, *lynch law* moved with it. At first, *lynching* sometimes meant bringing together the citizens of a community to hear a case and mete out punishment, and the punishment was rarely capital. But in the later nineteenth century, *lynching* usually meant mob action and death by hanging or even burning. And it was not confined to the frontier; lynchings took place in every part of the country except New England. While members of all races were lynched, lynching was particularly hard on blacks in the South, who had little recourse to the law; some three thousand were lynched between 1880 and 1960. Only then, with the success of the civil rights movement, did the practice finally die out.

1781 blue laws

During the American Revolution, Connecticutters were shocked—yes, shocked!—to learn that a book by a pro-British American traitor had been published in London that portrayed their early days as grim and gloomy. Rather than celebrating Connecticut for establishing the first English-speaking self-government entirely independent of the MOTHER COUNTRY (1617), the 1781 book by the Reverend Samuel Peters condemned the harshness of Puritan laws in the seventeenth-century Commonwealth of Connecticut. He called them "Blue Laws; i.e. bloody Laws; for they were all sanctified with whippings, cutting off the ears, burning the tongue, and death." The laws of early Connecticut included, for example, a five-shilling fine for absence from church on the Lord's Day. For a burglary committed on Sunday, in addition to the usual penalties the burglar had an ear cut off, and a third Sunday burglary meant the death penalty, there being no more ears. Lying or swearing earned time in the stocks. There were fines for playing cards, dice, or shuffleboard in public. Drinkers at inns were limited to half a pint of wine, and no alcohol was served after 9 P.M.

Peters says the early colonists spoke of laws like these as *blue laws,* but the term seems to be his own invention. It is thanks to his *General History of Connecticut* that *blue laws* entered the language as a term for laws that enforce a strict morality and godly behavior. Peters also set the tone of disapproval that *blue laws* conveys; to label a law a *blue law* is to imply that it is a vain attempt to enforce old-fashioned Puritan morality and is probably an invasion of privacy and infringement of liberty to boot.

Later authors adopted the term *blue laws* for their own criticisms of laws they saw as unduly harsh or moralistic, but some imagined a milder origin. *Blue,* they claimed, came simply from the blue paper on which the laws were supposedly printed, or the blue covers in which they were supposedly bound.

1782 belittle

In our infancy as a nation, to balance our sense of grandeur and moral superiority, we had a little bit of an inferiority complex. We lacked the corruption of the Old World, but also its sophistication. We were country cousins at the courts of Europe. But at least we had our grand spectacles of nature: forests and mountains, lakes and waterfalls, teeming herds and flocks of animals stranger and more numerous than any seen in the worn-out continents on the other side of the ocean.

Or did we? Our sense of American pride was especially stung by a condescending European notion that even our wildlife was inferior. Thomas Jefferson could not let this insult pass unchallenged. "So far the Count de Buffon has carried this new theory of the tendency of nature to belittle her productions on this side the Atlantic," Jefferson wrote in 1782 in his *Notes on the State of Virginia.* Jefferson then replied to the buffoonish count, expounding for many pages on the grandness of American animals, noting in particular the enormous bones of the mammoth, so much bigger than those of any Old World elephant. (In 1802 the MAMMOTH would come to life in the American vocabulary in a new way, thanks also to Jefferson.)

For this defense, Jefferson himself was belittled—because of his use of the very word *belittle.* Jefferson, apparently, was the inventor of *belittle,* and *Notes* was its first appearance in print. The *European Magazine and London Review* denounced the word so strongly that decades later American commentators on American English still claimed that nobody but Jefferson used it. They were wrong, however. *Belittle* had become an unobjectionable word on both sides of the Atlantic before the nineteenth century was half over. Today nobody belittles *belittle*.

1783 passenger pigeon

"Viewed from all angles, the passenger pigeon was the most impressive species of bird that man has known," wrote ornithologist A.W. Schorger in 1952. "Elegant in form and color, graceful and swift of flight, it moved about and nested in such enormous numbers as to confound the senses."

The name *passenger pigeon* appears first in a book probably written in 1783 and published in London in 1784: *Arctic Zoology* by Thomas Pennant. He was English, but the bird and the information about it unquestionably came from America, so we can claim *passenger pigeon* for our own. *Passenger* means "migratory," a distinguishing characteristic of the pigeons being their annual migrations in great flocks over great distances. As early as 1731 they were termed *pigeons of passage,* but that name was completely replaced in the nineteenth century by the more succinct *passenger pigeon.*

Long before 1783 or 1731, however, these creatures, going simply by the name of *pigeons* or *doves,* amazed newcomers to North America. They were hard to overlook. "I have seene them fly as if the Ayerie regiment had beene Pigeons," wrote a New Englander in 1624, "seeing neyther beginning nor ending, length, or breadth of these Millions of Millions."

In 1823 a skyful of passenger pigeons made a cameo appearance in James Fenimore Cooper's *The Pioneers,* a historical novel about upstate New York circa 1794. "Here is a flock that the eye cannot see at the end of," exclaims one character. "There is food enough in it to keep the army of Xerxes for a month, and feathers enough to make beds for the whole country." That novel also shows how the passenger pigeon could become extinct by 1914. For the fun of it, the pioneers slaughter as many of the pigeons as they can, using guns, arrows, rocks, and even long poles. The waste disgusts frontiersman Natty Bumppo, but the killing goes on.

Two centuries after Natty Bumppo, when astronomer Carl Sagan urged us to look up at the skies, there was no such migration to block the view. There are "billions and billions" of stars, Sagan told us. But the passenger pigeons, which also once numbered in the billions, were gone for good.

1784 poison ivy

You can look, but you'd better not touch. England knew ivy, but nothing so irritating. In 1784 the first volume of *Memoirs of the American Academy of Arts and Sciences* described Hedera or Poison Ivy as producing "inflammations and eruptions." The name *Hedera* did not stick, but *poison ivy* did.

Only the name was new in 1784. Captain John Smith, for one, had known of the plant in 1624 when he published his *Generall Historie of Virginia,* though he mentioned it in regard to Bermuda. To him *poison* seemed too strong a word: "The poysoned weed is much in shape like our English Ivy, but being but touched, causeth rednesse, itching, and lastly blisters, the which howsoever after a while passe away of themselves without further harme, yet because for the time they are somewhat painfull, it hath got itselfe an ill name, although questionlesse of no ill nature."

1785 bug

"Indeed," George Washington wrote in his diary in 1785, "some kind of fly, or bug, had begun to prey upon the leaves before I left home." The father of our country was not the father of *bug*. When Washington wrote that entry, Englishmen had been referring to insects as *bugs* for more than a century, and we Americans had already created LIGHTNING BUG (1778). But the English were soon to get rid of the *bugs* in their language, leaving it to the Americans to call a bug a *bug* in the nineteenth and twentieth centuries.

We got *bug* in our ears in other ways too. The American *bug* could also be a person, an enthusiast or fanatic, as the *Congressional Globe* records in 1841: "Mr. Alford of Georgia warned the 'tariff bugs'  of the South that . . . he would read them out of church." And although *fan* became the usual term, sports enthusiasts were *racing bugs* (1908), *baseball bugs* (1911), and the like. And a bug could be just plain insane (1884), confined to a bughouse (1899).

Or the bug could be a small machine or object: a telegraph key (1929); a clip used by a card sharp to hold cards under the table (1883); even a car, the small, bug-shaped, trademarked Volkswagen beetle (1960). The bug could also be a burglar alarm (1926), from which comes the expression *to bug*, that is, originally "to install an alarm," now a surveillance device like a hidden microphone. Since the 1840s *to bug* has long meant "to cheat," and since the 1940s it has been annoying.

We also know the bug as a flaw in a computer program or other design. That meaning traces back long before computers to the laboratory of inventor Thomas Edison. In 1878 he explained bugs as "little faults and difficulties" that require "months of anxious watching, study and labor" to overcome in developing a successful product. In 1889 it was recorded that Edison "had been up the two previous nights discovering 'a bug' in his phonograph."

Don't bug us for more definitions, or we'd have to fill the whole book with bugs.

1786 dime

A year before the Constitutional Convention determined what kind of government we wanted for the United States of America, we had already made up our mind about our money: dollars and dimes. On August 8, 1786, an ordinance of the

Continental Congress called for "Mills, Cents, Dimes, Dollars," with *dime* explained as "the lowest silver coin, ten of which shall be equal to the dollar."

Thomas Jefferson has been credited with proposing the names for the coins of the new nation. Among them was *disme,* based on the French word for "tenth," *dixième.* He suggested that *disme* be pronounced as if it were spelled *deem.* But the *s* was dropped by Congress, and the adopted spelling *dime* suggested pronunciation in keeping with *time* and *rime.*

Since then, *dimes* have been dropping all over our language. In the mid-nineteenth century, *dimes* was often a slang word for money, and the first of the sensational dime novels was published. In the twentieth century, *dime* has been used as slang for ten and even one thousand dollars, as well as for a ten-year prison sentence. We shopped at dime stores (1931). We learned to get off the dime (to get moving, 1925; originally of dancers in a dance hall) and to drop a dime (make a call on a ten-cent pay telephone, and hence to inform on someone, 1966). The latter is still current, even though phone calls cost more than a dime and are more and more often made on cellular phones.

1787 abolition

In the late eighteenth century, as slavery and the slave trade grew, so did the number of voices arguing against them. In the very year that the United States Constitution was drafted, with its euphemistic acceptance of slavery (slaves are designated as "all other persons" and counted in the census as three-fifths of a free person), a church synod in New York and Pennsylvania was calling for "the abolition of slavery." Before long the word *abolition* by itself came to mean the movement to end slavery. As arguments over slavery in the United States heated up in the early 1800s, so did the use and significance of *abolition.* In his 1845 autobiography, the escaped slave and renowned orator Frederick Douglass tells of the potency of the word for a twelve-year-old slave in Baltimore:

If a slave ran away and succeeded in getting clear, or if a slave killed his master, set fire to a barn, or did any thing very wrong in the mind of a slaveholder, it was spoken of as the fruit of abolition. Hearing the word in this connection very often, I set about learning what it meant. The dictionary afforded me little or no help. I found it was "the act of abolishing;" but then I did not know what was to be abolished. . . . After a patient waiting, I got one of our city papers, containing an account of the number of petitions from the north, praying for the abolition of slavery in the District of Columbia, and of the slave trade between the States. From this time I understood the words abolition and abolitionist, and always drew near when that word was spoken, expecting to hear something of importance. . . .

With the abolition of American slavery in 1865, this use of the word became just a historical footnote. *Abolition* could then have been taken up by the movement to abolish the sale of alcoholic beverages, but *temperance* was already doing that job.

1788 squatter

In 1788, while he was encouraging ratification of a Constitution that would "establish Justice" and "insure domestic Tranquility," future president James Madison took time to complain about those who set up households and farms without proper authorization: "Many of them and their constituents are only squatters upon other people's land, and they are afraid of being brought to account." To say the least, *squatter* was an undignified word, chosen presumably to express disapproval of the practice.

But such was life on the uncivilized frontier, and such was often the way the frontier became settled and civilized. "This settling on land which belongs to another person, and clearing and cultivating it without leave, is called Squatting," explained a writer in 1824.

And not everyone objected. "It is the fashion to speak slightly of these Pioneers, Squatters, Crackers, or whatever name it pleases them most to be called by," wrote a traveler in

1829, "but I must own that I was well satisfied with almost every one of them whom I encountered."

The fierce independence of the squatters led in the late 1840s to the notion of squatter sovereignty, by which settlers in a territory would be entitled to make their own laws. The Kansas-Nebraska Act of 1854 applied squatter sovereignty to those two states in the matter of slavery, resulting in six years of battles in "bleeding Kansas," a prelude to the Civil War.

Nowadays, with the frontier gone, squatters are more likely to be found in abandoned urban buildings than in the country, but they remain part of the American landscape.

1789 immigrant

The American-coined designation *immigrant* made its appearance in 1789 in Jedidiah Morse's book *The American Geography.* Referring to New York State, he noted, "There are in this state many immigrants from Scotland, Ireland, Germany, and some few from France." *Immigrate* was a verb already at home in English, but the noun *immigrant* was a new arrival.

It was the year of the founding of the modern United States, when the Constitution went into effect. *E pluribus unum,* "one from many," became not only motto but policy, as thirteen sovereign states made themselves one country, populated by immigrants or the descendants of immigrants. Even the American Indians could argue for being immigrants, the first to move to the Americas, thousands of years before the rest of us.

The number of immigrants to the United States has remained substantial throughout our history. In 1850, the first year the official census took notice of foreign born, they amounted to nearly 10 percent of the 23,192,000 inhabitants. In 1900 foreign born were more than 14 percent of 76 million inhabitants; in 1950 nearly 7 percent of 151 million; in 1990 nearly 8 percent of a total population of 248,710,000. Even in the twentieth century, with more restrictions than before, many hundreds of thousands of immigrants have arrived nearly every year.

The importance of immigrants to America was acknowledged in 1809 by Edward Kendall in his *Travels through the Northern Parts of the United States:* "*Immigrant* is perhaps the only new word, of which the circumstances of the United States has in any degree demanded the addition to the English language." In England, reflecting the Old World preoccupation with reasons for leaving a country, *emigrant* has been widely used for persons entering as well as leaving, but the United States looks to the future, not the past, of the immigrants who arrive.

1790 reservation

A seemingly routine use of the familiar word *reservation* in 1789 led to its acquisition of a new meaning a year or two later. Attempting to clear up questions of federal and state authority with regard to Indians, the First Congress of the United States under the new Constitution stipulated, "The reservation, in the treaty with the [Iroquois] Six Nations, of six miles square round the fort at Oswego, is within the territory of the State of New York, and ought to be so explained as to render it conformable to the Constitution of the United States."

That was the beginning. Soon *reservation* became an everyday word for the places to which Indian tribes were assigned to get them out of the way of onrushing settlers.

The new concept of reservation provided Americans of European descent with a legal justification for depriving Indians of most of the continent and confining them to remote areas considered less desirable by whites. Formerly Indians exercised sovereignty on lands to which the colonial governments made only minimal claims. Now the ultimate authority over all the land belonged to the United States. The reservations were often arranged by treaty, but the U.S. government retained the right to renegotiate treaties, and it almost never renegotiated them to benefit Indians. While some tribes were collected onto shrinking remnants of their traditional lands, many others were removed from their homes to a patchwork of reservations in the so-called Indian territory, now part of Oklahoma.

At the end of the nineteenth century the government passed laws that broke the reservations into individual homesteads, encouraging impoverished occupants to sell their property. As a result of this and other policies, Indian reservations shrank dramatically and now comprise roughly 2 percent of their original holdings.

Nevertheless, many Indian peoples have adapted to living on reservations and learned to see them as sanctuaries for their traditional culture and self-determination.

1791 fishing pole

Although in the eighteenth century Americans were busy asserting independence, inventing a new government, and rearranging the continent, we found time to go fishing too. And we were not entirely satisfied with the *fishing rod* of the English. Some of us preferred a *fishing pole,* as in New Englander

"Nailer Tom's" journal for 1791: "I broke my Fishing Pole Cought 4 Pickrel 3 Eels and 6 Trout." By 1834 we find *fish pole* too, this time in Texas.

1792 logrolling

It began as a down-to-earth pioneer word. Preparing a homestead in the wilderness meant chopping down trees to clear a field for planting. Neighbors would come for the day to roll the logs into a pile, either to burn them or to construct a log cabin. And it was a social occasion. From 1792 we have a remark that "The standard dinner dish at log-rollings, house-raisings, and harvest days, was a large pot-pie."

Logrolling was a way to get settled quickly. "A family comes to sit down in the forest," wrote an observer in 1835. "Their neighbors lay down their employments, shoulder their axes, and come in to the log-rolling. They spend the day in hard labor, and then retire, leaving the newcomers their good wishes, and an habitation."

Politicians have long recognized that logrolling is mutually beneficial in legislative halls too. The word was applied to the political practice of reciprocal backscratching as early as 1809.

1793 Anglophobia

The American Revolution had scarcely ended when the French tried one of their own. It began peacefully enough with the calling of the Estates General in 1788, but by 1793 the clergy and nobility had lost all privileges, the king had lost his head, and the National Assembly was calling on the peoples of Europe to rise up and regain their liberty. Naturally, the other European governments were at war with France.

Across the Atlantic, memories of our own Revolutionary War were fresh, when the British had been our enemy and the French our allies. So there were "peals of exultation" from the crowd in May 1793 when a French frigate arrived at the wharves of Philadelphia with a captured British ship. But

President George Washington recognized the importance of the United States remaining neutral so we could trade with all parties, and Secretary of State Thomas Jefferson agreed. With regard to discussions among the president's advisors, Jefferson wrote from Philadelphia on May 13, "We are going on here in the same spirit still. The Anglophobia has seized violently on three members of our council. This sets almost every day on questions of neutrality." Later in the letter, while again mentioning Anglophobia, or "fear of the English," he also complained of "secret anti-gallomany," or "opposition to France."

America's love-hate relationship with the MOTHER COUNTRY (1617) continued throughout the nineteenth century and would be reflected also in the use of *Anglophile,* meaning "admirer of things English," coined a century later (by the English).

The modern American use of *Anglo* (without a suffix) has little to do with England. In the southwestern United States, *Anglo* means anyone who is not of Hispanic or Indian descent. It is a word originally used by HISPANICS (1889) but now generally adopted in the region.

1794 cavort

Barely was our nation founded when we began what we called *cavorting.* And a curious word it was too, mentioned with something of an apology when it was used by a North Carolinian in a letter in 1794: "The Hon. J—e 'cauvauted', don't laugh at the expression, it suits the idea I meant to convey." Nobody knows where the word came from, but we know the idea it conveyed: acting up, prancing about, carrying on.

And there was plenty of cavorting as the country expanded westward. An Illinois magazine in 1830 said *cavort* "expresses the conduct of an individual who fancies himself the smartest and best man in the world." And a boasting speech of 1831 declared, "I'm a ring-tail roarer, all the way from Salt River. So, none of your cockloftical cavorting about me, or I'll be into you like a streak of lightning." The FRONTIER (1676) is gone now, but we still know how to cavort.

1795 progress

Ben Franklin couldn't stand *to progress,* but when the Father of our Country said it, again and again, what could we do but progress too?

To progress was nothing new to English or Americans. During the eighteenth century, however, the verb had fallen out of favor with the English, and also with Franklin.

Franklin disliked the verb that was "formed from the Substantive *Progress,*" as in "The committee, having Progressed, resolved to adjourn." This verb, Franklin declared, was "most awkward and abominable."

Meanwhile, however, President Washington was making great progress with that very verb. "Our country," he wrote in 1791 when the country was all of two years old, "is fast progressing in its political importance and social happiness." In 1796 he was still at it, writing of his pleasure at hearing that an acquaintance was progressing in his studies. Twenty years later, in 1816, in the first book devoted to the subject of American English, John Pickering could declare of "this obsolete English word" that it "has had an extraordinary currency for the last twenty or thirty years."

We have progressed ever since and have maintained our belief in the associated noun *progress.* The twentieth century has echoed to the advertising slogan, "Progress is our most important product."

1796 stenographer

No, we Americans did not invent shorthand, or *stenography.* The art of quick abbreviated writing was known to the ancient Romans and to the English of Queen Elizabeth's time, when in 1602 John Willis published a book called *The Art of Stenographie, teaching . . . the way of compendious Writing.*

But we can claim to have originated the job of stenographer. It is mentioned in the records of the Fourth Congress for 1796: "He also adverted to the attempt at the last session to introduce a stenographer into the House, which failed." Early in the next century, Washington Irving referred to the occupation in an issue of the *Knickerbocker* for 1809: "My predecessors, who were furnished, as I am told, with the speeches of all their heroes taken down in shorthand by the most accurate stenographers of the time." More recently, Americans also originated the slang abbreviations *stenog* (1906) and *steno* (1925) for the people who did the writing.

The nineteenth century begat an American invention called the *stenograph,* a machine for typing in shorthand. It was especially welcomed by court reporters. But even in the twentieth century, stenographers in business offices generally took notes by hand. By the end of the century, dictating machines and computers had begun to encroach on the work of stenographers, but voice-recognition software was not yet developed enough to render them obsolete.

1797 bogus

Around the time we were getting used to being a new nation, we Americans contributed something bogus to the English language. At first, apparently, it was only money. A glossary defining *bogus* as a "spurious coin" was published in 1798, indicating that the word must have been coined at least as early as 1797. Its origins are obscure, but one guess that is as good as any is that it is from *boko,* meaning "deceit" or "fake" in the Hausa language of west central Africa. The word then would have been brought over by Africans sold into slavery here.

Once it was introduced into our language, the word *bogus* circulated widely, and it began to count for more than coins. A machine to make bogus coins was also called a *bogus,* at least in Painesville, Ohio, in 1827. By 1848 *bogus* could be counterfeit paper money too. In fact, by midcentury, *bogus* could be anything fake, as it is nowadays. For example, we read of a bogus legislature in 1852, bogus lottery tickets in 1856, bogus life insurance companies in 1859, bogus jewelry in 1860, and a bogus piano tuner in 1887. Since the late nineteenth century it has also meant something that is simply no good, a use of *bogus* that persists in slang of the present day.

1798 veteran

After the American Revolution, a new meaning for the old word *veteran* helped us express our appreciation for the soldiers who had fought for our independence. Formerly *veteran* had just meant "someone with experience," as it can nowadays. But we began to use *veteran* also to designate ex-servicemen, those who had completed military service rather than those who were still in it. A book published in 1798 states in its preface, "The Author has gone near to offend the veterans of the American army who were present on the first night." Our new meaning for the word gave veterans a certain respect after their retirement from soldiering and earned them not only gratitude but practical benefits from their country.

Starting with the American Revolution, the federal government has provided veterans with pensions, land, hospital care, and preference in hiring, the particular benefits depending on the temper of the times and the lobbying of the veterans themselves. By 1848 we were using the affectionate abbreviation *vets.* In the twentieth century, the federal government established a Veterans' Administration to deliver benefits. November 11, the Armistice Day commemorating the end of World War I in 1918, was officially renamed *Veterans' Day* in 1954.

1799 revival

We Americans not only got religion, we got it again and again. We got it in the 1600s, when the New England colonies were founded for religious reasons. We got it again at the start of the next century, when in 1702 Cotton Mather of Massachusetts remarked on "a notable Revival of Religion." Yet again, in the 1730s, what would become known as the AWAKENING (1736) of religious spirit began in Northampton, Massachusetts, and for several decades spread throughout the colonies as far north as Maine and as far south as Georgia.

But something more immediate and practical was meant by *revival* when the word was first used by itself with a religious meaning in 1799. That was when the Presbyterian preacher James McGready took religion out to the wilderness of Kentucky. Instead of going from isolated cabin to cabin, he held revivals that lasted several days and attracted settlers from miles around. McGready would preach, baptize, and marry, while the settlers joined in the praying and singing and caught up on the neighborhood gossip. These gatherings were also called *camp meetings* because families would camp overnight rather than return to their homes during the days of the revival.

McGready's revivals were a great success and soon imitated throughout the country. The whole nineteenth century became a time of revivals in America, some of them lasting as long as two or three weeks. Even the more secular twentieth century has had its share of revivals.

1800 misstep

Was the new spirit of American independence making us kinder and gentler? Or were we merely anticipating the coming era of Victorian prudery on both sides of the Atlantic? Whatever the explanation, *misstep* was an American invention.

Misstep took the place of an older English term, *false step,* which in turn derived from French *faux pas.* Instead of being false, that is, the misstep was just a slip, a little mistake instead of something blatantly wrong. Forgiveness would be that much easier, and so would a new start.

And forgiveness might be needed, considering the meaning these words modestly concealed. In its early days, *misstep* was a euphemism for a euphemism. Like as not, *misstep* meant a young woman's "losing her virtue," as evidenced by her pregnancy. This is the *misstep* discussed in a publication of about 1800 from Walpole, New Hampshire. "The Squire," says *The Spirit of the Farmers' Museum, and Lay Preacher's Gazette,* "can Sit on the Sessions, and fine poor Girls for natural missteps." Similarly, at the end of the nineteenth century we find an article in *Harper's Magazine* that comments on Thomas Hardy's

Tess of the D'Urbervilles with a delicate mention of "the first misstep of Tess in the immaturity of her girlhood."

In the more sexually explicit twentieth century, that veiled meaning of *misstep* would be misunderstood. But we have plenty of ordinary slipups from which we hope to escape with the least possible amount of blame and embarrassment, so *misstep* finds itself still actively employed as a gentler alternative to *mistake*.

MAMMOTH

ENTERPRISE:

1801-1865

*B*y leaps and bounds in the first part of the nineteenth
century, the newly created slow-moving United States
that stretched along the Atlantic became the high-speed, coast-
to-coast nation we know today, its inhabitants traveling by
train and steamboat and communicating instantly by telegraph. By purchase, treaty, or just plain war we gobbled great
chunks of land formerly held by France, Spain, and Mexico, so
that the United States dipped down to the Rio Grande and
stretched all the way across to the Pacific. We grappled with
slavery, first watching it spread to its greatest extent, then de-
stroying it forever in the bloodiest war our nation has ever
known. At the end of it all, *United States* was a singular instead of a plural.

It was a huge undertaking, aptly characterized by the word
mammoth (1802), which referred to the giant prehistoric creature whose bones so fascinated Thomas Jefferson as proof that
nature was more robust in the New World than in the old. In
the 1800s, we learned to use *mammoth* for anything big. If we

were ill, we sought a *cure-all* (1821). We went *whole hog* (1828).

Other new words during the first part of the nineteenth century reflected this extravagance too. A whole new category of slang engaged our amused attention. We added *rowdy* (1808), for example, and *cuss* (1815), *ornery* (1816), *sockdolager* (1827), *high muck-a-muck* (1856), and *shindig* (1857). In politics, the famous *gerrymander* (1812) was invented, *bunkum* (1819) was spoken, and the *filibuster* (1852) got a name. And we had both *hoosiers* (1833) and *know-how* (1838).

As the West opened up, we talked of *pioneers* (1817) and the *tenderfoot* (1849) and borrowed from the Spanish the words *ranch* (1831), *rodeo* (1844), *hobo* (1847), *cafeteria* (1853), and *vigilante* (1860), among others.

Northern and Southern differences over slavery were reflected in *slave driver* (1807), *underground railroad* (1843), and the song *Dixie* (1859), sung for the first time at a minstrel show in New York City. The Civil War, ending and consolidating this period, brought us *greenback* (1862) and *deadline* (1864). Unfortunately, *Jim Crow* (1829) was only beginning to flourish.

Our customs and way of life changed, reflected in words like *cocktail* (1806), *cookbook* (1809), *drugstore* (1810), *editorial* (1830), *downtown* (1836), *Christmas tree* (1837), *bloomers* (1851), *bluejeans* (1855), and finally the *commuter* (1865). Even literary figures got into the act with their novel usages like *loaf* (1835) and *tintinnabulation* (1845).

This most expansionist of American eras also saw the birth of the most expansionist Americanism of all, *OK* (1839). Typically for this era, it began as an extravagant joke, a wacky misspelling of *all correct* in a Boston newspaper. From the start, *OK* went beyond the bounds of decent spelling and grammar. Is it a word? an abbreviation? an adjective, a verb, a noun, or an interjection? How do you spell it? But whatever *OK* is, it has succeeded more than any other American innovation in the vocabulary. A century and a half later, it punctuates not only our own conversations but languages throughout the world.

1801 spook

Ghosts have abounded in folklore and literature for centuries, but the English language was not troubled by *spook*s until we imported them from our Dutch or German neighbors at the start of the nineteenth century. We find the noun *spook* in an American poem with a Dutch or German accent, printed in the *Massachusetts Spy* for July 15, 1801:

> If any wun you heart shool plunder,
> Mine horshes I'll to Vaggon yoke,
> Und chase him quickly;—by mine dunder
> I fly so swift as any spook.

As a verb, too, *spook* was an American innovation, also making its appearance in a poem. This is from James Russell Lowell's "Fitz Adam's Story" (1867): "Yet still the New World spooked it in his veins, A ghost who could not lay with all his pains."

Thanks to *spook,* a host of related specters haunt our language now. We felt spooky as long ago as 1854. In the twentieth century, we speak of spooking animals, putting them in a state of mind to panic or stampede. During World War II Americans began using *spook* as slang for "spy." After the war, *spooky* was used by surfers to label a large dangerous wave.

1802 mammoth

Until the presidency of Thomas Jefferson, *mammoth* had been just the name of a huge extinct elephant-like creature whose bones had been discovered in many places on the continent. It was a Russian name, borrowed into English in the previous century for a similar animal whose remains had been found in Siberia. Jefferson was especially fond of our mammoth because it showed the superiority of nature in America over the runty creatures of Europe.

When he moved into the President's House—later known as the WHITE HOUSE (1811)—in Washington in 1801, President

Jefferson remarked that the large unfinished east room was big enough to hold a mammoth. And when the farmers of Cheshire, Massachusetts, in honor of the new president, used the milk of 900 "Republican cows" to create a cheese weighing 1200 pounds and delivered it to him on New Year's Day in 1802, he put it in that mammoth room of the President's House. To observers, it seemed like a mammoth cheese indeed. *Mammoth* thus became generalized as a word of great size, suited to the rapidly expanding nation. Appropriately, Jefferson had the mammoth cheese served on July 4, 1803, in celebration of the Louisiana Purchase, a mammoth addition to American territory.

In a non-election peacetime year, the mammoth cheese was big news. And thanks to the cheese, the long-extinct mammoth came to life in the popular imagination. A baker offered "Mammoth bread" for sale in 1802. In 1813, it was reported that "the Mammoth bank bill passed the senate this day on a third reading." In 1824, a Massachusetts newspaper declared, "The last load, as we Yankees say, was a 'Mammoth': . . . producing an aggregate of nearly twelve cords."

By 1842, an English traveler writing about the Southern states could report "the custom of this country to call every thing very large by the epithet of 'mammoth'; so that one hears of a mammoth cake, a mammoth pie, a mammoth oyster." There are examples of a mammoth advertisement in 1883, a mammoth dam in 1907, and so on to the mammoth sales of the present day. No other North American animal, living or dead, has had such mammoth success as an adjective.

1803 stud

The English language was studded with *stud*s long before anyone spoke it in America. There were wooden studs like those now used in framing houses and studs that were bumps, knobs, buttons, or nailheads. And as long ago as the year 1000 there were studs in England that were places for breeding horses.

But Americans can claim one proud innovation for *stud*: originating the sense "a stallion, a male horse used for breeding." An American, the Reverend Manasseh Cutler, LL.D., in 1803 wrote of "the famous white stud, an Arabian horse, called the Dey of Algiers, on the ground." In 1845 the *Knickerbocker* reported, "A very large stud broke from the line." In 1891 a visitor to America wrote, "He was a stud, and as fine a horse of his class as I ever saw."

Somehow also in the late nineteenth century our *stud* (or the related word *studhorse*) became the name for a variety of poker. In stud poker, every card after the first is dealt face up so the other players can see it. Perhaps its exhibitionistic quality suggests the stud, or perhaps it just requires horse sense.

Late in the nineteenth century, *stud* was used as a term for a "ladies' man," a sexually attractive or promiscuous man. And by the 1920s, black Americans had generalized the usage to refer to any young man, regardless of sexual behavior, as in the 1970 book *Positively Black*: "But who's this stud they call Billy?" We also learned to use *stud* as an adjective to mean "fine or outstanding," as well as "manly." Stud was one word that wouldn't be kept down on the farm.

1804 tornado

A tornado is a storm with a twist, and the word *tornado* took several twists before it landed with its current meaning in the United States. It comes ultimately from the Spanish for thunderstorm, *tronada,* turned into *ternado* by English sailors in the 1500s to mean "a violent tropical storm."

Americans brought it ashore to describe the destructive whirlwinds distinctive to our continent. In 1804 a newspaper in Fredericktown, Maryland, gave a precise description of a "Tornado" that went through a village: "Within the vortex before the cloud a column of thick vapour, very black, extending from the earth to the heighth of about 40 feet, and advancing rapidly in the direction of this place was discovered by several inhabitants."

In the twentieth century, such a storm has also been called a *twister,* as in the 1996 movie of that name, but *tornado* still carries more weight.

1805 artery

Thomas Jefferson did it again. He seems to have been the first to think of arteries not just as routes for flow of blood in the human body but as routes for flow of trade and transport through the body of a continent. Rivers, he thought, were arteries of transportation. In 1805 he wrote, "We shall delineate with correctness the great arteries of this great country." James Fenimore Cooper was not far behind. In his novel *The Prairie,* published in 1827, he wrote of "The mighty arteries of the Missouri and Mississippi."

Not content with nature's arteries, by the midcentury Americans were busy building their own artificial ones. In his 1850 journal of Army life, published later in San Francisco, one writer admired "those great arteries of commerce—the railroads."

In the twentieth century, this time to accommodate automobiles and trucks instead of trains, the United States developed yet another system of arteries, beginning with the U.S. highways and augmented by the Interstates.

1806 cocktail

Among the most notable of American inventions, ranking at least with Coca-Cola (1887) and homogenized milk (1904), is the concoction known as the *cocktail*. In 1806 a newspaper in Hudson, New York, defined it as "a stimulating liquor, composed of spirits of any kind, sugar, water, and bitters—it is vulgarly called *bittered sling,* and is supposed to be an excellent electioneering potion." The occasions for drinking a cocktail have expanded beyond political campaigns, and the recipe has varied ever since, limited only by the imagination of the bartender and the supply of liquor on hand. In the mid-twentieth century H. L. Mencken defined *cocktail* simply as "any hard liquor, any milder diluent and a dash of any pungent flavoring." By then it had became so renowned that, with tongue only slightly in cheek, Mencken could assert that "to multitudes of foreigners" the cocktail "seems to be the greatest symbol of American life."

Where the name *cocktail* came from is anyone's guess, but that has not stopped its devotees from imagining. Perhaps its source is *coquetier,* French for "egg cup." Perhaps its source is *cock ale*, an English drink said to consist of ale and chicken broth. Perhaps not.

The many kinds of cocktails have acquired their own names. The Manhattan (1890) was named for a hotel in the heart of New York City. The Martini (1894) reportedly gets its name from the well-known Martini brand of vermouth. And the Old-Fashioned (1901) uses the original (1806), now "old fashioned" cocktail recipe.

In the twentieth century, *cocktail* gained wider use in compounds like *cocktail hour* (1927), *cocktail party* (1928), *cocktail dress* (1935), and *cocktail lounge* (1939). The word also extended its meaning to encompass any stimulating mixture, evidenced by terms like *fruit cocktail* (1928), *shrimp cocktail*

(1960), and the explosive *Molotov cocktail* (1939). At the less hard-drinking end of the century, it is perhaps in such nonalcoholic combinations that the word will survive.

1807 slave driver

There was no ignoring slavery in early nineteenth-century America. In the North it was dying out, and abolitionists were beginning to speak against it; but in the South slavery was more profitable than ever, thanks to the growth of cotton plantations worked by slave labor. In 1807 the British abolished the import-export slave trade, and in 1808, after a twenty-year wait imposed by Article 1, section 9 of the Constitution, the United States did too, but the number of native-born slaves continued to increase and restrictions on them grew harsher.

As if to emphasize the inhumanity of slavery, just as there were drivers of cattle, so there were drivers of slaves, a word used as early as 1763 for those who literally whipped slaves to work. The combination *slave driver,* oddly enough, appears first in an 1807 satire by Washington Irving that seems to have nothing to do with American slavery. It is a purported letter "to Asem Hacchem, Principal Slave-Driver to His Highness the Bashaw of Tripoli" from his American agent. The letter directs its satire at the liberated women of New York City, not at slavery, but the ascription of "Slave-Driver" to a notorious realm of pirates implies a recognition of its barbarity.

It was an epithet to provoke a fight. In 1856, during the battle for "bleeding Kansas" between pro- and antislavery settlers, an abolitionist prayer in a Maryland newspaper asked, "Our Heavenly Father . . . help us to shiver the Union into atoms rather than to concede to Southern demons, in the form of slave-drivers, one inch of the disputed territory."

Slavery fortunately is long gone, but the slave driver lives on today in the form of the merciless taskmaster. And as Henry David Thoreau points out in the first chapter of *Walden* (1846), this person is not necessarily an employer:

"It is hard to have a southern overseer; it is worse to have a northern one; but worst of all when you are the slave-driver of yourself."

1808 rowdy

Nobody has been more rowdy than Americans. We have Kentucky lawyer and humorist William Littell to thank for the first evidence of it: "It seems to this court that the loss to him would be the same, as if he had lost it among those, whom his gentlemanship is pleased to call *rowdies*." This was in an 1808 collection called *Festoons of Fancy, Consisting of Compositions Amatory, Sentimental, and Humorous, in Verse and Prose*. His ironic treatment of the word implies that it is ungentlemanly, and his emphatic treatment of it suggests that it is new.

Soon, however, the nineteenth century was filled with American rowdies—especially in Kentucky. We have a report about "the Rowdies of Kentucky" in 1823, saying that they "frequently decoy travelers, supposed to have money, out of the road, and then shoot them." In that year an English traveler complained, "A line of houses on the lonely road to Missouri is ... kept up by these Rowdey robbers and murderers for the reception of travellers, and villains to rob them." In 1844 the *Lexington Observer* reported that "a gang of drunken rowdies attacked a Methodist Camp Meeting." Elsewhere, in 1842 the *Chicago American* warned, "Let the police be more energetic ... or we shall soon gain a reputation for rowdyism." That became a student problem, according to the *University of Chicago Weekly* in 1894: "A few of the 'Varsity students in a fit of pique allowed rowdyism to overcome their collegiate training." And in 1885, a century before the civilizing arrival of Walt Disney World, the Orlando, Florida, *Sentinel* wrote that "Every portion of Orlando ... [demands] protection from rowdies by our police."

To this day rowdy behavior is not unknown to college students and others, whether merrymakers or protesters. But *rowdy* has long lost its murderous edge, and now describes a milder form of disruption.

1809 cookbook

What has been commonly called a *cookery book* in England since at least 1639 has been known in America as a *cookbook* since at least 1809. The first evidence is in the writing of Royall Tyler, in his *Yankey in London:* "I can send you an assortment of culinary reviews, vulgarly called cook-books."

Whether the American term derives from its English forebear or is a loan translation from German, as in the form so widely used in eastern Pennsylvania, is uncertain from the evidence. *Kochbuch* from German and *kookboek* from Dutch both are possible sources.

Among the most famed of American cookbooks was *The Boston Cooking School Cook Book,* first published in 1896 by Fannie Merritt Farmer at her own expense. The publisher quickly seized upon her name as a prominent feature of authority and the book has been in print ever since. The last sentence of the preface to the first edition reads, "It is my wish that it may not only be looked upon as a compilation of tried and tested recipes, but that it may awaken an interest through its condensed scientific knowledge which will lead to deeper thought and broader study of what to eat. F.M.F." Through her cookbook, Fannie Farmer introduced to our language terms such as *level teaspoon* and *measuring cup.* For her, cooking was a science that relied upon careful measurement and cookbooks were reliable guides even for the inexperienced chef.

1810 drugstore

Apothecary had been used in England since the Middle Ages as a name for a purveyor of medication, and *pharmacy* was coined there too, but it took American marketing savvy to invent such a potent term as *drugstore.* This new compound combined American STORE (1721), rather than British *shop,* with a down-to-earth bluntness about what was sold using the simple word *drug* that has always fascinated Americans.

Early evidence of the appeal of our new term is an 1810 newspaper ad from Washington, D.C., that prefixed another effective four-letter word: "Cash Drug Store." Not long after that, drug stores were everywhere. In 1819 the book *Sketches of Louisville and Its Environs* stated, "There are at this moment, in Louisville . . . three printing offices, three drug stores."

These early drugstores were just apothecaries or pharmacies by another name. But thanks to soda water, they expanded their wares beyond medication to all things necessary for health and welfare. Naturally or artificially carbonated, the bubbly water was a health drink of the 1820s and 1830s, and by the 1840s it was dispensed at a soda counter in many drugstores. It was soon discovered that this "medicine" tasted better with flavoring from ginger and other roots. And so the soda fountain became a social center, not just a medical destination. It was at a soda fountain in Atlanta in 1887 that Coca-Cola got its start, and it was through soda fountains that this most famous of American beverages began its worldwide spread.

In the twentieth century shelves of bottled and canned sodas displaced drugstore soda fountains. The stores themselves grew in size and variety of goods to the point where *drugstore* was both inadequate to describe them and too old-fashioned. They had morphed into brand-name *superstores* on the one hand and *convenience stores* on the other, betraying their origins only by housing a pharmacy and extensive shelves of over-the-counter medication.

1811 White House

The residence of the president of the United States did not start out as the *White House*. In the early years of its occupancy by the Adamses and Jeffersons, it was called the *President's House*. It took a proclamation by Theodore Roosevelt in 1901 to officially designate it the *White House*.

Many early presidents had a hand in the establishment of this important government building. George Washington picked the site for the Federal City and even supervised some of the construction of the President's House. James Hoban, an architect, won the contest for the design, though it is said that Thomas Jefferson had submitted plans, too. The first to live there as president was John Adams, in 1800, even though it was at the end of his term and the building was far from complete. The first child born in the mansion was a grandchild of Jefferson, resident president from 1801 to 1809.

Legend says it got the name *White House* when it was rebuilt and painted white after the British burned it in 1814. In fact, it was known as the *White House* at least three years earlier. A letter of 1811 mentions a politician who went "to act as a sort of political conductor to attract the lightning that may issue from the clouds round the Capitol and the White House at Washington."

1812 gerrymander

One of the most famous inventions in the language of American politics was a result of the radical new form of government we adopted in 1789. We called for the election of representatives not from permanently established regions, as did the few other democracies of the time, but from districts of equal population. To account for changes in population and keep districts equal, we directed that a census of the nation be taken every ten years and districts adjusted accordingly.

Then as now, in the course of redistricting politicians liked to arrange boundaries to give themselves and their parties the advantage. More often than not, then as now, they pushed the ENVELOPE (1988) as far as they could, stretching and twisting district boundaries to include friends and exclude enemies. So it happened in 1812 during the second one-year term of Governor Elbridge Gerry of Massachusetts. His party—the Democratic or Anti-Federalist Party—redistricted the state legislature to its advantage, and Governor Gerry signed the bill. At the office of the Boston *Centinel,* when artist Gilbert Stuart sketched some lines on the map of the redistricting to make it look like a salamander, editor Benjamin Russell named the creature a *Gerrymander.* Stuart's cartoon was widely circulated, and *Gerrymander* came to mean "to redistrict to political advantage." In keeping with the spelling, it was pronounced with a *j* sound, even though Gerry pronounced his name with a hard *g*.

The actors in the Gerrymander drama were distinguished figures. Stuart was famous for his paintings of George Washington; one of his portraits is on our one-dollar bill. Gerry had served in the Continental Congress, signed the Declaration of Independence, participated in the Constitutional Convention of 1787, served in the United States Congress, and, after the governorship, finished his career as vice president under James Madison. To a politician, the ability to *gerrymander* clearly need not be a liability, despite the satire.

1813 airline

Long before heavier-than-air craft left the ground, Americans were thinking in terms of airlines. The first were just straight lines on the map, indicating the shortest distance between two places. Ignoring the inconvenience of mountains and valleys, forests and swamps, visionaries of nineteenth-century America zipped directly from one place to another in their imaginations. Legislators spoke loftily of air lines; one member of Congress is recorded as saying in 1813, "They will not rigidly observe any air-lines or water-lines in enforcing their necessary levies," and another in 1840, "The bill of the House supposed that they must travel through the air, for they were to charge for their mileage by an air line."

When railroads were built, if the topography did not intervene, developers aimed to follow the direct airline between two points. This was possible across the great plains of the West. But even when there was landscape to reckon with, *airline* was used to mean "the shortest way possible." In 1863, for example, the *Congressional Globe* reported "a proposition to construct an air-line railroad between Washington and New York." And *air-line* became an attractive name for a railroad, just as *instant* did for foods in the next century. There was the *Raleigh and Augusta Air-Line Railroad*, the *Selma & Peatville*

Air-line Railway, and the *Muscogee Air Line*, among many others.

The most long-lived of the air-line railroads was the *Seaboard Air Line* along the Atlantic coast. That name led to misunderstandings for the railroad when transportation lines involving airplanes began to use the name. An advertisement in an outdoors magazine of 1921 read, "The Air Line to the Big Woods . . . Cutting Days to Hours in Getting Into the Land of Lakes and Wilderness." Soon the meaning of *airline* was too elevated for a railroad, no matter how straight its tracks. Despite long tradition, the Seaboard finally dropped *Air* from its name well before the century was over.

1814 keno

What passes for lotto in many state is actually a version of keno. The term *keno* comes from French *quine,* meaning "five winning numbers." Players mark off numbers printed on a keno ticket and the keno caller draws numbers on keno balls from a keno goose in order to determine if there are any winners. Originally the keno goose was a wooden chamber with a long neck wide enough to emit one numbered ball at a time when tipped. Nowadays, the goose is often a chamber with numbered ping-pong balls which are forced up at random through a tube by a blast of air.

Keno, a relative of bingo, comes from the gambling halls of New Orleans, which explains the French connection. It is a de-

scendant of lotto, which originated in Italy in the sixteenth century. Originally, keno was intended for a large number of players, each paying the same price for a ticket, usually on a weekly schedule. A diary from 1814 makes the first mention of the game: "I employ'd in washing & mending my messmate playing keeno."

In present-day Las Vegas casinos, the game has been modified to some degree. It allows a smaller number of players to gamble a variable amount of money on a ticket in games that may be played several times in an hour. This has also been called *racehorse keno* because the ticket carried the names of horses rather than numbers in its early history.

1815 cuss

By the early nineteenth century, we knew how to cuss. In an 1815 book called *A Yankee in England,* we find a definition: "*Cuss,* curse."

As the definition indicates, *cuss* is nothing more than a variation of the spelling and pronunciation of *curse.* To *cuss,* the verb, comes from the identical noun *cuss,* a form that is attested as early as 1775 in the *Narragansett Historical Register:* "A man that . . . was noted for a damn cuss." Like BUST (1764) from *burst,* it reflects the *r*-dropping pronunciation of New England and the South, as heard by others who pronounced the *r.* But somehow the cussing was so emphatic it took on a life of its own.

Or perhaps it was a euphemism, available to those who did not want to utter a word that was as shocking as *curse.* Evidence for this is in Mark Twain's use of the phrase *cuss word* in his 1872 book *Roughing It:* "He didn't give a continental for anybody. Beg your pardon, friend, for coming so near saying a cuss-word."

For whatever reason, Twain found the word congenial. He used it in *Life on the Mississippi* (1883): "He got mad and jumped up and begun to cuss the crowd, and said he could lam any thief in the lot." And in *The Adventures of Huckleberry Finn* (1884): "He . . . cussed me for putting on frills and trying to be better than him."

Cussing continues nowadays. It can be therapy, as in a 1976 article "Failure Is a Word I Don't Accept" from the *Harvard Business Review:* "How do you deal with anger? If I'm mad at somebody, I just go in a room, close the door, and cuss him or her out where nobody can hear me. Sometimes I write a letter that I don't mail. I've done a lot of that."

1816 ornery

It was just an ordinary word. That is where *ornery* comes from, being a dialect or slang use of *ordinary,* and that is how it is used when we first meet it in Farmer Brown's journal for 1816, published later in the *Maryland Historical Magazine:* "The Land is old, completely worn out, the farming extremely ornary in general." But to an American, being called *ordinary* is hardly a compliment; in fact it is positively mean (another word meaning "ordinary"). So *ornery* soon developed a correspondingly negative connotation, as in this exchange from the *Massachusetts Spy & Worcester County Advocate* of July 28, 1830:

> Southerner: You ornery fellow! do you pretend to call me to account for my language?
> Yankee: I did but drop a hint.

And in this example from *Knickerbocker Magazine* in 1857: "That poor ornary cuss of a red-haired, cross-eyed grocerykeeper." And from Elizabeth Custer, the widow of George Armstrong, in *Tenting on the Plains* (1887): "He's a good enough fellow, only he's an ornery scamp of a Republican."

By 1899 we were using *orneriness* too, in the sense of "the quality of being positively mean." In *The Gentleman from Indiana,* Booth Tarkington wrote, "Sometimes they . . . let loose their deviltries just for pure orneriness."

1817 pioneer

America did not have pioneers until the nineteenth century. Or rather, for the first two centuries of English-speaking North America, the word *pioneers* meant something quite different than "people who settled the wilderness." In England, and in the American colonies, *pioneer* was a military term. Pioneers were laborers who went in advance of armies. They paved the way by clearing paths, building roads, and digging trenches. A South Carolina historian in 1741 wrote of an unsuccessful siege of St. Augustine, Florida, earlier in that century, involving "800 pioneers (Negroes or White Men), with Tools Sufficient for that number of men, Such as Spades, Hoes, Axes and Hatchets to Dig Trenches."

These pioneers did unglamorous grunt work, but they were also the ones in front, clearing the way for others. So when a nineteenth-century writer applied the word *pioneers* to the early land-clearing settlers in a new region, it caught on. Timothy Dwight, writing about his travels in New England and New York in 1817, said, "A considerable part of those, who *begin* the cultivation of the wilderness, may be denominated *foresters*, or *Pioneers*." And so they were throughout the rest of that century, as pioneers transformed the width of the continent into settled territory.

Pioneers in this sense are now historical or literary memories, as in novels like Willa Cather's *O Pioneers!* (1913). We (and the English) now apply the word to one who is first in discovery, exploration, or achievement in any field, especially science and medicine. But we also recall the nineteenth-century meaning with "pioneer days" in communities that were settled during a century of westward migration.

1818 cruller

Once again we have to thank the Dutch, who brought us COOK-IES (1703), for a tasteful innovation in our language and our cuisine. They had undoubtedly been baking crullers for well over a century in their settlements in the Hudson River valley, but it was by the early nineteenth century that their Yankee neighbors were taking note. Washington Irving mentions the cruller lovingly in his 1818 *Legend of Sleepy Hollow* as he describes the object of Ichabod Crane's affection:

> Fain would I pause to dwell upon the world of charms that burst upon the enraptured gaze of my hero, as he entered the state

parlour of Van Tassel's mansion. Not those of the bevy of buxom lasses, with their luxurious display of red and white: but the ample charms of a genuine Dutch country tea-table.... There was the doughty dough-nut, the tenderer oly koek [another kind of doughnut], and the crisp and crumbling cruller; sweet cakes and short cakes, ginger cakes and honey cakes, and the whole family of cakes.

A similar, though less eloquent sentiment was expressed in the *Boston Transcript* in December 1842: "The ole-kochen, crullers and cookies were of a quality that proved the skilful hand of some genuine Dutch housewife in the manufacture."

Crullers nowadays are familiar throughout the Northeast, the upper Midwest, and California. But what are they? An early recipe from Massachusetts for "Crullers, Matrimony or Love Knots" says to "Roll thin, cut in strips and tie in knots, or braid three strips together." Others use the term *cruller* for an unraised doughnut without a hole, also called a *fried cake* or *cake doughnut*. The author of *A Word Geography of the Eastern United States* (1949) found that the difference in usage "gives rise to many a lively discussion in New England." Among the opinions recorded there in the 1930s: "Cruller contains more egg and less milk than a doughnut" (Shrewsbury, Massachusetts); "Crullers are nothing more than doughnuts, only they're twisted" (Boston); "Anybody that would call a cruller a doughnut would be laughed out of court" (New Milford, Connecticut).

1819 bunkum

A congressman from western North Carolina was so mindful of the voters in his home county that he inadvertently made its name a household word. It was the Honorable Felix Walker, Representative from the county that includes Asheville, North Carolina, who in 1819 (or perhaps 1820) justified his long-winded remarks on the nearly deserted House floor by saying that his constituents had elected him "to make a speech for Buncombe."

That was all it took. Evidently the country was in need of a word more colorful than *nonsense* for the rantings and ramblings of politicians and boosters. With the disrespectfully simplified spelling *bunkum,* the word soon established itself in the jargon of politics. "Talking to Bunkum!" exclaimed an article in 1828. "This is an old and common saying at Washington, when a member of congress is making one of those humdrum and unlistened to 'long talks' which have lately become so fashionable."

Meanwhile, there came into existence around the same time another *bunkum* meaning just the opposite: "excellent, outstanding." Starting in 1834, we find bunkum candy and cakes, a Buncombe fence, and a bunkum politician—supposedly a first-rate one. These two opposite meanings for one word made it exceptionally useful by allowing a speaker to damn with seeming praise.

Later developments accentuated the negative implications of the word. In the 1870s, a San Francisco gambler introduced a new game with the Spanish name *banco.* When it was discovered that the banco dice were loaded, the first vowel was humorously changed to suggest an affinity with *bunkum.* Soon enough *bunco* came to stand for any kind of swindle.

By 1900 a further shortening had reduced *bunkum* to modern *bunk,* ready for application to the plentiful nonsense of the twentieth century, as in Henry Ford's famous "History is bunk." And in 1923 the author of a book about *bunk* felt the need to coin a word for getting rid of it: *debunk.*

1820 shanty

There is a French word *chantier* meaning "a stand or place," and an Irish word *sean-tig* meaning "a hut." Maybe one of those is the ancestor of *shanty.* Whatever the case, we find *shanty* in our American English in 1820 in a journal kept by one Zerah Hawley as he traveled in Ohio. He observed people who "lived in what is here called a shanty. This is a hovel of about 10 feet by 8, made somewhat in the form of an ordinary cow-house."

After that, shanties show up all over the landscape. A shanty appears in James Fenimore Cooper's *The Prairie* in 1827 and in a story of Davy Crockett's exploits in Texas in 1836: "When we entered the shantee, Job was busy dealing out his rum." George Ruxton wrote in 1847 of touring the Rocky Mountains: "Scattered about were tents and shanties of logs and branches of every conceivable form." And there was also the shanty family (1872), a family living in a shanty; shanty cake (1846), eaten by those who lived in shanties; and shanty villages (1858) and shanty towns (1888).

Sometimes a shanty was a LOG CABIN (1770). But whereas the log cabin gradually gained in sentimental and political value as the birthplace of sturdy pioneers, the shanty was always mean and disreputable, at best the next best thing to no shelter at all. Nobody boasted of being born in one.

1821 cure-all

In the early nineteenth century, seeing a doctor could be hazardous to your health. Under the influence of Dr. Benjamin Rush of Philadelphia, doctors were causing more casualties than had the American Revolution. To cure hypertension, the supposed root of all illnesses, they would literally bleed their patients, in extreme cases removing as much as 80 percent of the blood. Then, to clear out the intestines, they might finish off their patients with stiff doses of mercurous chloride. Mercury does help cure infections, but we also now know it can have deadly long-term effects.

No wonder, then, that many Americans preferred self-medication. Besides, we lived in a democracy. Why bother with authority? Skip the doctor, heal yourself.

That was where patent medicine came in, so called because its manufacturers supposedly patented the ingredients. (In fact, usually all they had was trademark protection for the label.) It was obligingly provided by the new nation's pioneers in advertising and marketing. One of the patent medicines, launched by William Swain in 1820, was immodestly named *Panacea.* In plain English, that was *Cure-all,* a term we find in a newspaper of 1821. Expounding on "Popular Remedies against External and Internal Fogginess," the *Journal* of Lancaster, Pennsylvania, listed "Cure-all" as well as "rum and brandy."

In an era of great enterprise and ambition for the newly expanded nation, anything seemed possible. So why not a cure-all for everything that ails you? Swain's *Panacea* claimed to cure cancer, scrofula, sore throat, rheumatism, gout, hepatitis, diseases of the bones, liver complaints, and the early stages of syphilis. And it was potent. It contained sarsaparilla, oil of wintergreen, and "corrosive sublimate," a form of mercury. The first of these was a healing herb, the second pleasant-tasting, the third poisonous. Those who missed both the doctors and the cure-all had the greatest chances for survival.

In the twentieth century, pure food and drug laws put the cure-alls out of business. Now we know better than to expect a cure-all; we just hope for an arsenal of magic bullets (1940) to destroy diseases without harming the patient.

1822 paleface

We can thank Euro-American author (to use today's lingo) James Fenimore Cooper for this one. True, there is an earlier instance than any in Cooper. It is an 1822 report of a frontier masquerade party where a white man dressed as an Indian chief says to another, "Ah, *Paleface!* What brings you here? you seem to take pleasure in saying rude impertinencies." And there is no "paleface" in the first of Cooper's best-selling "Leatherstocking" novels, *The Pioneers* (1823).

But *The Last of the Mohicans* (1826) made *paleface* a household word. There the Mohawk chief Chingachgook, who spoke of "whiteskins" in *The Pioneers,* now uses "pale-face": "What say your old men? do they tell the young warriors, that the pale-faces met the redmen, painted for war and armed with the stone hatchet and wooden gun?"

Why *paleface* but not *redface*? A possible explanation is that Cooper's whites dress to cover their whole bodies, except for their faces, while the Indians cover very little. Hence *face* is used only in the word for the whites.

Whether Cooper is to be trusted with regard to the language of the Indians is open to question. For that matter, whether he is to be trusted with regard to the language of the English-speaking characters is also open to question. All use a formality rarely encountered in real life, like this speech from the lips of his frontiersman hero Hawkeye, a.k.a. Leatherstocking: "I did believe there was no cry that Indians or beast could make, that my ears had not heard; but this has proved that I was only a vain and conceited mortal!"

1823 flunk

American enthusiasm for the trappings of higher education has been evident since colonial days in the college words we have contributed to the English language, such as ALUMNUS (1696) and *alumna* (1882), *fraternity* (1777) and *sorority* (1900), *campus* (1774) and VALEDICTORIAN (1759), not to mention later innovations like *coeducation* (1852) and *multiversity* (1963). But we were also the first to flunk.

It happened at least as long ago as 1823, when the editors of a Yale College magazine, the *Crayon,* made a plea for subscribers: "To joke in earnest, gentlemen, we must have, at least, as many subscribers as there are students in College, or 'flunk out.'" And once we started to flunk out—or just plain flunk—in our lives and our courses, we never stopped. Back in 1856, to be sure, a dictionary of college words was hesitant about it, claiming that "The phrase 'to flunk out' was formerly used in some American colleges as is now the word 'flunk.'" Perhaps that underestimation was because *flunk out* then had something of a vulgar connotation, as explained in an 1873 dictionary: " 'He flunked out' is low. 'He sneaked out,' or 'He backed out,' are better expressions to denote a mean or cowardly abandonment of an enterprise."

Much other language of that time, especially slang, has become outdated. For instance, we no longer use *rush* as in this

1877 essay on social life at Yale: "At the close of the daily morning service, which is held at ten minutes past eight o'clock, the students gather in the recitation-rooms, where they 'rush' or 'flunk,' according as they have studied the night before or been 'out on a lark.'" But to this day *flunk* has remained the slang word for academic failure.

From *flunk* comes *flunky* (1838). Originally a flunky was someone who flunked, that is, who failed, academically or otherwise. Then it was used for an ignorant new investor in the stock market. Those meanings led to the modern one of a person who holds a servile or menial position or who merely runs errands for someone else.

1824 you-all

Now listen, you-all, if you want to understand how *you-all* became the most important word in the Southern vocabulary and the easiest way to tell a southerner from a Yankee. *You-all* is the Southern solution to a problem that arose in the seventeenth and eighteenth centuries when the English language became too polite. We had been using *thou* in speaking to one person and *you* to more than one, but *you* seemed more polite, so by the time the United States came into existence, we (and the English) said *you* to one person too. The only *thou*s left were in prayers, poems, and in the plain talk of the Quakers.

But when *you* became singular, referring to just one person, what could we say to more than one? We could still say *you*, of course, but we could also do something to *you* to make it plural. Some people just added the *s* we usually use for plurals, making the word we spell *youse*. Others spoke of *you-uns*. Today many say *you guys,* regardless of the gender of the guys.

The South had a different solution. Americans in the South added *all* to form the plural, making *you-all*. And while the Northern plurals never made their way into polite society, always sounding a little uncouth, *you-all* became the essence of Southern good manners.

People from the North sometimes think southerners use *you-all* all the time, even when speaking to one person. That just ain't true. When southerners ask "How y'all?" they are being polite, including a person's whole family in their inquiry. No, *you-all* is just a nice Southern way to make distinctions of person.

1825 blizzard

In frontier territory, *blizzard* was "a knock-down blow," delivered at first by a fist or gun rather than by the weather. It must have been in use by the mid-1820s. We encounter it in an 1829 glossary in the *Virginia Literary Museum*: "Blizzard. 'A violent blow,' perhaps from [German] *Blitz*, lightning. *Kentucky*." Whatever its origin, the word was familiar to frontiersman Davy Crockett, who wrote in his 1835 *Tour Down East* that at dinner, asked by a parson for a toast, "Not knowing whether he intended to have some fun at my expense, I concluded to go ahead and give him and his likes a blizzard." In this case it was a blizzard of words.

Blizzard went to college too. A writer in 1881 recalled, "In 1836 I first heard the word 'blizzard' among the young men at

Illinois College, Jacksonville. If one struck a ball a severe blow in playing town-ball it would be said 'That's a blizzard.'"

Meanwhile, back on the frontier, *blizzard* began to be the term for the severe blow struck by a snowstorm. An 1862 book called *Forty Years on the Frontier* recorded this entry: "Snowed in the forenoon. Very cold in afternoon. Raw east wind. Everybody went to grand ball given by John Grant at Grantsville and a severe blizzard blew up and raged all night. We danced all night; no outside storm could dampen the festivities."

During the particularly severe winter of 1880–81, this kind of blizzard struck the whole country, as a writer in the *Nation* of New York City commented in 1881: "The hard weather has called into use a word which promises to become a national Americanism, namely 'blizzard.' It designates a storm (of snow and wind) which men cannot resist away from shelter." In general usage ever since, the blizzard of snow has knocked out the former meaning of mere human violence.

1826 pothole

Instead of causing travelers to swerve away, the first potholes attracted them. Found in rock formations rather than roads, they were curiosities of nature: holes with the shape of pots. In 1826 the superintendent of the Bureau of Indian Affairs, T. L. McKenney, traveling to Wisconsin to negotiate treaties, wrote in his *Sketches of a Tour to the Lakes,* "The waters once were, in many places, some fifty feet above their present level; for their action upon the rocks is plainly seen in the *pot holes*, as the excavations are called, which are made by the action of pebbles upon the rocks." Half a century later a writer for the *American Naturalist* described "well-worn cavities in the sides of the mountains, showing how the running waters ... formed the cavity much as a 'pot hole' is made in our streams at the present time."

It took the ingenuity of modern road construction to create the potholes that we complain about nowadays. The gentle asphalt roads we are accustomed to today are particularly vulnerable to the undermining actions of water and ice; these create deep holes with steep sides like potholes in rocks, and thus are similarly named. The first of these potholes is mentioned along with the first of these roads in the early days of the twentieth century. Smooth modern roads and fast modern cars have managed to transform the pothole from tourist attraction to travel hazard.

1827 sockdolager

Entering the vocabulary by at least 1827, *sockdolager* was already well enough established in American slang to be included in a glossary published in the *Virginia Literary Museum* on January 6, 1830: " 'sockdolager,' 'a decisive blow'—one, in the slang language, 'capable of setting a man thinking.'" It also could mean something or someone big. "There is but one 'sogdollager' in the universe," James Fenimore Cooper wrote in 1838, "and that is in Lake Oswego."

Sockdolager was just one of the outrageous ten-dollar words coined early in the nineteenth century that sprang from the exuberance of the expanding new country. Others were *absquatulate* for "depart," *callithumpian* for "a noisy parade," *hornswoggle* for "cheat," and other *s*-words like *slumgullion* for "something disgusting," *snollygoster* for "a political jobseeker," and *slangwhanger* for "a partisan speechmaker," as well as *skedaddle* and SHINDIG (1857), which both survive today.

On April 14, 1865, *sockdolager* was a key word in a tragic moment of American history. The Englishman Tom Taylor used it in his comedy, *Our American Cousin,* to Americanize the play's hero when he spoke the line that got the most laughs: "Well, I guess I know enough to turn you inside out, you sockdologizing old man-trap." As the audience roared, John Wilkes Booth pulled the trigger. Those were the last words President Abraham Lincoln ever heard.

1828 whole hog

It was 1828. Andrew Jackson, who had received the most popular votes in the election four years earlier but lost all the same, was running for president of the United States again. In a letter that year, Daniel Webster, a senator from Massachusetts, remarked that Jackson "will either go with the party, as they say in New York, or go the whole hog, as it is phrased elsewhere."

As it turned out, Jackson did go whole hog, and so did his party: He did it all. This time Jackson won not only a majority of the popular vote but also 178 electoral votes to John Quincy Adams's 83. On Inauguration Day in 1829, the first day of his presidency, he went whole hog by letting the "rabble" into the White House. He went whole hog as a politician, too, bringing in the spoils system and appointing fellow Democrats to government offices. The era of the Founders was over (John Adams and Thomas Jefferson had died on July 4, 1826), and Jacksonian Democracy had begun.

Perhaps the Jacksonian appetite for political power and expansion made *whole hog* such a prominent phrase in the Jackson years. There was no desire to compromise. Jackson went whole hog to get rid of the Bank of the United States, withdrawing federal funds from the bank and putting them in "pet banks" belonging to his friends. In 1832 a Kentucky newspaper remarked, "You will universally find them belonging to one of two classes: either *whole-hog* Jackson men, or *half-way* Clay men." And in 1835 a travel writer claimed that "in Virginia originated *Go the whole hog*, a political phrase marking the democrat from a federalist."

The Jackson era is history, but American politicians, criminals, athletes, businesspeople, and hobbyists may still be observed following Old Hickory's example by going whole hog.

1829 Jim Crow

A hopeful sign of racial progress in present-day America is that we no longer know the origin of *Jim Crow*. Unfortunately, however, the term deserves a place in this chronology because for more than a century Jim Crow guided white Americans' thinking about race.

He began, so the story goes, in 1828, in Louisville, Kentucky, where a young actor and musician, Thomas D. "Daddy" Rice, introduced on stage a character he called *Jim Crow.* As we look back from what we hope is a more enlightened time, it is repugnant to see the caricature of the black man presented by Jim Crow, and it is even more embarrassing that by 1829 audiences were so delighted with a white man who blackened his face with burnt cork, outlined his lips in white, and then sang and danced like a happy fool that Rice's "Jim Crow" became the most popular song in the country:

> First on de heel tap, den on de toe,
> Ebery time I wheel about I jump Jim Crow.
> Wheel about and turn about and do jis so,
> And ebery time I wheel about I jump Jim Crow.

Legend has it that Rice imitated the singing and the shuffling dance of a crippled slave tending horses near the theater in Louisville. Whatever the origin, his act was a forerunner of the hugely popular minstrel shows.

But his caricature of African Americans as ignorant, laughable folk also prepared the way for Jim Crow segregation laws. From the end of the nineteenth century through the middle of the twentieth, Jim Crow laws in the South and Jim Crow customs throughout the country separated blacks from whites and kept blacks from voting and from holding positions of responsibility.

During World War II, a sixteen-year-old African-American girl won an essay contest in Columbus, Ohio, on "What to Do with Adolf Hitler" with her proposal that he be put in a black skin and required to spend the rest of his life living in the United States of America. If there is hope for better race relations in our country today, it is at least in part because *Jim Crow,* like Adolf Hitler, is finally dead.

1830 editorial

The newspaper is not an American invention, nor is the magazine, but we can claim credit for an important step in the development of both: the editorial. This is not to say that Americans were the first to think of letting the editor's opinion appear in print. Quite the opposite: until the advent of the editorial, the editor's opinion permeated the publication, mixing inextricably with the news. Journals of the day did indeed report news, but they did so in the service of propaganda for a particular party or policy. In that way they were like most present-day newsletters.

Early in the nineteenth century, however, Americans began to develop the notion of journalistic objectivity. It was not only possible, but perhaps advantageous, to separate the news from the editor's opinion. There were idealistic reasons for this: the reader would get the news without fear or favor, and opinion would be labeled as such. But there were also practical reasons, without which the idealistic could not have prevailed. To present the news as plain fact makes it of interest even to those who do not share the editor's opinion. And, as we in the "information age" know well, it is information that people will pay for, not opinion. The labeling of opinion to separate it from news is now so ingrained in American MEDIA (1921) that lapses are targets for criticism.

Editorial was the label we used as long ago as 1830 to designate a statement of the editor's opinion. "The great green table in the centre groaning under the weight of editorials, and friendly correspondence," was mentioned in the *Collegian* of Cambridge, Massachusetts, in 1830. Even earlier, in 1802, we find reference to "the editorial part of the paper."

By the turn of the twentieth century, newspapers had designated a separate editorial page for editorials and letters to the editor. Even the location of the editorial page is distinctive: it is always a left-hand page, usually in the front section. Modern newspapers have expanded this space by using the facing page for lengthier opinions by columnists and guest writers.

They call this *op-ed,* that is, opposite the editorial page, a feature introduced by Herbert Bayard Swope in the *New York World* of the 1920s.

1831 ranch

The roots of the American nation were in the farm. The "embattled farmers" of Concord, Massachusetts, in Ralph Waldo Emerson's words "fired the shot heard round the world" to start the war of independence; and several gentleman farmers from Virginia, notably Thomas Jefferson and George Washington, articulated the new country's principles and made the nation a reality. As the United States expanded to the west, new settlement was marked by clearing the forests and PRAIRIES (1773) for more farms.

But when settlers reached the wide open spaces of the Southwest, *farm* no longer fit. Spanish speakers had arrived there first and adapted from the Indians distinctive ways of making a rural living in the arid land, and their *ranchos* are what new settlers found there. "At a ranch," wrote James Ohio Pattie in a book published in 1831, "I procured a horse for three dollars." When English-speaking settlers began making their homes on the range, they took the word *ranch* as well as their land titles from Spanish *ranchos,* and instead of farmers, they called themselves *ranchers* (1836).

The typical ranch was far more spacious than an Eastern farm, and it was used primarily for grazing rather than growing crops. But *ranch* became such a dominant word in the West that it was also used for places that looked like the farms of the East. A writer in 1853 noted, "The old Texan has no farm, it is a *ranche.*" In addition to cattle ranches, Montana in the 1880s had hay ranches, grain ranches, milk ranches, and chicken ranches. There have also been bee ranches, fruit ranches, grape ranches, and orange ranches. Richard Nixon grew up on a lemon ranch in Whittier, California. In the 1950s, a survey asking what the word was for "a small country place where crops are grown" got the answer *ranch* from 56 percent of those interviewed in California and Nevada.

East and West finally met in the twentieth century with the invention of the dude ranch (1921), a cattle ranch where city slickers could pretend to be cowboys (see DUDE 1877).

1832 bark up the wrong tree

Americans have coined entire expressions as well as individual words. At first *bark up the wrong tree* meant exactly what it said, the *bark* being that of a hunting dog pointing at the wrong tree. In *Americanisms Old and New* (1889), John S. Farmer explains, "The Western huntsman found that his prey gradually became more and more wily and cunning in eluding pursuit, and frequently he and his dogs were at fault, supposing they had 'treed' their game when in reality, especially in the case of opossums and squirrels and such-like animals, it had escaped by jumping from the boughs of one tree to another."

But we have found the expression useful even when there are no hunters, trees, or barking dogs involved. In 1832, we encounter it in James Hall's *Legends of the West:* "It doesn't take a Philadelphia lawyer to tell that the man who serves the master one day, and the enemy six, has just six chances out of seven to go to the devil. You are barking up the wrong tree, Johnson."

Davy Crockett seems to have been fond of the phrase. In the *Sketches and Eccentricities of Col. David Crockett, of West Tennessee* (1833), we find, "I told him . . . that he reminded me of the meanest thing on God's earth, an old coon dog, barking up the wrong tree." And *A Narrative of the Life of David Crockett*, published a year later, contains the sentence, "I began to think I was barking up the wrong tree again." The 1836 story of *Colonel Crockett in Texas* includes the remark, "Job, little dreaming that he was barking up the wrong tree, shoved along another bottle."

To *bark up the wrong tree* basically means "to follow an incorrect assumption." Two other related expressions are also American: *be all wet* (1792) and *fire into the wrong flock* (1848).

1833 Hoosier

Next door to the Buckeye State of Ohio, the Bluegrass State of Kentucky, the Wolverine State of Michigan, and the Prairie State of Illinois, behold the Hoosier State of Indiana. *Hoosier*? That would be like referring to the Hillbilly State of Kentucky or the Gangster State of Illinois. Not very likely!

And yet the natives of Indiana have been proud to name themselves after "a hillbilly or rustic; an unmannerly or objectionable person," to use the definition of *Hoosier* in the *Dictionary of American Regional English*. *Hoosier* has had this meaning, and Indiana this nickname, since the late 1820s. The nation learned about it in a poem called "The Hoosier's Nest" by John Finley, published January 1, 1833, in the *Indianapolis Journal* and soon copied everywhere. Of "blest Indiana!" he wrote that

> hosts of Preachers, Doctors, Lawyers,
> All independent as wood-sawyers,
> With men of every hue and fashion,
> Flock to this rising 'Hoosher' nation.
> . . . .
> With equal tact the 'Hoosher' loons,
> Hunt offices or hunt raccoons.

Finley describes a visit to a Hoosher cabin:

> One side was lined with skins of 'varments'
> The other spread with divers garments,
> . . . .
> Two rifles placed above the door,
> Three dogs lay stretched upon the floor,
> In short, the domicile was rife,
> With specimens of 'Hoosher' life.

He also regrets that

> My pockets are so shrunk of late
> I can not nibble "Hoosier Bait."

According to an 1859 dictionary of Americanisms, the latter is "a sort of coarse gingerbread, which . . . is the best bait to catch a hoosier with."

1834 goober

The Southern nickname for the peanut, *goober,* came to us by way of Africa, along with the goober itself. The original home of the plant, however, was South America. Early trans-Atlantic explorers brought the peanut from there to Africa, where it spent a century or two before it reached our part of the world. In west-central Africa, where various Bantu languages were spoken, the peanut acquired Bantu names that were the ancestors of *goober.* The Kongo, noting its shape, called it *nguba,* the word for kidney in their language. In Kimbundu, a related language, the word was also *nguba.* And in Umbundu, another related language, it was *olungupa.*

Many Africans, and many African words, perished on the "middle passage" from Africa to North America in the nearly three centuries of the slave trade. But *nguba* made it across, perhaps because goobers themselves were brought from Africa along with the slaves. A Louisville advertisement of 1833 announces bags of "Gouber Pea" for sale. *Goober* by itself first appears in 1834 in the *Cherokee Phoenix and Indians' Advocate,* published in Georgia, in language attributed to a black speaker: "But he so mean I frade of he, I guess he steal my goober."

Although it never displaced *peanut, goober* remains widely known and used today, especially in the southern states. It also lives on in the old Civil War song, "Lying in the shadow underneath the trees, Goodness how delicious, eating goober peas!"

1835 loaf

No, this is not the *loaf* of bread, the staff of life that has been with the English language from the beginning. Our distinctive American contribution is the loaf that does nothing. It took true American genius to invent a new way of passing the time: loafing.

A Philadelphia newspaper declared in 1835, "The propensity to loaf is confined to no rank in life." While workers accused of shirking their duties are often said to loaf, the term can just as easily be applied to those of the leisure class who laze about. So in *Uncle Tom's Cabin* (1852), *loaf* is used to critical effect, for while slaves are confined on the lower deck of a steamboat, the horror of their fate is heightened by the fact that above them "all went on merrily, as before. Men talked, and loafed, and read, and smoked. Women sewed, and children played, and the boat passed on her way."

And an American genius, Walt Whitman, celebrated loafing in *Leaves of Grass* (1855):

> I loafe and invite my soul,
> I lean and loafe at my ease observing a spear of summer grass.

The related word *loafer* is even earlier, attested in Utica, New York, in 1830 and New York City in 1835, as well as New Orleans in 1839. *Loafer* in turn comes from *land loper* (1785), later *land loafer* (1836), also meaning "an idle person." It is probably related to German *Landläufer,* meaning "one who runs along the land."

It is time to loaf a little and bring this entry to a close.

1836 downtown

Maybe it began in New York City. Circumstantial evidence certainly points there, for the only direction in which rapidly expanding New York could grow was up the island of Manhattan. Someone heading that way would be going up from town—and New York was still something of a town at the start of the nineteenth century. By the early 1830s, the term *uptown* was used for the desirable new residential district away from the business center. An 1833 article states, "The property-holders up-town would have the site of the building a mile or so from the present chief seat of business."

"Chief seat of business" is ponderous next to glamorous *uptown;* in fact, it makes the central business district sound positively old-fashioned. So it is not surprising that some central-city booster thought of changing *up* to *down* and balancing *uptown* with its brisk opposite, *downtown.* A diarist noted in 1836, "This, at least, is the opinion of the best judges of the value of down-town property." By 1844 New York's *Evening Mirror* could comment, " 'Up-Town' and 'Down-Town.'—We see that these names of the different halves of the city are becoming the common language of advertisements, notices, etc."

Both *uptown* and *downtown* spread beyond New York to practically every city and town in America. But most cities have not been constrained by geography into a single direction for expansion, so single-direction *uptown* is less satisfactory as a word for the newer residential areas. Geography and transportation have worked together to give us the suburb, which has replaced uptown in the twentieth century as downtown's polar opposite. But downtown has had more staying power. For better or worse, for renewal as well as decay, every city still has a downtown central core, even when it sprawls as much as present-day Los Angeles.

1837 Christmas tree

Both England and America learned about the Christmas tree in the 1830s. Their source was the same: Germany, where the custom of decorating evergreens at Christmas time had long been established. But the English didn't quite get it, as attested by the *Oxford English Dictionary,* which explains this custom as "a famous feature of Christmas celebration in Germany, frequently but imperfectly imitated in England, especially since its introduction into the royal household in the early years of the reign of Queen Victoria."

Victoria came to the throne in England in 1837. By then, Americans were learning about Christmas trees not from royalty but from German-American neighbors. Harriet Martineau, in her 1838 *Retrospect of Western Travel,* declared, "I was present at the introduction into the new country of the spectacle of the German Christmas-tree." Americans, who had already enthusiastically adopted Santa Claus (1773), eagerly embraced the tree. By 1855 an article in the *Rural New Yorker* could remark, "The last thing attended to is the selection and adornment of the Christmas tree."

And the present-day sentimentality of the tree was well established a year later when the *San Francisco Call* wrote, "Who can think . . . of the anxious children gathered round the Christmas tree—the fabulous visits of Santa Claus . . . without feeling that man has other ends than those that characterize every day life?" Although artificial trees are increasingly replacing real ones, electric lights now take the place of candles, and we are careful to say *humans* or *people* instead of *man,* that editorial would not be much different in a newspaper of the present day.

The tree is so important to our celebration of the season that in parts of the country, especially the South and New England, *Christmas tree* also stands for a Christmas party held at home around the tree, complete with carols and presents.

1838 know-how

"I know how to curse," says the savage Caliban in Shakespeare's *The Tempest* (1611–12). Indeed, the English knew how to say *know how* well before they sent colonists to America. But we Americans were first with the noun *know-how,* as in this oath of office published in the *New Yorker* of 1838: "I promise . . . to do the duties of the office to the best of my know-how." American know-how cleared the wilderness (and is now protecting what's left of it), made communication instantaneous (and is now trying to protect our privacy), built universities and colleges everyone could attend (and is now trying to figure out how to afford them), sent people to the moon and back again, and brought American products to every corner of the globe. Who knows where our know-how will get us in the twenty-first century.

For a few years in the 1850s, Americans were also known for the opposite of know-how, represented by a political party known as the *Know-Nothings*. They got their name because all members were sworn to secrecy. Asked about their party, they had to answer, "I don't know." Opponents seized on this oddity and labeled them *Know-Nothings*, not just to point to their secrecy but also to criticize the ignorance of Know-Nothing anti-immigrant and anti-Catholic policies. Those called *Know-Nothings* had previously been the first to use the term *Native American*, not for the original inhabitants of the North American continent, but for themselves—descendants of European immigrants who wanted to keep future immigrants out.

Fortunately, few Americans were content to be Know-Nothings, and the party came to an end in 1855. It is instead for our know-how that Americans are known today.

1839 OK

Is it a word, a phrase, an abbreviation, an acronym? Do you spell it *O.K., OK, o.k.,* or *okay*? Any way, it's OK. This most uncategorizable of Americanisms is categorically the most successful of all time. *OK* is "all correct."

That was its original meaning, an in-your-face misspelling of the first letters of *all* and *correct*. In 1839, when we first come across it, *O.K.* was just one of many humorous abbreviations in the newspapers of Boston, like *O.F.M.* (our first men), *S.P.* (small potatoes), and *R.T.B.S.* (remains to be seen), and like these other abbreviations, *O.K.* was usually spelled with periods. The modern expert on *OK*, Columbia University professor Allen Walker Read, found the epidemic of abbreviations then spread to the newspapers of New York City, Philadelphia, and New Orleans, not to mention Chicago and the small town of Peru, Illinois. When the fad for abbreviations faded a few years later, only two of them, *N.G.* (no go, no good) and *O.K.*, took permanent hold. But *O.K.* took off like a rocket.

Why? Because the following year, 1840, was a presidential election year, and Martin Van Buren, a.k.a. "Old Kinderhook" because of his birthplace in Kinderhook, New York, was up for reelection. His supporters, the Democrats, formed an *O.K. Club* in New York City that attained notoriety not only with torchlight parades but also by disrupting rallies of Van Buren's Whig opponent, William Henry Harrison. Although *O.K.* the politician lost the election, *O.K.* the expression doubled its strength. From that time on, America was O.K.

After these humorous and political beginnings, *O.K.* settled in to make itself indispensable, sometimes losing its periods in the process and becoming simply *OK*. *OK* was quickly recognized as a brief, distinctive, universally understood annotation to indicate approval of a document, and a brief, distinctive, universally understood spoken response to indicate understanding and acceptance of a request or order. Its brevity, simplicity, and distinctiveness have commended it to languages the world over. *OK* is America's most successful linguistic export.

1840 keep the ball rolling

The rip-roaring (1834) presidential campaign of 1840, renowned for the "O.K. Clubs" of incumbent Martin Van Buren and the "LOG CABIN (1770) and Hard Cider" of successful challenger William Henry Harrison, also introduced the ball that we have kept rolling ever since. One of the features of the 1840 campaign was the rolling of an enormous decorated ball in a political parade. A line in the pro-Harrison *Log Cabin & Hard Cider Melodies,* published in Boston in 1840, alludes to this practice: "Virginia will keep her ball rolling."

Partisans of the Democratic Party and Van Buren kept their ball rolling too, propelled by men known as *ball rollers*. "This gang of loafers and litterateurs," wrote one contemporary observer that year, "are said to number 1,000 braves, being the picked men of the old 'huge paws'—'butt enders'—'roarers,' and 'ball rollers.' " Butt enders were enthusiastic young men of the fire department in New York City; roarers were boasters as well as boosters.

The actual ball was soon rolled aside, and *ball roller* is no longer an avocation, but *keep the ball rolling* has rolled along with our language to the present day.

Later expressions involving *ball* came from our twentieth-century enthusiasm for sports other than politics. Americans were the first to keep our eyes on the ball (1907) and to be on the ball (1939).

1841 deadhead

Long before Jerry Garcia was even born, there were deadheads in America. We read of them as far back as 1841, as reported by *Spirit of the Times: A Chronicle of the Turf* in New York City: "The house on Tuesday was filled as far as $300 could fill, barring the 'dead heads.' " Two years later, with regard to a less successful performance, the *Knickerbocker,* also of New York City, noted "tickets numbered as high as twelve hundred, and not fifty persons in the room? —and half of those 'dead heads.' " Who were these dead heads who lived more than a century before the Grateful Dead played their first note? They were freeloaders—whose heads did not count in the receipts.

No one knows who first invented the word. But it met an evident need for an expression that was both descriptive and sarcastic, to be used by proprietors who got no income from deadheads and by paying guests envious of those who got in free. And soon deadheads were spoken of everywhere, not just in the theaters of New York City. In an 1848 glossary of American words, John Russell Bartlett explained: "Persons who drink at a bar, ride in an omnibus or railroad car, travel in steamboats, or visit the theatre, without charge, are called *dead heads*. These consist of the engineers, conductors, and laborers on railroads; the keepers of hotels; the editors of newspapers, etc."

The meaning of *deadhead* as "one who gets something for nothing" was extended before long to include "one who is good for nothing, an idler, a shiftless person." Or, to use another American term of the time, a deadbeat (1863). In the later nineteenth century, *deadhead* took on the technical meaning of "a trip by train, truck, or other vehicle without cargo or passengers."

So in the 1970s, when *deadhead* with its connotations of freeloading, idling, and taking empty trips met the new sense of *head* meaning "drug user," as in *pot head,* it was not so surprising that fans of the Grateful Dead would identify themselves as *Dead Heads* as they followed the rock band from concert to concert around the country from the early 1970s until Garcia's death in 1995.

1842 underground railroad

It was neither underground nor a railroad, just as nowadays an underground newspaper does not come from under the ground and the information superhighway is not a highway for cars to drive on. But railroads were the new technology of the 1840s and the fastest way of getting from one place to another, so when Southern slaves were whisked almost invisibly across the North to freedom in Canada, it seemed as if a railroad had been operating somewhere under the ground.

Underground railroad was used as early as 1842 in a publication known as the *New York Semi-Weekly Express:* "We passed 26 prime slaves to the land of freedom last week. . . . All went by 'the underground railroad.' " And the name caught on quickly. To the escaping slaves and the abolitionists who helped them, *underground railroad* implied mystery, speed, and power. To slaveholding southerners, it likewise implied mystery, speed, and power, thus justifying their demonizing of the radicals who attacked their peculiar institution (1840). The term was, however, somewhat misleading to both sides in that it made the clandestine journey seem more organized and systematic than it actually was.

Those involved in the underground railroad soon elaborated on the railroad language. There were passengers, the escaped slaves themselves. There were stations, the houses and barns along the way where the slaves were hidden by sympathetic Northern whites and free blacks. And there were conductors who took the passengers from station to station. A ride on the underground railroad was indeed a ticket to freedom.

1843 suffrage

A vote is just a vote, but suffrage is a vote with high purpose. Thus it is no surprise that the high-purposed radical movement to extend the vote to women adopted the term *suffrage* to sum up its goal. *Suffrage* was already enshrined in the United States Constitution, where it applies to a right so fundamental it cannot be amended away. According to Article 5, the Constitution can be amended with approval of the legislatures of three-fourths of the states, except that "no State, without its consent, shall be deprived of its equal suffrage in the Senate."

This was the first use of *suffrage* to mean "voting as a right rather than a privilege." In the earlier sense of "privilege," *suffrage* had been in the English language since the Middle Ages. Suffrages originally were prayers. Then the meaning was extended to requests for assistance, then to assistance itself, then the assistance provided by a supporting vote, and finally the vote itself. So it stood when in 1787 the Constitution used *suffrage* to mean "an inalienable right to vote."

And the right to vote, not merely the condescending permission to do so, was what advocates of women's equality sought. Hence they used *suffrage,* either in the phrase *female suffrage* or simply by itself, with the understanding that *suffrage* referred to the vote for the half of the adult population that had been excluded. By the early 1840s there was a Suffrage Party with this mission.

Even beyond its legal meaning, *suffrage* had connotations that helped the cause. The word evokes dual meanings of *suffer:* "to allow," but also "to endure pain and hardship," here for the sake of achieving a goal. By a quirk of spelling, *suffrage* also concludes with the "rage" that might be felt toward those who would deny suffrage to women.

The goal of the suffrage movement was accomplished in 1920 with the Nineteenth Amendment to the Constitution: "The right of citizens of the United States to vote shall not be denied or abridged . . . on account of sex." With that, the word *suffrage* was retired too. Since then, campaigns to extend the vote have simply called for "voting rights."

1844 rodeo

We learned of it from the Spanish-speaking settlers of the Southwest: the *rodeo,* or "roundup" of cattle, was conducted once a year to brand the calves and count the herd. "In the spring," wrote Thomas Farnham in his 1844 *Travels in the Californias,* "yearling calves are collected by an appointed *rodea* of cattle." This rodeo was so important to the maintenance of order that the new state of California made it mandatory, passing a law in 1851 that declared, "Every owner of a stock farm shall be obliged to give, yearly, one general rodeo."

The rodeo brought together COWBOYS (1779) as well as cattle, giving the cowboys an audience and a chance to demonstrate their skills. American enterprise soon made show business out of the event; before long the competition mattered more than the roundup, and rodeos became unabashed contests in cowboy skills.

The Americanization of the rodeo also gave it an American accent. In most of the United States, *rodeo* now is pronounced with emphasis on the first syllable, *ro.* Southern California is an exception; there the word still has emphasis on the second syllable, an *e* that rhymes with *day.* But Southern California has given a further twist to *rodeo.* The best-known rodeo there is not a cowboy show but the state's most glamorous and expensive shopping street, Rodeo Drive in Beverly Hills.

1845 tintinnabulation

While uncouth boosters and boasters on the frontier were adding the likes of *skedaddle*, SOCKDOLAGER (1827), and *splendacious* to the American vocabulary, members of the literary elite contributed an invention of their own: *tintinnabulation*. It doesn't exactly ring a bell with Americans today—except, perhaps, with readers of Edgar Allan Poe. "Hear the sledges with the bells— / Silver bells! / What a world of merriment their melody foretells!" begins Poe's poem "The Bells." In the night, Poe says, the stars twinkle, "Keeping time, time, time, / In a sort of Runic rhyme, / To the tintinnabulation that so musically wells from the bells, bells, bells, bells, / Bells, bells, bells. . . ." Only these sleighbells tintinnabulate; the wedding bells, fire bells, and funeral bells later in the poem make other sounds.

The poem was published in 1849, the year Poe died. But *tintinnabulation* was already making the rounds of the American literary community in 1845, when a theology student at Princeton, W. W. Lord, having just published a book entitled *Poems*, wrote to the literary critic Elizabeth Kinney in nearby Newark, New Jersey, "Others bore a distinct resemblance to the tintinnabulations of jingled cow bells." Poe was not one of Lord's admirers; in a review in the *Broadway Journal* of May 24, 1845, he said that Lord's *Poems* showed "a very ordinary species of talent." And Lord's letter to Kinney was not published, so it is unlikely Poe would have read *tintinnabulation* there. The word must have been in the air when he wrote his own poem on bells a few years later.

Similar words had been used in England before this time: *tintinnabular* and *tintinnabulary*, "pertaining to bells," since the eighteenth century, and *tintinnabulant* for "ringing or tinkling" since early in the nineteenth. But *tintinnabulation* was an American invention. Thanks to Poe, it has been ringing in our ears ever since.

1846 Podunk

It is said to have been a real place in Massachusetts, Connecticut, Long Island, upstate New York, Michigan, and Nebraska, but only faint traces of it still exist in the twentieth century. One authentic vestige is just to the northeast of Hartford, Connecticut, where the little Podunk River appears on the map to this day. Another is a rural area some dozen miles west of Worcester, Massachusetts, encompassing Quaboag Pond and Quacumquasit Pond, long known to the people in the vicinity as *Podunk*. And for a few years in the nineteenth century, a town in Nebraska officially bore the name *Podunk* until the railroad came through and changed it to *Brock*.

The power of *Podunk* to stir the American imagination was not the fame of any such place, however, but its very obscurity. The turning point came in 1846, when "R.P.," a columnist for the Buffalo, New York, *Daily National Pilot*, wrote a series of eight humorous articles titled "Letters from Podunk" about the supremely uneventful life of that mythical small town, "Podunk," which was "a little world of itself . . . high up on the Big Pigeon." Whether or not R.P. originated the notion of Podunk as the ultimate backwater town, his articles, reprinted in other newspapers, were the means of spreading its fame across the country. The lack of identifiable geographic references in the articles made it possible for *Podunk* to be used as an epithet for a sleepy small town anywhere.

Podunk was a name known to New Englanders two centuries before the writings of R.P. In the Algonquian language spoken by a tribe of Indians then living in Connecticut, *Podunk* meant "a neck or corner of land." Hearing the name from those Indians, English speakers applied it to the place where these Indians lived, the river that ran through it, and the tribe itself. The place was small, the river was small, and the tribe was small, making *Podunk* an apt choice for R.P.'s fictional "little world."

For two centuries, in both England and America, homeless wanderers from place to place had been known as *tramps*. Then an unknown American came up with a new word for them: *hobo*. Researcher Barry Popik has found it used in a breezy letter from New York City in the *New Orleans Picayune* of August 19, 1848: "Well, here I am once more in Gotham, after three years' absence—three years which have passed as agreeably as time usually passes with people in this digging world. During that period I have floated about and circulated round to some considerable extent. . . . a year's bronzing and 'ho-boying' about among the mountains of that charming country called Mexico, has given me a slight dash of the Spanish."

Where this odd word came from nobody knows for sure, but the "slight dash of the Spanish" gives a hint. It could be borrowed from the Spanish *hobo*, or *jobo*, a word which appeared in print as far back as 1516. This word, in turn, comes from the Taino Indian language spoken in the West Indies and refers to a tree that grows there. How could a tree become a tramp? Well, over the centuries Spanish *jobo* acquired other more relevant meanings. In Mexico *jobo* can refer to a Guatemalan; in Cuba, *correr jobos* means "to play truant." So to avoid the taint of the term *tramp*, an American wanderer might be happy to adopt the exotic *hobo*.

In American English, it has continued to imply relatively higher status than *vagrant* or *tramp*. The exact definition has depended on who was using the word, but *hobo* has generally meant "a wanderer who is willing to work."

1848 grapevine

First came the telegraph, then the grapevine. In fact, one led to the other. This would seem to reverse the natural order, in that Mother Nature grew grapevines long before Samuel Morse strung the first telegraph wire from Washington to Baltimore in 1844. And Americans talked of grapevines long before then too; there is mention of "grape Vines" in Rhode Island in 1654. But it was the likeness—and unlikeness—of grapevines to telegraph wires that inspired the modern use of *grapevine* to refer to the means by which unofficial news and rumors are spread.

In contrast to the straight copper wire of the telegraph, a grapevine is gnarled and twisted. So the *grapevine telegraph,* as it was originally called, was also gnarled. Like Morse's telegraph, it was speedy and carried news, but unlike the Morse telegraph, it operated privately and by word of mouth. Public and official news zipped along the telegraph wires; nearly as quickly went the person-to-person reports of the grapevine.

Since the grapevine was clandestine, we do not know when it was first used, but the late 1840s is a safe guess. There is a printed report in 1852 declaring, "By the Grape Vine Telegraph Line . . . we have received the following." In *Up from Slavery* (1901), Booker T. Washington marvels at how rapidly slaves in the South got news about the abolition movement, Lincoln's campaign for the presidency, and the Civil War through the "grape-vine telegraph."

Coming from unofficial and often unknown sources, news on the grapevine was properly viewed with skepticism. Soldiers in the Civil War used *grapevine* to mean "gossip" and "rumor," news that was not to be trusted. Around the same time, out in California, *grapevine telegraph* meant "a BOGUS (1797) or tardy source of information." A newspaper that suspected a rival publication of inventing fictitious reports would accuse it of using the grapevine telegraph instead of the real thing.

The telegraph now is in disuse, but in this era of instant electronic communication, the grapevine is stronger than ever, efficiently circulating news, gossip, and rumor in an organization or community outside of official channels.

1849 tenderfoot

The California gold rush enriched the American vocabulary with *forty-niner* and with mining terms like *pay dirt, placer, sluice,* and *tailings.* It also brought in the kind of person known as a *tenderfoot*. This was a beginner or newcomer, someone unaccustomed to mining and the West. Outfitted for mining, the newcomer was likely to be costumed in his first pair of cowboy boots, which would soon make the feet tender. Another word for the phenomenon was *rawheel,* as we learn from a young miner, Tommy Plunkett, who was recorded in a friend's diary in 1849 as saying, "We saw a man in Sacramento when we were on our way here, who was a tenderfoot, or rawheel, or whatever you call 'em, who struck a pocket of gold."

Tommy's second term, *rawheel,* is not elsewhere recorded, but *tenderfoot* became an enduring legacy of the gold rush. Pointing to the sore spot in a newcomer's adaptation to the rugged life, it has proved its usefulness. For example, Elizabeth Custer, the general's widow, used it in an 1890 memoir: "The frontiersman had then, as now, a great 'despise,' as they put it, for the tenderfoot."

The twentieth century gave new life to the word when it gave birth to the Boy Scouts. The English founder (in 1910) of the Boy Scouts, Sir Robert Baden-Powell, could think of no better word than the American *tenderfoot* for the first and lowest of the ranks in his outdoor program for boys. The American Boy Scouts, founded a year later, used the same designation. As a result, throughout much of this century, many young American boys of all races, religions, and social levels have experienced first hand the meaning of *tenderfoot*.

1850 prohibition

Prohibition has lurked in the English language since the fourteenth century, when it was borrowed from the French of the ruling classes and law courts. But until modern times it was a rare word, confined for the most part to legal documents. So was the related verb *prohibit;* most English speakers preferred the Anglo-Saxon *forbid.* Shakespeare uses both *prohibit* and *prohibition* only once, the King James Bible not at all. They are forbidden territory.

A reform movement in mid-nineteenth-century America changed all that. The temperance movement borrowed *prohibition* from lawyers and legislators as a one-word summary of its goal: to pass laws that would rid the country of alcoholic beverages. So, for example, the 1851 annual report of the American Temperance Union declared, "The State of Vermont has struggled arduously to arrive at the summit level of entire prohibition."

Temperance, misleadingly, hinted at compromise, implying that moderate drinking was the desired end, as Benjamin Franklin had stated for the virtue of Temperance: "Eat not to Dulness. Drink not to elevation." But the movement wanted total abstinence, and it needed absolute language to make its goal clear. Here it must have been influenced by the antislavery movement, which often involved the same individuals. ABOLITION (1787) was the word chosen to conjure the end of slavery. If *abolition* had not already been adopted for that purpose, it could have been used against alcohol; then again, if it had not been in use against slavery, those against alcohol might never have thought to adopt a word ending in *–tion*. By its similar sound *prohibition* echoes *abolition*'s ring of absolute war against evil.

The battle over prohibition intensified during the remainder of the nineteenth century and the early part of the twentieth. By 1919, if alcohol was not on the tip of everyone's tongue, *prohibition* was, with the passage of the Eighteenth Amendment to the United States Constitution. It inaugurated the "noble experiment" that lasted thirteen years, till the

Twenty-First Amendment undid it officially, as bootleggers and gangsters had undone it already. Those events of the early twentieth century made *Prohibition* the word for a dry moment of American history.

1851 bloomers

Mrs. Amelia Bloomer, an early feminist, was delighted to be able to publish articles in her magazine *The Lily* about a new, liberating costume for women. Conventional fashion of the mid-nineteenth century was a long dress with skirts that scraped the ground, collecting mud and dust. The new costume raised the skirt to knee length, preserving modesty by encasing the lower limbs in a kind of loose pantaloons, snug around the ankles—not unlike the lower part of today's jogging suit. To complete the outfit, the modern woman wore a short jacket and a broad-brimmed hat.

Because it was associated with Mrs. Bloomer, the outfit with short skirt and pants became known as a *Bloomer suit* or *Bloomer costume*. The distinctive and shockingly visible pants themselves soon acquired the name *bloomers,* though Mrs. Bloomer protested that she wasn't the inventor. The *Boston Transcript* reported in May 1851, "The first 'Bloomer' made its appearance in our city yesterday." And *Harper's* magazine for September of that year communicated, "The ladies seem determined to reduce the volume of their dresses. This is manifested . . . at home by the general favor in which the 'bloomers' are held."

1852 filibuster

It began with pirates. The Dutch had a descriptive term for them: *vrijbuiter,* which roughly translates into English as *freebooter*—that is, someone free of national allegiance who sought booty. Other languages borrowed *vrijbuiter* too. The French translated it as *filibustier,* the Spanish *filibustero.* And from the Spanish we derived the American English *filibuster.*

Why Spanish? Because a new kind of filibuster was taking place in the Spanish-speaking parts of North and South America in the nineteenth century, and citizens of the United States were among the most involved. This new piracy occurred on land rather than at sea, and it aimed at capturing whole countries rather than ships. After the revolutions of the 1820s had swept most of Latin America free of Spanish control, the weak new governments provided tempting opportunities for adventurers seeking to bring democracy, or do business, or both. One such adventurer was William Walker of Nashville, who tried unsuccessfully to capture Lower California in 1853–54 and successfully installed himself as president of Nicaragua in 1856. Our government was not amused; the U.S. Navy routed him out one year later. He died in 1860 while attempting to conquer all of Central America.

By 1852 this adventuring was much discussed in Washington, D.C. In January of 1853 one U.S. senator was recorded as accusing another of "filibustering" against the United States. The term then began to be applied to a particular tactic: taking advantage of the Senate's privilege of unlimited speech to delay action on a bill. A senator can speak on any topic for as long as he or she wishes. This provided a way for the minority party, a small group, or even one determined individual to prevent the majority from having its way. In the mid-twentieth century southerners used this kind of filibuster to block civil rights laws that would end the legality of discrimination based on race. An overwhelming majority of the Senate (formerly two-thirds, now three-fifths) can vote to cut off debate, and that finally happened in 1957 to pass the first civil rights bill.

1853 cafeteria

As the *cafe* ("coffee") indicates, a cafeteria was originally just a coffee shop of one kind or another. But by the time English speakers in California borrowed the word from Mexican Spanish in the 1850s, the menu seems to have included alcohol too. "It is rather a place for drinking than for eating," one such Californian explained in 1853, "and in this respect, the name has little of the meaning current in parts of Mexico where a 'cafeteria' is a small restaurant serving ordinary alcoholic drinks and plain meals."

Whatever the origin, *cafeteria* was a quiet part of the Western vocabulary until the 1890s, when a new kind of cafeteria sprung up in places like Chicago as well as California. This new cafeteria was a restaurant that distinguished itself by having patrons serve as their own waiters.

In the twentieth century, cafeterias gained in importance in American life, while *cafeteria* gained in importance in the American vocabulary as we helped ourselves to the suffix *–teria* for other self-service or simply up-to-date establishments like the basketeria, caketeria, chocolateria, groceteria, and furnitureteria in the 1920s and 1930s, and the booketeria in the 1940s. In the 1950s, the first part of *cafeteria* was blended with the last part of *auditorium* for the architectural innovation called the *cafetorium*, where patrons could eat and be lectured to at the same time.

And though cafeterias have largely been supplanted by FAST FOOD (1954) establishments, and *–teria* no longer is a freely added suffix, *cafeteria* lives on in the late twentieth century in the cafeteria plan for fringe benefits that allows employees to choose their own.

1854 peter out

Like the gold in the hills of California, American English had begun to peter out by 1854, as in the novel *Puddleford and Its People* by Henry H. Riley, published that year: "He 'hoped this 'spectable meeting war n't going to Peter-out.'" Abraham Lincoln used the phrase too, according to an 1865 biography: "The store in which he clerked was 'petering out'—to use his own expression."

Peter out, as a literal mining term and a figure of speech meaning "dwindle" or "give out," derives from *peter,* attested as early as 1846 in Quincy, Illinois: "When my mineral petered why they all Petered *me.* If so be I gets a lead, why I'm Mr. Tiff again." Where that *peter* came from, no one knows. In any case, plain *peter* soon petered out in favor of *peter out,* as in the words of Riley and Lincoln, and this 1884 dialogue from *Century Magazine:* "We'll have a blank good time, . . . anyhow, as long as the whisky don't peter out."

A technical mining definition of *peter out* appears in the *Century Dictionary* (1889–91): "to split up into branches and become lost: said of a vein which runs out or disappears, so that it can no longer be followed by the miner." But Americans have kept *peter out* from petering out by using it in all sorts of contexts having nothing to do with mines; a feud, a road, a river, a crop, a hurricane, even a BOOM (1871) for a political candidate all can be said to *peter out.*

1855 bluejeans

The life of an ordinary citizen at the time of the American Revolution could involve extraordinary events—hunting and farming in the wilderness, whaling, fighting in the war, and in one case, being captured by the British and held in England for forty-eight years, then returning a forgotten hero. This last was the case for one Israel Potter, whose partly imagined biography was written in 1855 by Herman Melville, who makes this remark towards the end of the book: "For a time back, across the otherwise blue-jean career of Israel, Paul Jones flits and re-flits like a crimson thread. One more brief intermingling of it, and to the plain old homespun we return."

Melville's statement is evidence that bluejeans were recognized in those days as the everyday wear of everyday Americans. More evidence comes from the career of James Douglass Williams, governor of Indiana (1876–80). He was known as "Blue Jeans" Williams because he wore bluejeans to cultivate the rural vote.

More Americans now wear jeans (not always blue) on more occasions; women and men, rich and poor, in college classrooms and at parties, and to night clubs as well as to work. Designer jeans (1966) were a successful twentieth-century attempt to make jeans fashionable as well as down to earth, thus raising their humble prices.

Jeans themselves are not an American invention. The word *jean* dates at least from the 1560s, referring to cloth of Genoa, Italy, and by the 1840s in England we read of workers in stables wearing jeans. But the association of bluejeans with cowboys and miners, and the success of the San Francisco manufacturer Levi Straus & Co., has given *bluejeans* and *jeans* an American accent known around the world.

1856 high muckamuck

Americans scorned the tired old titles of Europe. We had no emperors or kings, no princes or dukes. Instead, we invented our own fanciful names for leaders, borrowing freely from Indian languages. Somehow, however, dignified Indian titles like *sachem* (1622) when applied to not-so-noble American politicians seemed more mocking than reverent.

The grand mockery of them all was an utter and probably deliberate mistranslation. It was from the Chinook Jargon, a mixture of Chinook Indian language, English, and French that was used as a trade language throughout the Pacific Northwest. Thanks to researcher Charles Lovell, we know exactly where *high muckamuck* came from. *Muckamuck* means "food"; *high* means "much or plenty"; so *high muckamuck* means "lots of food." It was used to advertise a grocery store in the Portland *Oregonian* in 1853: "Thomas Pritchard, General Store: Hiou Muckamuck of all kinds."

That was enough for one California wag, who wrote in the *Democratic State Journal* of Sacramento for November 1, 1856, "The professors—the high 'Muck-a-Mucks'—tried fusion, and produced confusion." Not surprisingly, Mark Twain picked up the phrase, writing in a letter of 1866, "Not if I was High-You-Muck-a-Muck and King of Wawhoo." There have been many variations, including *high mucky-muck, high muckety-muck,* and *high-monkey-muck,* and they all refer to a person who assumes an air of importance.

1857 shindig

On the American FRONTIER (1676), the partying sometimes grew strenuous. During the course of the nineteenth century, we came up with an appropriate name for it: *shindig.* The word may well have come from *shindy,* meaning "a row or commotion," known since the 1830s. To *cut shindies* was "to make a ruckus." By the late 1850s, someone evidently had mistaken *shindy* for a mispronunciation of *shin dig,* a kick in the shins, such as might happen during the course of a shindy. An 1859 dictionary of Americanisms indeed defined *shindig* as "a blow on the shins. Southern."

Shindig in the sense of "a boisterous dance or party" made its way to the West, appearing in a Bret Harte story in 1871: " 'Is this a dashed Puritan meeting?' 'It's no Pike County shindig.' " We are more laid back about the shindigs we hold nowadays; no matter how noisy, they rarely involve bruises.

1858 piker

Pike County, Missouri, is located on the Mississippi River north of St. Louis and just south of Mark Twain's Hannibal. It is still a quiet rural county, noted for the Stark Brothers Nursery and not much else. But its name is known nationwide, thanks to Pikers, who followed the gold rushes to California and Colorado in the mid-nineteenth century. By the late 1850s they were so prominent in these adventures that *Piker* became the nickname for anyone from Missouri, not just from Pike County. We find them in a Marysville, California, newspaper of 1860: "Pillbox said they were there for the benefit of the 'Pikers,' that they might learn to read."

The Pikers were not noted for quickness of wit or spectacular success at finding gold, but they did gain a reputation for frugality. A Piker would not gamble, drink, or spend his money to excess. Thus he was viewed by the free-spending majority as a timid cheapskate. And so *piker,* having lost its association with a particular place and thereby its capital letter, came to mean someone of no boldness or ambition, someone who ventures little and always plays it safe. The term applied first to small-stakes gamblers, then to small-stakes investors in the stock market, then to slackers in any enterprise. Missouri nowadays has no more pikers than anyplace else.

1859 Dixie

On a frosty morning in February 1859, *Dixie* was born singing. It was first heard not in the South, however, but in New York City. The name appears in a minstrel song written and performed by Dan Emmett, a man from Ohio who imitated the language of black slaves in the South: "Gib me de place called Dixie Land, wid hoe and shubble in my hand." That song passed into obscurity, but *Dixie* did not, thanks to another song Emmett wrote and first performed on April 4, 1859, also in New York City. This song took *Dixie's Land* as its subject and title, and contains the still familiar lines "In Dixie Land whar I was born in" and "I wish I was in Dixie."

Where Emmett got *Dixie* is still anyone's guess. It may derive from *Mason and Dixon's Line,* the name of the boundary separating North and South. Or it may come from *dix,* the French word for "ten," which was printed on the back of ten-dollar bills issued by the Citizens' Bank of New Orleans. In any case, Emmett's song made *Dixie* the sentimental nickname for the South. Its tunefulness and Southern patriotism ("In Dixie land I'll take my stand to live and die in Dixie") were heard when *Dixie's Land* was played on the frosty morning of February 18, 1861, in Montgomery, Alabama, as Jefferson Davis was inaugurated as president of the Confederacy. Four years and two months later the Confederacy surrendered not only its armies but also its song. "I insisted yesterday that we fairly captured it," President Lincoln said on April 10, 1865. "I presented the question to the Attorney General, and he gave his opinion that it is our lawful prize. I ask the band to give us a good turn on it."

Although *Dixie* was not invented in Dixie, *Dixieland* was. It is the name for a style of jazz first heard in New Orleans in the 1920s.

1860 vigilante

"Eternal vigilance is the price of liberty," declared the antislavery orator Wendell Phillips in 1856. But the vigilantes of the Western states had something different in mind: not liberty, but keeping order in unruly towns. They enforced the law—or rather, they took the law into their own hands and enforced it as they chose, answering to no higher authority.

The story of the vigilantes begins not in the West but in the South. Vigilance committees were formed there, starting in the 1830s, to keep blacks and abolitionists in their place: that is, silent and obedient to the proslavery majority. In response, northerners founded their own vigilance committees to help fugitive slaves.

A different kind of vigilance was called for in the West of the Gold Rush days. On the waterfront of San Francisco, a "Barbary Coast" of disreputable service industries had sprung up, providing intoxicating beverages, games of chance and skill, houses of ill-repute, and generous opportunities for violence and mayhem. To bring the Barbary Coast under control, respectable citizens formed a Vigilance Committee in 1851. By 1860, members were being called by the Spanish name *vigilantes.*

Groups of vigilantes were organized in other Western cities too. In an 1865 account of a visit to Montana, we are told that "the power is vested in the 'Vigilantes,' a secret tribunal of citizens, organized before civil laws were framed."

Sometimes the motives of vigilantes were honorable, but sometimes they merely dispensed their own version of LYNCH LAW (1780), also an American invention. Citizen initiative in maintaining order, if not always law, has persisted to the present day, but now it usually takes the milder form of a neighborhood watch (1972).

1861 caboose

Only in America did a cookstove turn into a railroad car. That was the fate of the caboose. We find it thus transformed as far

back as 1861, in *Reminiscences in the Life of a Railroad Engineer:* "I never prepared myself for another midnight ride in the 'Caboose' of a freight train by telling horrid stories before I started." By then it was the name for the small car at the end of a freight train that served as the conductor's office and crew quarters.

The word ultimately comes from the Dutch. Long before railroads, it went to sea as the name for a cookstove on a sailing ship, or the chimney for it. Thomas Jefferson knew that meaning of the word; in 1791 he proposed distilling fresh water "on board of vessels at sea, by the common iron caboose (with small alteration,) by the same fire and in the same time which is used for cooking the ship's provisions." Meanwhile, on land, *caboose* was occasionally used to mean a small dwelling or shack. There is an 1839 congressional reference to a "little caboose of a post office."

A few years later, when American railroads began to haul freight over long distances, they contrived a special car for the train crew, something like a caboose shack, with a caboose style cookstove to keep warm. Soon the car itself was called a *caboose.* Train crews called it by many other names as well, including *waycar* (1879), *conductor's car* (1895), *crummy* (1916), and *hack* (1916).

For more than a century the little red caboose was a distinctive feature of American railroading, but work rules were changed and crews reduced in the 1970s, and cabooses were consigned to museums, playgrounds, and scrap.

1862 greenback

The beginnings of many words are obscure, but we know exactly when *greenback* entered the vocabulary of American English. It was in the Civil War year of 1862, after a year of fighting had made it clear to officials in Washington that there would be no quick victory and vast additional resources would be needed. Paper money was already in circulation, issued by state banks, but the federal government had restricted itself to coins, and coins were fast disappearing under the pressures of war. On February 25, therefore, for the first time in history, the United States Congress approved the issue of paper money backed not with gold or silver but simply with the full faith and credit of the government, and valid for all debts, public and private (except duties on imports and interest on the public debt).

But why *greenback*? Because of a precaution against the common practices of altering and counterfeiting paper money. To prevent these, a patented ink had been devised that was difficult to erase and also difficult to imitate because it had a secret formula. Being green instead of the usual black, it was also difficult to photograph. The Secretary of the Treasury ordered this special ink to be used for one side of the new notes. Because of the distinctive color on the back of the notes, the Union soldiers who received them in pay began calling them *greenbacks,* and soon everyone else called them *greenbacks* too. The blue or gray Confederate money similarly became known as *bluebacks* and *graybacks.*

From that time to the present, all U.S. paper money has had a green back, making green the color of money. So we have coined terms like *green* itself meaning "money" (1898), *green handshake* (1975), "a bribe or tip," and GREENMAIL

(1983), a play on *blackmail*. In recent years, *green* has also been used for a quite different purpose: to describe those who have concern for the natural environment (1971), but the connection of *green* with money will remain as long as the green stuff (1887) is in circulation.

1863 AWOL

Americans on both sides in the Civil War sometimes skedaddled (1861, a Union term), not only from the battlefield but from their assigned posts. The phrase *absent without leave* was used to designate those who were gone for a relatively short time, as opposed to permanent deserters. In the Army of the Confederacy, such a soldier was punished by being draped with a sign bearing the initials "A.W.O.L." to signify his crime, that is, being *a*bsent *w*ith*o*ut *l*eave.

At first *A.W.O.L.* was pronounced letter by letter. This is evident in the humorous World War I variant *A.W.O. Loose,* meaning the same thing as *A.W.O.L.* By the start of World War II, however, the pronunciation had changed to "AY wall," as if the initials constituted one word rather than an abbreviation. Humorously contrived attributions of the letters in World War II included "A Wolf On the Loose" and "After Women Or Liquor." In our century, it has also been possible to be AWOL from a pursuit in civilian life.

1864 deadline

It began as a real line, drawn in the dirt or marked by a fence or rail, restricting prisoners in Civil War camps. They were warned, "If you cross this line, you're dead." To make dead sure this important boundary was not overlooked, guards and prisoners soon were calling it by its own bluntly descriptive name, the *dead line.* An 1864 congressional report explains the usage in one camp: "A railing around the inside of the stockade, and about twenty feet from it, constitutes the 'dead line,' beyond which the prisoners are not allowed to pass."

Nothing could be more emphatic than *dead line* to designate a limit, so we Americans happily applied the term to other situations with strict boundaries. For example, the storyteller O. Henry wrote in 1909 about crossing "the dead line of good behavior." But it was the newspaper business that made *deadline* more than just a historical curiosity. To have the latest news and still get a newspaper printed and distributed on time requires strict time limits for those who write it. Yet many are the excuses for writers to go beyond their allotted time: writers' block, writers' perfectionism, or just plain procrastination. (Perhaps the writer is a deadbeat (1863)—another *dead* word invented by Americans during the Civil War.) Seeking the strongest possible language to counter these temptations, editors set deadlines, with the implication that "Your story is dead—*You* are dead—if you go beyond this time to finish it."

Our urgent twentieth century has made such deadlines essential not just for reporters and other writers but in every kind of activity; there are deadlines for finishing a job or assignment, for entering a contest, for ransoming hostages, or for buying a product at the special sale price.

1865 commuter

Americans did not invent the suburbs, but they did create the commuter—someone who shuttles from a home in the suburbs to a job in the city and back again every day. Residing at a considerable distance from work was made possible by the invention of the railroad, and the name for someone who did so was made possible by the invention in the 1840s of a ticket good for multiple rides, the commutation ticket. Here *commutation* means "an exchange of one thing for another," especially if the new thing is a consolidation or reduction of the old. That is what the commutation ticket did: it exchanged individual tickets for a collective one at a lower price. The holder of such a ticket, being involved in the commutation, was thus called a *commuter*. Here is an 1865 exerpt from the *Atlantic*

Monthly about railroads: "Two or three may be styled com-muters' roads, running chiefly for the accommodation of city business-men with suburban residences."

In that statement we already see the modern connection of *commuter* with a lifestyle rather than a kind of ticket. Soon it no longer mattered whether the person held a commutation ticket, only where the person lived and worked. A commuter could ride a trolley, subway, cable car, or ferry as well as a train. In the twentieth century the commuter turned to the bus and automobile. While public transportation still carries com-muters, the modern image of the commuter has become the lone driver on the freeway (1930), expressway (1944) or inter-state (1968), enduring gapers' blocks and GRIDLOCK (1980), talking on a cell phone (1984) to a drive-time talk radio (1985) host.

END OF

THE

FRONTIER:

1866-1900

The westering was as big as God, and the slow steps that
made the movement piled up and piled up until the
continent was crossed.

Then we came down to the sea, and it was done. . . .

There's no place to go.

—JOHN STEINBECK, "The Leader of the People"

At the end of the Civil War in 1865, the English language was spoken in North America from the Atlantic
to the Pacific. With the purchase of Alaska in 1867, the boundaries of the continental United States stretched to their full
present-day extent. As Steinbeck said, we could go no further.
We as a nation were all grown up. But we were not yet civilized, or at least not yet citified. So during the rest of the nineteenth century, we worked on what we took to be improve-
ments to the land we already owned. As the *frontier* (1676),
that former fixture of American life, retreated to the Western

deserts and then vanished altogether, we directed more and more of our attention to city life and its new amenities like the electric light, the telephone, and the automobile.

Our words for these years have little to say about nature or rural life, about the challenges of the frontier, or even about government and politics—except for *carpetbagger* (1868) in the aftermath of the Civil War. Instead, we centered on urban matters: economic *boom* (1871) making possible the first *sky-scrapers* (1883); *country clubs* (1891) for some urban dwellers and *sweatshops* (1892) for others; the threat of *gangsters* (1894) and concern for the *underprivileged* (1897). We created respectful terms for *Hispanics* (1889) and *Afro-Americans* (1890). We said *hello* (1885) on the telephone and used *credit cards* (1888) for the first time. For entertainment, we went to *Chatauquas* (1873), or the *midway* (1893) of a fair, or became baseball *fans* (1886) eating *potato chips* (1878), *hamburgers* (1884) and *hot dogs* (1895). We tried to hit the *jackpot* (1879). For our health, we drank *moxie* (1876) and ate *cereal* (1899).

We tried *lipstick* (1880)—used by actors at first. Some urban *dudes* (1877) wore *sideburns* (1887). And we watched out for what was *phony* (1900). We were fascinated by *yellow journalism* (1898). The modern world was rushing toward us.

1866 nifty

Sure, we had been engaged in a great Civil War, but some Americans were managing to have a nifty time in spite of it. One of them was Mark Twain, who used *nifty* in his depiction of slang used in Virginia City, Nevada, in the early 1860s. "As all the peoples of the earth had representative adventurers in the Silverland," Twain wrote in *Roughing It* (1872), "and as each adventurer had brought the slang of his nation or his locality with him, the combination made the slang of Nevada the richest and the most infinitely varied and copious that had ever existed anywhere in the world, perhaps, except in the mines of California in the 'early days.' Slang was the language of Nevada. It was hard to preach a sermon without it, and be understood."

Twain continues with the story of Buck Fanshaw's funeral. A fireman, Scotty Briggs, making arrangements for the funeral, says to the puzzled minister, "We are going to get the thing up regardless, you know. He was always nifty himself, and so you bet you his funeral ain't going to be no slouch—solid silver door-plate on his coffin, six plumes on the hearse. . . ."

Another writer of the gold- and silver-fevered West, Bret Harte, employs *nifty* in a poem written in the 1860s, "The Tale of a Pony." He sets his humorous story in far-away Paris, but uses the American slang word to describe his young heroine's "new turn-out," or horse-drawn carriage: "Smart! You bet your life 'twas that! Nifty! (short for *magnificat*)." Harte's explanation of *nifty* is not meant to be taken seriously (in fact, the word's origins are unknown), but the word he and Twain presented to the public has found many nifty uses ever since.

1867 maverick

It was all the fault, or the bright idea, of Samuel Augustus Maverick, who lived from 1803 to 1870. Descended from an old and notable New England family, he sought his fortune in Texas and there inadvertently made a name for himself. He took up cattle ranching, which was quite a different proposition from raising livestock back East. In Texas cattle grazed on the open range, without fences to keep one herd separate from another, and thus there was much opportunity for theft and disputes over ownership. To identify their cattle, ranchers branded them, rounding up the calves each year for this purpose.

But Maverick put no brand on his cattle. Stories about "old man Maverick" give various reasons for his abstinence: he was lazy; he objected to the cruelty of branding. Whatever the reason, if he had been an ordinary citizen, this practice would have put him at the mercy of other ranchers, who would have appropriated his cattle and marked them with their own brands. But Maverick was influential: mayor of San Antonio, member of the Texas legislature, and holder of 385,000 acres, he was able instead to claim that any unbranded calf was his. And so, either in earnest or in jest, the name *maverick* was applied to all cattle without brands. In 1867 a writer complained, "The term maverick which was formerly applied to unbranded yearlings is now applied to every calf which can be separated from the mother cow—the consequence is, the fastest branders are accumulating the largest stocks."

It was too good a word to leave to the cattle. What better word to use for a politician who was "unbranded" by a party label, not "owned" by special interests? In 1886 a San Francisco publication called the *California Maverick* defined it: "He holds maverick views" means "his views were untainted by partisanship." A Massachusetts politician declared in 1905, "I am running as a maverick; I have no man's brand upon me." *Maverick* accords with our American inclination to admire someone who goes his or her own way. A loner (1947) may be loony, but a maverick is an independent thinker.

1868 carpetbagger

Before the grip (1879), the suitcase (1902), the tote bag (1900), and the BACKPACK (1914) had their days as travel accessories of choice, Americans traveling light packed their belongings in carpetbags, invented in the 1830s. Long before Samsonite, the carpetbag was valued for its durability, for it was made of two sturdy pieces of carpet sewn together to which handles were attached.

It was this carpetbag that Northern adventurers brought with them to the South after the Civil War, having little in the way of luggage to slow them down as they sought political office and profit in the land of their defeated enemy. North and South, carpetbaggers were denounced. "A great deal of bitterness has been shown in all the conventions in regard to the presence, and great prominence as members, of what the Louisiana people call 'carpet-baggers'—men, that is, who are new-comers in the country," wrote a Northern reporter in 1868. "I would sooner trust the Negro than the white scalawag or carpet-bagger," declared one unreconstructed white southerner in that same year.

Carpetbagger has outlived the carpetbag. It still refers to someone who has newly come to a place with pretensions to take charge, especially a politician.

1869 showboat

Not that anything like the melodrama of *Showboat,* the musical based on Edna Ferber's bestselling 1926 novel, ever actually happened on the rivers of nineteenth-century America. Nobody ever sang "Old Man River" until Oscar Hammerstein II and Jerome Kern set *Showboat* to music on the Broadway stage in 1929. But for a century there really were floating theaters, what we now call *showboats,* on the great waterways of middle America. The rivers steamed with them, especially after the Civil War.

The first "Floating Theatre" was built in Pittsburgh in 1831 for the Chapman family of English actors. It was a narrow box on a narrow barge, 100 feet long and just 16 feet wide, but it was a real theatre, complete with a stage at one end, a pit in the middle, and a gallery at the other end. The Chapmans floated it down the Ohio and Mississippi rivers, going from landing to landing during the fall and winter season. At the end of their journey, in New Orleans, they sold it for firewood and returned to Pittsburgh to build another for the next season. In 1836 they were able to afford a steamboat of their own to use as a permanent floating theatre.

Other boats followed, offering everything from serious drama to circuses. The most spectacular was Spaulding and Rogers's *Floating Circus Palace,* with 3400 seats, which was launched in Cincinnati in 1851. After interruption by the Civil War, such boats flourished as never before, and we find the word *showboat* used to describe them in 1869. These showboats continued to carry fancy names, including *New Sensation* (1878), *Twentieth Century* (1882), Dan Rice's *Floating Opera* (1886), *Theatorium* (1889), Robinson's *Floating Palace*

(1893), and *Cotton Blossom* (1909). *Showboat* itself was too pedestrian ever to be the actual name of a boat.

Sometimes instead of *showboat* the word *boat-show* was used for these waterborne temples of the muses, but the musical *Showboat* has kept the former in our vocabulary long after the disappearance of the boats themselves. In recent years, to *showboat* has been used to mean "to show off," and a *showboat* is someone who tries to get noticed.

1870 bathtub

Mark Twain seems to have invented the bathtub. Well, not the object itself. Baths, and wooden tubs for bathing, sometimes called *bathing tubs,* had been around for centuries. But Twain appears to be the first to join the two one-syllable words *bath* and *tub.* In *Innocents Abroad* (1869) he wrote, "They were going to put all three of us in one bath-tub." And in "A Ghost Story" of 1870 he wrote, "I . . . was sorry that he was gone . . . and sorrier still that he had carried off my red blanket and my bath-tub." By 1870, then, we can say that the bathtub had been installed in our language.

The new word coincided with the introduction of indoor plumbing, when bathtubs of cast iron were permanently

located in bathrooms. In the late nineteenth and early twentieth centuries, bathtubs had feet to hold them off the floor. Gradually, the built-in style of bathtub surrounded with ceramic tiles became the fashion.

During Prohibition, when people resorted to home distillation of grain to make gin, it was quickly dubbed *bathtub gin.* The bathtub also figures in nautical slang, including *bathtub weather* (1894) for fine sailing weather and *bathtub sailor* (1944) for a sailor based on land.

1871 boom

Boom and bust has been the roller-coaster pattern of the American economy. Or at least *boom* and *bust* have been used as snappy labels for the great expansions and contractions of business activity as the country has grown. The terms have also been used for small expansions and contractions, for a new town booming with construction or a player going bust in a card game. BUST (1764) actually came long before *boom,* the first appearance of *boom* in the business sense apparently due to Mark Twain: "My popularity is booming, now," he wrote to his publisher in 1871.

But *boom* quickly made up for its late start toward the end of the nineteenth century and the start of the twentieth. This was the great era of boom towns (1900) and boom cities (1904), of real-estate booms (1887), cotton booms (1880), immigration booms (1890), oil booms (1907), even presidential booms (1887). Encouraging all this activity were boomers (1880), people who spread enthusiasm for a project, an investment, a town, or a candidate. Those who did this for a living were the forerunners of those we now call by the more polite names of *promoters* or *public relations people.*

The later twentieth century had a boom of its own, a baby boom (1941). The boom in births in the United States began after the end of World War II and continued until the early 1960s. Some references to the baby boom were made during those years, but it was only in 1974, well after the baby boom was over, that those born during the boom were first labeled *baby boomers.* Because of their numbers, the supposedly self-indulgent boomers stayed in the public eye as they aged, acquiring new fads and tastes and contrasting with the members of the leaner, supposedly less-privileged Generation X (1990) that followed.

1872 jambalaya

The word *jambalaya* in English dates from 1872 as a borrowing from the French of the Cajuns in Louisiana. It appears in the *New Orleans Times* for June 28, 1872: "Those who brought victuals, such as gumbo, jambalaya, etc., all began eating and drinking." The word is from Provençal, the Romance language of southwestern France, where *jambalaia* is composed mostly of rice and chicken or other fowl.

In Cajun culture jambalaya is a staple of everyday cooking. Its contents are so varied that it has been said, if you have it in the kitchen you can put it in the pot. Popular ingredients besides rice and chicken include sausage, seafood, tomatoes, celery, onion, and green peppers. And don't forget the cayenne pepper, garlic, thyme, and rosemary.

The traditional way to cook it, as with most stews, is for a long time. But like everything else, it is available nowadays as FAST FOOD (1954) too.

In Louisiana, *jambalaya* is used figuratively too, for "a mixture of ingredients." The *Times-Picayune* of New Orleans noted in 1951, "A Creole beauty, a murder in a fashionable French home, an illicit love affair . . . —these are the ingredients of the movies' latest jambalaya."

1873 Chautauqua

It was, and still is, just a little town, a long lake, and a county at the far western end of New York State, all bearing the Indian name *Chautauqua*. In the Seneca language *Chautauqua* is said to mean "foggy place" or "one has taken out fish there," but it was the fishers of men who made *Chautauqua* a household word. The lake became a religious and educational summer resort. In 1873 the Chautauqua Lake Camp Meeting Association was formed, and the improving began in earnest. Ministers and scholars, politicians and musicians, even exercise experts came to the healthy summer air of Chautauqua to better their audiences in mind and body, and to assuage any worries the audiences might have had that they were frivolously taking a mere vacation. The name of the place became identified with a system of self-improvement.

By the 1880s the Chautauqua idea of combining relaxation and edification had caught on as far west as Dakota Territory. Speakers and performers went on a Chautauqua circuit from resort to resort giving Chautauquas, usually in tents or just the open air. There was even a Chautauqua salute, waving a white handkerchief, first used in appreciation of a pantomime lecture given by a deaf man at Lake Chautauqua in 1877.

Chautauquas lasted until well into the twentieth century, but they were eclipsed starting in the 1930s by the Depression, radio, movies, television, and air conditioning. Towards the end of the century, however, Chautauquas saw a modest revival, once again bringing noted speakers to towns and resorts for a combination of fresh ideas and fresh air.

1874 canning

The important method of preserving food by heating it and sealing it in a jar or can was developed throughout the nineteenth century by the French and the English as well as the Americans. In midcentury, we introduced some of the terminology that developed with the method to the English language. Canned vegetables were mentioned in America in 1859, while in 1861 the Illinois Agricultural Society discussed fruit that "will be dried, or canned, for export."

The year 1874 can claim our attention here simply for the use of *canning* as the name of a process or business. In Oregon that year, there was a notice that a "Capt. West . . . has adventured into the canning of beef and mutton." And a U.S. Department of Agriculture Report for 1874 stated, "In 1873 there were in Maine thirty-three canning-factories. . . . The canning establishment of Mr. William Archdeacon . . . occupies 13 acres of land."

In the years before refrigeration, home canning in Mason jars (1858) was an important household activity. In the present day, it remains a popular avocation.

1875 P.D.Q.

Throughout the nineteenth century, initials touched the American sense of humor. A Boston newspaper playing with misspelled initials in 1839 concocted *O.K.,* the most successful of American linguistic innovations. And in 1875, a play featuring a similar use of initials became a great hit, touring the country for more than 2,500 performances in the next fifteen years.

The play was *The Mighty Dollar* by Benjamin E. Woolf. Its initializing character is the money-hungry M.C., or Member of Congress, Judge Bardwell Slote, who punctuates his speeches with "by a large majority" and uses more than two dozen initialisms in the course of the play. The only one that has stuck in our vocabulary is *P.D.Q.,* from his line, "That's right, you'd better step P.D.Q., pretty damn quick."

The judge, who is annoyed when another character does not "speak straight United States," also plays with *K*'s, in "the K. of his M., the color of his money" and "You are K.K., quite correct." He uses initials in his complaints: "a D.D.S., a damn dirty shake"; "a P.A., a perfect ass"; "my R.I., sir, my righteous indignation"; "the W.T., the worthless traitor!"; and "H.M., Holy Moses!" He also uses initials to fawn: "the D.O., the distinguished honor"; "the P. P., the particular pleasure"; "H.S., your humble servant"; and "O.B.I., our beauteous idol." And he manages to have "an H.O.T., a high old time" and "a T.T.T., a tip top time" until "G.I.C. Our goose is cooked!"

All these, and others like the Judge's "J.C., gin cocktail," failed to step out of the play into our general American vocabulary—all but *P.D.Q.* Why would that abbreviation be the one to succeed? Perhaps because it is the very first spoken by the Judge during the play. Or perhaps because we were in a hurry and needed a new term for it—pretty damn quick!

1876 moxie

The twentieth century may pride itself on miracles of modern medicine, but it's not the first; the nineteenth century was not shy about medical miracles of its own. It was the great era of the CURE-ALL (1821). *Moxie* had its beginning as the name for a medical marvel of this kind, invented in 1876 by Dr. Augustin Thompson of Union, Maine. If we are to believe the label on its 26-ounce bottles, this Moxie worked better than any twentieth-century wonder drug (1939): it claimed to cure "brain and nervous exhaustion, loss of manhood, imbecility and helplessness. . . . It gives a durable solid strength, and makes you eat voraciously; takes away the tired, sleepy, lifeless feeling like magic, removes fatigue from mental and physical overwork at once."

According to the label, Moxie was named after a Lieutenant Moxie, who discovered the active ingredient, "a simple sugarcane-like plant grown near the Equator and farther south." But Frederic Cassidy, editor of the *Dictionary of American Regional English,* suspects that both the lieutenant and the plant may be inventions. Dr. Thompson could have gotten the name of his tonic much closer at hand, from a plant called a *moxie-berry* that was used in Maine by Indians, and then by settlers, to make medicinal tea.

In the twentieth century, federal drug laws removed the extravagant claims from the Moxie label. But a Boston soft-drink manufacturer took over the Moxie name in the 1920s, applied it to a fizzy drink made with gentian root, and perpetuated its vigorous connotations so successfully that by the 1930s *moxie* had acquired a new life independent of the beverage. It had become a slang synonym for strength, energy, courage, and mental sharpness combined.

1877 dude

As the frontier of the Wild West began to be tamed, a certain kind of young American male turned his attention eastward, to the frontier of the civilized world of fashion. Instead of the somber black worn by his forefathers, he chose checks and bright colors. Instead of full-cut outer garments, he wore skin-tight hip-hugging pants, snug shirts and short jackets. His collar was tall, stiff and starched. His conversation was . . . well, consider this from an article on "The American 'Dude'" in 1885: "He may talk with a lisp, but when he converses on his favorite topic—woman—his conversation is peculiarly juicy. He is coldly doubtful and suspicious and ignorant of everything which the solid portion of the community regards as of great importance, but of actresses, wine and horses he can discourse feelingly." As for his costume, "his nether integuments fit like knit underwear."

Dude is recorded as early as 1877 in the words of those who were not impressed. "Don't send me any more [drawings of] women or any more dudes," grumbled the young Frederic Remington at school in 1877, preparing for his career as a Western artist. "Send me Indians, cowboys, villains or toughs." In 1879 a book titled *Fighting Indians* says that the garrison of Fort Snelling, Minnesota, "was at that time composed of dude soldiers, pets of dress parade officers." In the next century, however, westerners got theirs back from dudes at dude ranches (1921).

Early in 1883 the dude became the rage of New York City, starting with a poem in the newspaper *The World* on "The True Origin and History of 'The Dude.'" That word was said to be a great improvement on *masher* (1875) by another writer, who added that "The discovery or invention of Dood should be hailed with joyous acclaim."

The African-American use of *dude* as a synonym for "man" seems to be a descendant of this nineteenth-century character. From that usage it entered general American conversation, especially among young people, meaning "man" in the 1960s and as a general exclamation in the 1980s.

1878 potato chip

A quarter century before it got its current name, what we now know as the *potato chip* was invented, supposedly by an American Indian chef at Moon Lake Lodge in Saratoga, New York. By slicing potatoes to utmost thinness before frying them, we are told, Chef George Crum transformed a humble native American tuber into the quintessential American snack. His gourmet creations were copied throughout the resort town, and they came to be known as *Saratoga chips*. An English visitor wrote in his diary in 1865, "These potatoes are the *specialité* of the place—the 'maids of honour,' the whitebait of Saratoga. . . . They are eaten with game, they are eaten with sherry-cobblers, and they are eaten with ice-creams."

The appeal of the chips spread far beyond Saratoga, and after a while they lost the name of their birthplace in favor of a generic designation. So *The American Home Cook Book* of 1878, by "Ladies of Detroit and Other Cities," simply stated, "Put around potato chips."

For many years after their invention, potato chips remained a delicacy. Whether in a restaurant or at home, they had to be prepared fresh in the kitchen. Finally, however, with the invention of the mechanical potato peeler at the end of the nineteenth century and the development of cellophane packaging in the 1920s, potato chips became the snack food we know today, available in every grocery store and beyond.

The single word *chips* has been understood to mean *potato chips*, as in *chips and dip*, until recently, when potato chips have been rivalled in popularity by corn-based tortilla chips (1977). The tortilla chip had a predecessor in the corn chip, developed in the 1930s from a recipe by a street vendor of Mexican food in San Antonio, Texas.

Chips are known in England, too, but they are not the same thing. To this day the English use *chips* for what we know as *French fries* (1947). Our thin American product is known in England as the *potato crisp*.

1879 jackpot

Poker, an American invention of around 1830, was the game by which the West was won—and lost. During the nineteenth century, poker helped shape our vocabulary as well as our character. In poker we learned to BLUFF, making use of an innocent word from 1666, to ante up (1845), and to stand pat (1882). And we learned the pleasures and perils of going for the jackpot.

A jackpot is the betting pool in a version of draw poker that requires a pair of jacks or better to "open the pot" and start the betting. "The money up is called the pot," explained a gambler to an Indiana court in 1879, "and the man who holds jacks can require the others to bet him or to drop out." With a progressive jackpot the standards get higher: if a pot is not opened with jacks or better, then next time a pair of queens or better is required, and so on up.

Playing jackpot poker thus "jacks up" the quality of the competition and the value of the pot. If you "hit the jackpot" (1944), you have gained yourself a rich pot indeed. The jackpot increases the risk of staying in and bluffing with a poor hand because at least one player has at least minimally good cards. But it may also increase the boldness of the bluffing, and thus the size of the pot, because it takes a higher bet to persuade a player with a decent hand to drop out of the betting.

So *jackpot* has acquired two meanings beyond the realm of poker. One kind of jackpot is serious trouble. "You're probably already in the jackpot for taking a duty car out of Dade County," says a character in a mystery novel by Carl Hiaasen. But the other kind is the more familiar jackpot we hope to win, or rather to hit—in a competition, a lottery, or a lifetime.

1880 lipstick

Painting the lips was not an American invention. Our Puritan predecessors came to the New World to escape such vanities, and as the American character developed, it had a sturdy down-to-earth quality that hardly made us leaders in either urban sophistication or urban decadence. But we were inventors, so it is not surprising that the convenient modern way of painting the lips, the lipstick, appears first in the United States.

Originally lipstick was a convenience for actors, advertised for example in an 1880 catalog of supplies for minstrel shows. But in the twentieth century it became a convenience offstage too—which was a little shocking at first. "Metta was even using a lip stick!" exclaims a character in H. L. Wilson's 1919 story *Ma Pettengill.* The Roaring Twenties made lipstick familiar enough that we could read in a 1926 *Ladies' Home Journal,* "She had recently lipsticked a red mouth into startling contrast to her natural pallor." We have had lipstick, lipsticking, and lipsticky kisses ever since.

1881 bandwagon

The date 1881 is admittedly just a guess for an as yet undocumented transition: the moment when the circus bandwagon, first mentioned in 1855, became a figurative expression for a burgeoning political movement, a sense seemingly well established in 1893. Making the transition smoother, but also harder to detect, is the similarity between circus and politics.

Phineas T. Barnum (1810–91) was the first great publicizer of the original bandwagon, as he was of so many other acts in the nineteenth-century circus of American life and politics. He is supposed to have said, "There's a sucker born every minute," and he did his best to attract every one of them first to his American Museum in New York City and later to his traveling circus. He exhibited the first Siamese twins (Cheng and Eng, from Siam), the singer Jenny Lind from Sweden, and Jumbo the elephant. And to stir up enthusiasm for the circus, he paraded the performers through town, using a bandwagon to call attention to them and rouse enthusiasm.

Barnum mentions the bandwagon in his youthful autobiography of 1855. It was no ordinary wagon, but was brightly and elaborately decorated on its tall paneled sides. Behind these decorations, but on a platform high enough to be easily visible to bystanders, sat the brightly and elaborately costumed members of the band.

The later figurative uses of *bandwagon* may be observed, for example, in the *Congressional Record* for August 25, 1893: "It is a lamentable fact that ... our commercial enemy ... should come along with a band wagon loaded with hobgoblins." And in 1906: "Many of those Democrats," warned the *New York Evening Post,* "who rushed into the Bryan bandwagon ... will now be seen crawling out over the tailboard."

In William Safire's definition, the modern *bandwagon* is "a movement appealing to the herd instinct of politicians and voters to be on the winning side." Those who join such campaigns are said to be *jumping in* or *hopping on the bandwagon.* Though literal bandwagons are now to be found only in circus museums, figurative ones roll through American politics as merrily as ever.

1882 graham cracker

Sylvester Graham (1794–1851), by the standards of his day, was a crackpot. In the early 1800s, when Americans believed good eating meant as much meat and fowl as one could consume, the fatter the better, Sylvester preached a diet that would do a 1990s nutritionist proud. The base of his food pyramid was whole wheat flour, coarsely ground and not sifted. He would allow bread made of this flour, provided the bread was not too fresh; it had to stand for at least twelve hours after baking. Graham's menu also included other grains, likewise coarsely ground, and vegetables and fresh fruits. To drink? Water, of course.

Grahamism and Grahamites flourished in the 1830s in the wake of popular lectures by Graham, a minister who was general agent for the Pennsylvania Temperance Society. Aside from the plain diet, Graham also, according to the *Dictionary of American Biography,* "recommended hard mattresses, open bedroom windows, cold shower baths, looser and lighter clothing ... and cheerfulness at meals."

It was not through these lectures, however, or his books *Treatise on Bread and Bread-Making* and *Lectures on the Science of Human Life,* that Graham made his lasting contribution to American English. It was rather an invention some thirty years after his death, a cracker made out of Graham flour (1834), the coarse whole wheat flour he had prescribed, with a touch of sweetener added. In 1882 this graham cracker was touted as "easy of digestion." Aside from being wholesome, it had enough taste appeal to maintain its popularity to the present day.

Cracker (1739) is an American word too. Although *cracker* was known in England to signify a biscuit that is hard and thin, to this day the English prefer the generic word *biscuit* instead. So it is only in America that we have water crackers (1825), soda crackers (1830), and oyster crackers (1879), as well as the healthful and nutritious graham crackers.

1883 skyscraper

Before it became a building, Americans knew *skyscraper* as "a high-flying bird" (1840), "a tall hat or bonnet" (1847), or "a high fly ball in baseball" (1866). But in 1883, a visionary writer in *American Architect and Building News* declared that "a public building should always have something towering up above all in its neighborhood.... This form of sky-scraper gives that peculiar refined, independent, self-contained, daring, bold, heaven-reaching, erratic, piratic, Quixotic, American thought ('young America with his lack of veneration'). The capitol building should always have a dome. I should raise thereon a gigantic 'sky-scraper,' contrary to all precedent in practice, and I should trust to American constructive and engineering skill to build it strong enough for any gale." We have built skyscrapers ever since.

In early America, the steeples of the churches reached closest to the heavens. In the mid-nineteenth century, the state capitols raised themselves ever higher. Even county courthouses attained new heights. But by the end of the century, both church and state stood in the shade of the commercial skyscraper.

And for commercial developers it was not enough to take conventional construction to its upper limit, ten or eleven stories with thick load-bearing walls. American "constructive and engineering skill" enabled us to reach higher. We used iron to reinforce the masonry walls, then to support the floors, then to support both floors and walls. Finally we scrapped the iron entirely and replaced it with a riveted steel skeleton, and buildings were at last free to rise to any height.

In the 1890s, fifteen stories was high for a skyscraper, but the twentieth century soared much higher. In 1913, the Woolworth Building in New York City reached sixty stories. That was overshadowed by New York's Empire State Building in 1931, at 102 stories, which in turn yielded in 1974 to Chicago's Sears Tower, at 110 stories—1454 feet tall.

1884 hamburger

From the city of Hamburg, Germany, in the late 1800s Americans learned the fine art of grinding or chopping beef into tiny pieces and forming the pieces into a patty for cooking like a steak. At first it was simply called a *Hamburg steak*. But frequently there was an *–er* at the end of *Hamburg* because that was the way the Germans would say it; they add *–er* to the name of a city to indicate something or someone belonging to it. Thus the kind of sausage used in a hot dog was called a *frankfurter* (1894) after the city of Frankfurt am Main, Germany, from which it came, and thus President John Kennedy in 1963 said to the citizens of divided Berlin, "Ich bin ein Berliner." (Contrary to legend, his words did not mean "I am a creampuff," any more than "I am a New Yorker" would mean "I am an issue of a well-known weekly magazine.")

The nutritional value of the hamburger steak was promoted in the early 1900s by a Dr. Salisbury, from whom it acquired the more elegant name of *Salisbury steak*. But the popularity of hamburger really soared when the convenient practice of putting it in a bun became widespread. This was at first called the *hamburger sandwich,* but when it became the usual way of serving ground beef it was simply called the *hamburger,* and the bunless version had to be distinguished by terms like *hamburger meat* or *hamburger patty.*

As the hamburger gained in popularity, variations were invented. In the 1930s, someone who added cheese invented the name *cheeseburger.* That hybrid ended the patty's association with the city of Hamburg. Nowadays the hamburger is one of America's favorite fast foods, and plain *burger* is the usual term for it. A prefix can be added to call attention to a topping, ingredient, or style. The results have included names for chiliburgers, frankburgers, pickleburgers, and oliveburgers; lamburgers, hashburgers, nutburgers, and veggieburgers; California burgers, bar-b-burgers, twinburgers, and circus burgers.

1885 hello

Alexander Graham Bell's much-talked-about invention gave us not only the new word *telephone* (1876) but also the greeting *hello.* To be sure, something like *hello* had been with us for a long time as a shout that the English had learned from the French in the Middle Ages. *Ho là!* they would say. It meant both "stop" and "pay attention," or in the words of an early translator, "hoe there, enough, soft soft, no more of that; also, heare you me, or come hither." In various English shouts and reshouts over the centuries, this became *holla* (1523), *hollo, hollow* (1542), and *hillo, hilloa* (1602). For long-distance shouts the ending was lengthened to *–oo*, leading to *halloo* (1568) and *hulloo* (1707). By the nineteenth century the variants included *hallo, halloa* (1840) and *hullo, hulloa* (1857).

It is not surprising that a call to stop and pay attention should become associated with the first telephones. But with all the possible ways of saying it, why should telephones call for a different pronunciation, that of the present-day *hello*? Because it is rude to shout, and *hello* discourages shouting. The short *e* keeps the mouth more closed than *o* or *a*, and *–lo* makes a quieter ending than *–loo*. Telephones badly needed this civilizing because the first ones required people to shout and the first telephone exchanges were manned by boys who enthusiastically shouted right back. "Nothing could be done with them. They were immune to all schemes of discipline," noted one author. So within a few years, in the mid 1880s, "In place of the noisy and obstreperous boy came the docile, soft-voiced girl"—often called a *hello girl* in recognition of her civilized calling word. In 1889, Mark Twain's *Connecticut Yankee in King Arthur's Court* included this tribute: "The humblest hello-girl along ten thousand miles of wire could teach gentleness, patience, modesty, manners, to the highest duchess in Arthur's land."

The telephone *hello* soon became a face-to-face greeting too. It could take the place of *How are you?* and *How do you do?*, although it did not replace the informal *hi* and *howdy* derived from those expressions. At the end of the twentieth century, there was also a *hello?* that expressed surprise and a *Hello-o-o* with an exaggerated up and down of the voice that implied, Wake up! What do you think you're doing?

1886 fan

While fanatics abounded in the Old World, we Americans can claim credit for inventing a kinder, gentler version: the baseball fan. It happened in the 1880s, apparently thanks to Ted Sullivan, manager of the St. Louis Browns. According to an 1887 article in *Sporting Life,* a Philadelphia publication, "It was Ted who gave the nick-name of 'fans' to base ball cranks. You never hear a man called a 'fiend' out in the Western League cities. 'Fan' is the word that is invariably used. It is a quick way of saying 'fanatic.'"

A few years later, in 1896, Sullivan himself explained how he came up with the term: "The first season I was with [Chris] Von der Ahe [the team owner], Chris had a board of directors made up of cranks who had baseball on the brain, and they were always interfering with me and telling Chris how the team ought to be run. I told Chris that I didn't propose to be advised by a lot of fanatics. 'Vat dat you call it? Fans, eh?' said Chris. 'Yes, fans for short. They're a lot of fans, Chris,' I said. The expression was a hit with me. Comiskey and the players took it up, and then the newspapers."

By the turn of the century, the *fiend*s (1865) and *crank*s (1882) were gone. A 1901 glossary noted that *fan* was "common among reporters," perhaps for its innocuous sound and breezy humor. *Fan* would also appeal to headline writers, hungry for short words.

As the first American sport to turn professional, baseball modeled fandom (1903) for the others. And fans were too useful to confine to sports. From early in the twentieth century, entertainers of all sorts, especially movie stars, cultivated their fans, leading to such phenomena as fan mail (1924), the fan letter (1932), and fan clubs (1941). Even science fiction got into the act with fan magazines in the 1930s, known also since 1940 as *fanzines.*

1887 sideburns

Who says America has not been a leader in men's fashion? Not only have we provided the world with BLUEJEANS (1855), cowboy boots (1895), leisure suits (1975), and baseball caps, but we have also defined two distinctive styles of facial hair.

One cropped up in the 1840s. It became fashionable then for men to trim their chin whiskers into a shape that looked like the beard of a goat and thus earned the designation *goatee*. "A few individuals," remarked an 1844 book on Oregon, "have what is called, by some of their politer neighbors, a 'goaty' under the chin."

Even more significant was the facial fashion statement of Ambrose Burnside, who came to prominence as a general in the Union Army during the Civil War and later served as governor of Rhode Island and U.S. senator from that state. Burnside had mixed success both in battle and in fashion. He was named commander of the Army of the Potomac but was relieved of his command after losing the battle of Fredericksburg in 1862. He wore a soft hat with the crown pushed out, a style that survived for a decade or two after the war with the name *Burnside*. But he was most renowned for a kind of beard that was the opposite of the goatee: side whiskers and moustache, with a clean-shaven chin. The style was known, naturally, as *Burnside's*.

By itself, this word for his hairstyle had no meaning other than the name of its originator. But as memory of the general and senator faded, *Burnside's* was mistakenly heard as *burnsides,* a plural, seeming to refer to the two prominent sides of hair. With that interpretation, *side* was in the wrong place; *burn sides* is puzzling, *side burns* a perfectly understandable phrase. Isn't that right? Etymologically, no; logically, yes. "McGarigle has his mustache and small side burns still on," announced the *Chicago Journal* for August 1, 1887. And so, through the effort of making a word make sense, *sideburns* entered American English and remained, allowing us to describe the look of Elvis Presley and others in the century to come.

1888 credit card

Long before the first credit cards were issued in California in the 1950s, an American visionary of the nineteenth century imagined them. Not only that; he envisioned that a cashless society, using credit cards for purchases, would exist at the end of the twentieth century. Falling asleep in 1887, the narrator of Edward Bellamy's novel *Looking Backward,* published in 1888, wakes in the year 2000 to an America whose problems have been solved by getting rid of buying and selling. Instead, "A credit corresponding to his share of the annual product of the nation is given to every citizen on the public books at the beginning of each year, and a credit card issued him with which he procures at the public storehouses, found in every community, whatever he desires whenever he desires it." It works for travel abroad too: "An American in Berlin [for example] takes his credit card to the local office of the international council, and receives in exchange for the whole or part of it a German credit card, the amount being charged against the United States in favor of Germany on the international account."

Bellamy's credit card is actually what we nowadays would call a *debit card,* one that draws from an established account. The plastic credit card first issued by California's Bank of America in 1956 was more radical. It did not require prepayment but offered the bank's own credit, instantly, for purchases at a great variety of participating businesses. With credit cards, businesses could offer customers the convenience of credit while the bank took the risk (and a percentage of the price).

We have a long way to go before reaching Bellamy's vision of a cashless society, and we are farther than ever from his vision of a society without banks, retailers, and advertising, but the end of the twentieth century has put credit cards in nearly everyone's hands, with accounts immediately accessible by computer almost anywhere in the world.

1889 Hispanic

The first European language spoken in North America in modern times was a Hispanic one, the Spanish language brought over in Columbus's three ships in 1492. St. Augustine, Florida, the oldest city in what is now the United States, was Hispanic too, founded in 1565 by Pedro Menéndez de Avilés. And of course what is now the southwestern United States was

Hispanic for several centuries, an outpost first of Spain and then briefly of independent Mexico.

Not that anybody used the word *Hispanic* in the English language then, however. As a designation for the heritage of Spanish language and culture in our hemisphere, it is newer. We find English writers as far back as 1584 using *Hispanicall* to refer to Spain. But it was only in about 1889, as nearly as lexicographers can determine, that we realized *Hispanic* would be a suitably descriptive designation for residents and citizens of the United States who traced their immediate ancestry not necessarily to Spain but to the Spanish-speaking lands to our south.

In the 1970s, with renewed awareness that the United States was peopled from many more directions than England alone, *Hispanic American* gained popularity—along with similar terms such as *Native American*, AFRO-AMERICAN (1890) or *African American,* and *Asian American*—as part of our burgeoning lexicon of diversity. *Hispanic American,* generally shortened to *Hispanic,* displaced the often misleading *Spanish* as well as the impossibly awkward *Spanish-surnamed person.* It also recognized a growing sense of community among a varied population whose roots were in many different soils south of the border but whose language and culture gave them much in common.

In the present day, *Latino* (1946) has emerged as an alternative to *Hispanic.* It is preferred by many, in part because it acts more like a Spanish word and also because it invokes cultural ties with Latin America rather than Spain.

1890 Afro-American

Of all the peoples who migrated to the present-day United States after European discovery, those whose ancestors came from Africa against their will have had the longest and most difficult struggle for recognition of their rights as citizens and their dignity as humans. In all likelihood, they have also been called (and have called themselves) by more different names than any other American group in their search for respectful terminology.

When first brought here from Africa in the 1600s, they were naturally called *Africans,* an ancient word in English that came ultimately from the Romans. The African slaves were also called *Negroes,* a word borrowed from the slave-trading Portuguese in the 1500s and known in North America by the mid 1600s. This led to a variant pronunciation spelled *Niger* or *nigger,* at first neutral in connotation but gradually becoming more derogatory. Also in use before the end of the seventeenth century was the simple descriptive *black.*

By the end of the eighteenth century, with the emergence of a small but growing community of freed slaves and the start of the ABOLITION (1787) movement, black Americans began to seek new ways of referring to themselves—ways that would shake off the oppression of the past and command respect. *African* was the early preference, reflected in the name of the Sons of the African Society founded in Boston in 1798. But *colored people* also began to be used then, a term that met with such favor that it was the choice of the National Association for the Advancement of Colored People when it was founded more than a century later.

In the year 1890, *Afro-American* was the term of choice in the African-American publication *Advance,* which advocated "obtaining for the Afro-American an equal chance."

The twentieth century saw a succession of preferred terms, from *colored* to *Negro* to *Black* and then, with increasing emphasis on heritage rather than color, to *Afro-American* and *African American,* the latter widely adopted after a speech by the Reverend Jesse Jackson in 1988. In the 1960s and 1970s, *Afro-American* was prominent along with related terms such as *Afro-American studies* (1970), *Afroism* (1971), the hair style known as the *Afro* (1968), and music known as *Afro-beat* (1974) and *Afro-rock* (1977).

1891 country club

In the early 1890s a new cultural force was at play, and after a few years of development it was noted in one of the nation's most respected publications. "Although Philadelphia prides itself upon being the home of the oldest known club," said *Harper's New Monthly Magazine* in 1894, "it is not essentially a club town—that is, in the sense that London and New York are. It is true that a certain number of bachelors in Philadelphia regard their club as their home, but . . . Poor Richard's city has never looked leniently on the rich idler."

Enter, then, a new alternative to the staid clubs of *Harper's* article, the recently established Philadelphia Country Club. This alternative organization was still, perhaps, for the rich, but it was definitely not for the idler, and it was not just for men. Let *Harper's* describe it: "Besides the adornment of its beautiful house and very extensive grounds, which are much affected by the women-folk of Philadelphia, it has gone in for pony-racing, golf, and polo. . . . The Country Club is either very restful and bucolic, or very athletic and exciting, just as one chooses to take it."

In the cities and towns of America, many chose to take it. A country estate was beyond the means of most urban Americans, but the upper middle class happily organized country clubs that would afford them the healthy air and exercise of the country as well as social connections for their families.

Ponies and polo lost favor as Americans swapped horses for cars, but the golf course continued to keep the country in the club. And in the country, with proper planning, golfers would be far from the embarrassment described in Sarah Cleghorn's little poem of 1917:

> The golf links lie so near the mill
> That almost every day
> The laboring children can look out
> And see the men at play.

1892 sweatshop

A century ago, a *sweater* was not just an outer garment to keep out the cold. It could also be a person who sweated others by employing them at low wages in bleak conditions, in a place that was consequently called a *sweatshop*. The article "Among the Poor of Chicago" in an 1892 issue of *Scribner's Magazine* gives this explanation:

> The *sweat-shop* is a place where, separate from the tailor-shop or clothing-warehouse, a 'sweater' (middleman) assembles journeymen tailors and needle-women, to work under his supervision. He takes a cheap room outside the dear and crowded business centre, and within the neighborhood where the work-people live. . . . The men can and do work more hours than was possible under the centralized system, and their wives and children can help. . . . Even the very young can pull out basting-threads.

Like slavery, the sweatshop had defenders in its time. "Division of labor is good," the *Scribner's* reporter concluded. "Scattering of workers from great groups into smaller groups is good; . . . prevention of theft is good, and cheapness of garments is good." But then: "Unwholesome atmosphere, moral

and material, is bad; insufficient wages is bad; possibility of in-
fection is bad, and child-labor is (usually) bad. How shall the
good be preserved and the bad cured or alleviated?"

The twentieth century gave its answer by establishing the
minimum wage, workplace regulation, and the abolition of
child labor. The sweatshop now exists as an illegal, hidden
operation and as a word for a place with oppressive working
conditions.

1893 midway

Before it became the place for the sideshow, the Midway began
as an elegant example of urban planning. Ambitious to improve its ambiance as well as its reputation, Chicago in the
late nineteenth century adopted the motto *Urbs in Horto*
("City in a garden") and developed an extensive system of
parks and lakes. Six miles south of the city center, the Park
Commission laid out Jackson Park on the waterfront and
Washington Park inland, with a park one mile long and just
one block wide connecting the two. Envisioning grand boule-
vards and waterways along this link, the planners in 1871
named it the *Midway Plaisance.*

For twenty years *Midway* remained an obscure local designation. But in 1893 it caught the attention of the world thanks
to its association with America's most successful world's fair,
the Columbian Exposition belatedly celebrating the 400th an-
niversary of Columbus's first voyage. All of the grand white
electric-lit buildings in Greek and Roman styles, exhibiting the
world's accomplishments and cultures, were located on hand-
some lagoons in Jackson Park. If you just wanted to have fun,
you went to the tents on the Midway. There, away from the
grounds of the fair proper, and thus without scandal, you
could watch the belly dancer known as Little Egypt, who was
said to take off all her clothes as she danced the Coochee-
Coochee. You could also ride the world's first Ferris wheel.

Ever since, the avenue of games, rides, and other sideshows
at a fair, circus, or carnival has been known as the *midway*.
The name still carries associations of down-to-earth pleasures

and naughtiness, as well as the grand feeling of being in the midst of things. But while the original Midway Plaisance still exists, it has long since reverted to a city park and is now surrounded by the University of Chicago. Stripped of its pleasure tents, drained of its canals, and crisscrossed by streets, it is now a long grassy playground for the games and sports of university students and other neighbors.

1894 cold feet

At some time between the 1893 first edition and the 1896 second edition of his novel *Maggie, a Girl of the Streets,* Stephen Crane added the earliest known instance of *cold feet:* "I knew this is the way it would be. They got cold feet."

The new slang term, referring to loss of courage or enthusiasm, appears also in George Ade's *Artie,* another novel of 1896: " 'I see. He turned out to be a boodler [corrupt politician], eh?' 'I don't see no way o' gettin' past it. I like Jimmy. He's one o' them boys that never has cold feet and there's nothin' too good for a friend, but by gee, I guess when it comes to doin' the nice, genteel dip he belongs with the smoothest of 'em. And he learned it so quick, too. Ooh!' "

By the turn of the century, college students were getting cold feet too. A glossary of college terms published in 1901 includes this definition from Cornell University in Ithaca, New York: " 'To get *cold-feet* in a subject,' abandon it for weariness."

In the West in the twentieth century it has also been possible to call a person *cold-footed,* as in an example from New Mexico, "you are cold-footed on this proposition of marriage." The term was noted by Elsie Warnock in her rhetoric classes in 1914–17 when she asked them to list twenty disparaging terms used in everyday speech.

An echo of *cold-footed* comes from a book with a Texas setting in 1920: "We were not allowed to cross the cattle on the bridge, so we had to swim for it. Two of my men stayed with me, and the third, a 'cold-footer,' crossed on the bridge."

1895 hot dog

It was an old joke, with some truth to it: meat for sausages was said to come from dogs. In 1836 a New York newspaper declared, "Sausages have fallen in price one half, in New York, since the dog killers have commenced operations." Towards the end of the nineteenth century, clever students at Yale University in New Haven, Connecticut, began referring to the sausages themselves as *dogs*. A lunch wagon that operated there at night was called "The Kennel Club" because dogs were its specialty. A poem about it appeared in the *Yale Record* for October 5, 1895:

ECHOES FROM THE LUNCH WAGON
" 'Tis dogs' delight to bark and bite,"
Thus does the adage run.
But I delight to bite the dog
When placed inside a bun.

It remained only for the Yale wits to add *hot*. They did this in the October 19 issue of the *Record,* in a tall tale about abducting the "dog wagon." The proprietor supposedly woke up in the relocated lunch wagon at chapel time "and did a rushing trade with the unfortunates who had missed their breakfast. . . . They contentedly munched hot dogs during the whole service."

Even earlier, in 1894, *hot dog* was used as slang for a well-dressed young man. With the new meaning, *hot dog* soon showed up at other colleges and at ballparks, and by the early twentieth century it had become the standard name for a sausage on a bun, despite competition from *red hot* (1896) and the more polite *frankfurter* (1894) and *wiener* (1900). (Despite persistent legend, the hot dog was not named in a baseball cartoon by T. A. Dorgan of the *New York Journal.* No such cartoon exists.)

In the twentieth century, rather than an ingredient, the dog became the sausage itself, so today we can speak of *turkey dogs* and *cheese dogs.* The other meaning of *hot dog* persisted too, but now it refers more to daredevil behavior than to spiffy clothing.

1896 gangster

Groups of people who work or hang out together have been with us since the dawn of humanity, and *gang* or something like it (*ging*) has been an honorable word used to refer to them since the dawn of the English language. Around the time when English speakers were beginning to settle in North America, *gang* also acquired the specific meaning of "a group up to no good," as in a gang of housebreakers or thieves. It was apparently an American idea, though, to use the negative connotations of *gang* in reference to politicians. John Quincy Adams wrote bitterly of "the united gang of Calhoun and Jackson conspirators against me" in 1833.

But the great American invention related to *gang* was *gangster.* We find it in an editorial in the *Columbus* [Ohio] *Dispatch* in 1896: "The gangster may play all sorts of pranks with the ballot box, but in its own good time the latter will get even by kicking the gangster into the gutter."

The prohibition of alcoholic beverages enacted in 1919 as the Eighteenth Amendment offered expanded opportunities for gangsters to make money and come to the attention of the public. In Chicago, Al Capone wielded such ruthless power that to this day, throughout the world, the city is associated with gangsters. Gangster stories and movies became a favorite genre. The most recent development of the word identifies the genre of rap music known as *gangster rap* (1989) or *gangsta rap* (1990).

1897 underprivileged

The notion of privileges for favored people—the wealthy, or those in the know, or those connected to the government—has been around as long as civilization. But the democratic notion of privileges for everyone came into its own in America with our adoption of the word *underprivileged.* To say someone is underprivileged is to imply that there is a standard of privileges to which everyone is entitled, privileges that have been unjustly withheld from the underprivileged. We find the word in the *Princetonian* in 1896: "It was very quiet in the little square that was filled with nurse-maids and children moving about inside the railings—several little underprivileged ones peering in at them from the outside." By 1897, we can assume that *underprivileged* was well on its way to establishing its place in our vocabulary.

A century later *underprivileged* itself began to seem too privileged. In the politically correct 1990s, *underprivileged* sounded too condescending, too accepting of a privileged point of view, and *needy* is now more likely to be used.

1898 yellow journalism

The color wasn't new. Yellow has been a primary color in our language for thousands of years. But this yellow was in a new place, in comic strips on the front page of some of New York's Sunday newspapers. And the newspapers were fighting the fiercest circulation war in American history by clamoring for real war against Spain. In disgust, rival editors called it *yellow journalism*.

The explosive mixture began with Joseph Pulitzer's purchase of the *New York World* in 1883. With stories of sensational crime and crusades against corruption, aiming to be "just a bit breezy while at all times honest, earnest and sincere," the *World* soon reached the highest circulation of any American newspaper. It published the first comic strip, R. F. Outcault's "Hogan's Alley." And when the *World* added the first color to a Sunday supplement, "The Kid of Hogan's Alley," a boy, appeared in a bright yellow dress. (Yes, a dress; little children of both genders were clothed in dresses in those days.)

Then in 1895 William Randolph Hearst hired away the *World*'s top staff for his new acquisition, the *Morning Journal*. Hearst hired Outcault too and began running "The Yellow Kid" in his Sunday edition. The *World* retaliated by hiring another artist and continuing its own front-page "Yellow Kid."

In 1898 the circulation war of *World* vs. *Journal* reached its climax as both papers used huge headlines for the war with

Spain: "The Whole Country Thrills With the War Fever"; "Declaration of War!"; and "Manila Ours!" Edwin Lawrence Godkin's denunciation of that sensationalism in his weekly *The Nation* was one of many that used the term *yellow journal:* "The fomenting of war and the publication of mendacious accounts of war have, in fact, become almost a special function of that portion of the press which is known as 'yellow journals.'" In his *New York Evening Post* Godkin added, "A better place in which to prepare a young man for eternal damnation than a yellow-journal office does not exist."

The "Yellow Kid" and those two yellow journals are gone, but sensational reporting has been criticized as *yellow journalism* ever since.

1899 cereal

If it comes in a colorful cardboard box, if it is poured into a bowl and doused with milk, if it snaps, crackles, and pops, if it provides fiber and a substantial part of the day's nutritional needs, and if it is advertised all over the Saturday morning cartoons, it must be cereal. Or so we think nowadays, thanks to the work of America's nutritional pioneers a century ago.

The word for today's divine breakfast treat has a divine origin: *Ceres,* the Roman goddess of agriculture. Her name was invoked by English scientists and officials in the nineteenth century when they wanted a dignified, poetic word for "grain." So when Charles Darwin in 1868 wrote about "the slow and gradual improvement of our cereals," he was referring not to the development of breakfast food but to the development of domesticated grain.

It was Americans, however, who transformed plain grain into the modern miracle breakfast cereal. During the nineteenth century, the American aspiration for moral perfection and scientific improvement began to include the food we ate. The whole country seemed to suffer from dyspepsia (1706), and dietary as well as spiritual reformers gathered in the little city of Battle Creek, Michigan, hoping to cure the problem.

Notable among them was Dr. J. H. Kellogg, who founded a Health Reform Institute there in 1866, and his son W. K. Kellogg, who developed methods of preparing grain that became cereal as we know it today. The plain cereals were wholesome food, but not particularly appetizing to meat-eating Americans. So to make them more digestible and tasty, W. K. rolled out the grains and toasted them.

By 1899 Americans were using *cereal* to refer to these processed and packaged grains. An advertisement in the *Chicago Daily News* in May of that year offered "Free with 6 packages of Hazel Cereals, any assortment, a handsomely decorated tea canister." Later inventors added milk and sugar to the cereals, fortified cereals with vitamins (1912), gave them new shapes, textures, and colors, put premiums in their packages, and topped them off with celebrity testimonials.

1900 phony

We began the 1900s in a phony way, at least in our slang. The first instance of *phony* meaning "fake" or "not genuine" is from journalist George Ade in his book *More Fables In Slang,* published in 1900: "The Sensitive Waitress hurried Away, feeling hurt. 'Overlook all the Phoney Acting by the Little Lady, Bud,' said the Fireman to the Advance Agent. 'She's only twenty-seven.'" Then in 1902, in the even more extreme slang of C. L. Cullen's *Six Ex-Tank Tales*, we find another instance of *phony:* "If youse tinks f'r a minnit dat youse is goin' t' git away wit' a phony like dat wit' me youse is got hay in y'r hemp, dat's wot."

Before the new century was much further advanced, *phony* became sufficiently dignified to appear in more standard contexts as well, although it still had a strong colloquial flavor. In the *Saturday Evening Post* of 1909 we find a character saying, "I gave the sucker my name and address (both phony of course) and promised to send two hundred dollars as soon as I got home." And in the 1949 *Chicago Tribune,* "Stop moaning about that phony blonde and her phonier lawsuit."

The origin of *phony* is obscure, but it has been linked to the English cant expression *fawney rig* (1754), a swindle in which a brass ring or other piece of jewelry is dropped before a victim. The cheat then retrieves the expensive-looking ring and offers it to the victim at a supposedly bargain price. *Fawney* is attributed to Irish *fáinne,* meaning "ring," as it was a ring that was most popular in this scam.

MODERN

TIMES:

1901-1944

*W*hen we reached the 1900s, we had arrived in the modern world. Americans of 1901 lived closer to the way we do now, nearly a century later, than to the way our common forebears did a century earlier. Homes with central heating, rapid transportation by rail, and instant communication by telephone were all familiar in 1901. So were mail order, professional sports, and mass-circulation newspapers. Within another decade, Americans were familiar with airplanes and radio, and the automobile was making the horse obsolete. Welcome to the twentieth century!

Just as the two initials *OK* (1839) were the most significant addition to the American vocabulary in the nineteenth century, another pair of initials, *IQ* (1916), could be argued to be the most important in the twentieth. Those initials changed our minds, altered our system of education, and gave supposedly scientific support to certain theories of race and gender.

During this dawn of the modern era, influenced by the *media* (1921), we started going to *motels* (1925) and *supermarkets* (1933). We wore *T-shirts* (1919) and got *athlete's foot*

(1928). And, with profound consequences for civilization and culture, we learned that some of us were *teenagers* (1938).

We tried to reform our politics, going to the *grass roots* (1901), being moved by *muckrakers* (1906), and criticizing *pork barrel* (1909) legislation and *boondoggles* (1935). We believed that the American *melting pot* (1907) made us one culture from many, although we also began to notice that the world we lived in was *multicultural* (1941).

Our language grew in response to the ways we entertained ourselves, whether we were *highbrow* (1903) or not. We sang *barbershop* (1910) and watched *movies* (1912). We put our coins in *jukeboxes* (1939). We listened to *blues* (1911) and *jazz* (1913), introduced to the rest of us by African Americans. Sometimes entertainment was *groovy* (1937).

Most of us were farther away from nature than ever before, so we appreciated it in new ways. To get sentimental about it, we hugged *teddy bears* (1906). To get back to it, we would go hiking with a *backpack* (1914).

As we modernized, we were jolted by two world wars before the century was half over. The first brought us *GI* (1917) and *D-Day* (1918) and the second brought us *jeep* (1940), *gizmo* (1944), and *snafu* (1942). After World War I, we hoped for *normalcy* (1920); after World War II—that's another story.

1901 grass roots

Americans have been on the cutting edge of business and politics in the twentieth century. We were the first to get down not only to brass tacks (1897) but also to grass roots. The latter we originally talked about in regard to mining. An 1876 book about the Black Hills says that "gold is found almost everywhere, in the bars, in the gravel and sand of the beds, even in the 'grass roots,'" that is, the soil just below the surface. But by the turn of the century we thought of grass roots as more than just a place to dig. Beneath the visible blades of grass, keeping the grass alive and making it grow, are the simple roots. Getting down to grass roots meant looking at the "underlying principles or basic facts of a matter," in the words of Charles

Earle Funk, the lexicographer, who remembered the phrase from his Ohio boyhood in the late 1800s. It was in the grass roots where you could truly understand a situation and effectively respond to it.

Politicians often presented themselves as getting down to grass roots. They also talked about themselves, and the measures they favored, having support from the grass roots, that is, from their constituents—ordinary people, the salt of the earth. Grass roots lobbying takes the form of letters, phone calls, and visits from these constituents.

Politicians occasionally being unscrupulous, it has sometimes chanced that an artificial grass roots movement has been planned and put into action by the very politician or interest group that it seems to spontaneously support. In the 1990s, fake grass roots were labeled by their opponents with the trademarked name for artificial and rootless grass, *AstroTurf.*

1902 goo

The twentieth century got off to a gooey start. There was goo in the colleges and goo in the inventor's workshop. A survey of slang at a hundred colleges and universities, published in 1900, found *goo* used at twenty of them to mean "any liquid" and at one, Elmira College, "anything sticky."

The American inventor Lee De Forest (1873–1961), later called "the father of radio," must have had those meanings in mind around the year 1902 when he invented a paste to coat the ends of wires and named it *goo,* as reported a year later. He also invented and patented the Audion, forerunner of the vacuum tube long used in radio and television. But while De Forest's Audion is obsolete, his goo has stuck with us.

Gooey was also reported in the 1900 college survey, but only from Ithaca College, where it was explained as "weird, making one creep." By 1903, however, *gooey* had adhered to *goo* and had taken on the meaning "sticky, not easily handled."

In fact, *goo* words seem to have been the rage in the 1900s. *Goo-goo eyes,* probably developed from the baby's *goo-goo* of the 1860s, is first recorded in 1897. *Googly* eyes, large and round, date from 1901. Those words are apparently unrelated to the liquid or sticky *goo,* but they seem to have become entangled. Sometimes goo itself, when especially gooey, was called *goo-goo,* as early as 1903. During World War I it began to be called *goop* as well.

1903 highbrow

Americans can claim credit for both *highbrow* and *lowbrow,* the upper and lower levels of culture and cultivation. *Highbrow* seems to have come first, most likely around 1903, but *lowbrow* is close on its heels. In 1906 we have examples of both. That year the writer O. Henry refers to "the $250 that I screwed out of the high-browed and esteemed B. Merwin during your absence." As for *lowbrow,* we find it in S. Ford's *Shorty McCabe:* "The spaghetti works was in full blast, with a lot of husky low-brows goin' in and out." In *Collier's* the next year is a reference to "the overwhelming majority of Low Brows, who never read 'Peer Gynt.'" And in the *Saturday Evening Post* for 1908, we see *highbrows* again: "It takes all sorts of men to make a party, and Mr. Hearst apparently led in a few prize-fighters with the other high-brows and reformers he accumulated."

From the start, both terms were applied with tongue in cheek. They referred to the discredited phrenological notion that a person of superior intellect and culture would have a high forehead while an ignorant boor would have a low one.

A 1916 reviewer in *The Nation* took the distinction more seriously. *Highbrow* and *lowbrow,* he said, "stand for more genuine differences than Democrat and Republican. The one class has ideals, but no experience; it has flowered in an unfruitful transcendentalism. The other class has experience, but no ideals; its finished product is the millionaire. Each class looks with contempt, or rather with indifference, upon the other." The reviewer lamented this split, but in fact the two extremes of American culture seem to have prevented either side from taking itself too seriously. In the rest of the twentieth century both highbrows and lowbrows have had such success that American science, scholarship, and art on the one hand and practical inventions and popular culture on the other have swept throughout the world.

1904 cut the mustard

In the twentieth century, Americans were able to cut the mustard, that is, "to do what is needed." The first evidence comes from O. Henry in 1904: "So I looked around and found a proposition that exactly cut the mustard."

It is one of our most puzzling expressions. Does it have to do with cultivating or harvesting the mustard plant? Does it have to do with the slang expressions *be the proper mustard,* that is, "be the real thing," or *be all to the mustard,* "be very good"? Or might it mean "exceed the standard," where *cut* means "surpass" or "excel," and *mustard* is really the *muster,* or "examination," as in the old expression *pass muster*? All these explanations have been seriously advanced by those who cut the mustard in lexicography, but they are only guesses.

Here are examples of other *mustard* expressions of the time. From Andy Adams, *The Log of a Cowboy* (1903): "For fear they were not the proper mustard, he had that dog man sue him in court for the balance, so as to make him prove the pedigree." And from H. McHugh, *You Can Search Me* (1905): "Petroskinski is a discovery of mine, and he's all to the mustard."

1905 jellybean

The earliest evidence of the word *jellybean* seems to have appeared in an advertisement in the *Chicago Daily News* on July 5, 1905: "Jelly beans, assorted, per lb., 9c." It was years in the making. A precursor of the jellybean was advertised as early as 1861 as a gift for soldiers in the Civil War. A candy manufacturer had joined the confection known as *Turkish delight* and the French fashion of coating almonds with a sugar shell to produce a candy with a crisp shell and a soft center, the essential structure of today's jellybean.

The tradition of giving jellybeans in Easter baskets arose in the 1930s during the recovery from the Great Depression of 1929. Of seasonal candies, jellybeans at Easter rank with candy canes (1936) at Christmas and candy corn at Halloween. The National Confectioners Association reported that over thirteen billion jellybeans were sold for Easter in 1996.

President Reagan was particularly fond of jellybeans, to the point of keeping a jar of them on his desk in the Oval Office of the White House.

The epithet *jellybean* is used for people too. On the one hand, it has been used as a derogatory term for someone weak or timid, as in this example from 1919: "Mary is such a jellybean that she never gets her lessons." On the other hand, it can mean a young man dressed like a DUDE (1877), noted as early as 1921, and here in a 1937 example: "It made them all feel glowingly united, not just flappers and jellybeans, but a new young generation capable of facing the serious things of life."

1906 teddy bear

Our most cuddly companion for children got its inspiration and its name from the least cuddly of our presidents. Or perhaps more precisely, it was named for the president who seems least likely to have thought of himself as cuddly. Theodore Roosevelt deliberately cultivated the rugged outdoor life after growing up in wealth and comfort and frail health in the East. In between political positions in New York and Washington he retired to his ranch in the Dakota Territory. He also went on exploring and hunting expeditions in Africa, South America, and the American West. On such trips he brought along only difficult books to avoid the temptation of relaxing with easy reading matter.

Teddy Roosevelt favored a strong navy and a strong military position for the United States in world affairs. His "Rough Riders," a cavalry regiment consisting mostly of Western

ranchers and cowboys, was the star of the invasion of Cuba in the Spanish-American War of 1898. As president from 1901 to 1909, he was equally rough as a crusader against trusts and as an advocate for pure food and drugs and for conservation of national resources. And if not cuddly, he was widely admired, winning the 1904 presidential election with 60 percent of the popular vote.

So it happened that when the great hunter spared a bear cub in 1906, a cartoon celebrating the event was widely printed. And in the spirit of American enterprise, a commercial product soon followed: the plush toy teddy bear, cuddly enough for babies to enjoy while able to serve (at least in the minds of parents) as an inspiration to rugged individualism.

Teddy Roosevelt's brand of big-game hunting is now in disfavor, as is his gunboat diplomacy, but his legacy of government regulation of big business remains with us, along with the conservation movement and the soft stuffed toy that makes the lives of children around the world more bearable.

1906 muckraker

(No, this is not a mistake. The year 1906 introduced two new words so notable that each deserves consideration by itself. Here is the second.)

The noble journalistic profession of muckraker emerged from the ooze on April 14, 1906, at the laying of the cornerstone for the House of Representatives Office Building, when President Theodore Roosevelt denounced it: "The men with the muck-rakes are often indispensable to the well-being of society; but only if they know when to stop raking the muck, and to look upward to the celestial crown above them, to the crown of worthy endeavor. There are beautiful things above and round about them; and if they gradually grow to feel that the whole world is nothing but muck, their power of usefulness is gone."

Roosevelt's listeners knew exactly what he meant, but for a modern audience his words require explanation. A muckraker is one whose job is to rake up fresh manure. The "man with a muckrake" is a famous character in Part II of John Bunyan's allegorical *Pilgrim's Progress,* a bestseller since it was first published in 1684. During the pilgrim's journey, a man named the Interpreter shows "a room where was a man that could look no way but downwards, with a muck-rake in his hand. There stood also one over his head with a celestial crown in his hand, and proffered to give him that crown for his muck-rake; but the man did neither look up nor regard, but raked to himself the straws, the small sticks, and the dust of the floor. . . . it is to let thee know that earthly things, when they are with power upon men's minds, quite carry their hearts away from God."

Roosevelt was annoyed with writers like Lincoln Steffens, Upton Sinclair, and Ida Tarbell who exposed corruption and greed in government and business. Or rather, he was pleased when they exposed his enemies and annoyed when they exposed his friends. *Muckraker* was intended to smear the crusading writers, but they adopted the term as a badge of honor and kept on with what we nowadays would call *investigative reporting.*

1907 melting pot

We have always been a nation of immigrants, but throughout American history the earlier arrivals have wondered whether newcomers will degrade our national character or enrich it. And among newcomers as well as long-established citizens there has also been the persistent question of whether each ethnic group will maintain its own customs and character, or whether the different nationalities and races will amalgamate to a common American type.

Melting pot was a Jewish contribution to the discussion. It was apparently first used by Rabbi Samuel Schulman, who spoke of America as "the melting pot of nationalities" in a 1907 Passover sermon at his New York temple. But the term owes its popularity to a Jewish playwright, Israel Zangwill, whose drama *The Melting-Pot* opened in Washington, D.C., in October 1908 and was soon published and performed to applause throughout the country. The hero of the play is a young Jewish composer who falls in love with the daughter of an anti-Semitic Russian nobleman. Since the young couple lives in America, old-world animosities are overcome, thanks to the melting pot. This is how the young man explains it to his beloved:

> There she lies, the great Melting-Pot—listen! Can't you hear the roaring and the bubbling? There gapes her mouth—the harbor where a thousand mammoth feeders come from the ends of the world to pour in their human freight. Ah, what a stirring and a seething! Celt and Latin, Slav and Teuton, Greek and Syrian, —black and yellow—Jew and Gentile—Yes, East and West, and North and South, the palm and the pine, the pole and the equator, the crescent and the cross—how the great Alchemist melts and fuses them with his purging flame! Here shall they all unite to build the Republic of Man and the Kingdom of God. Ah, Vera, what is the glory of Rome and Jerusalem where all nations and races come to worship and look back, compared with the glory of America, where all races and nations come to labor and look forward!

1908 asleep at the switch

If the yard goose or switch monkey (railroad jargon for a switchman) happened to doze off for a minute during a slack period of traffic, he was said to be *asleep at the switch*. That literal description became a phrase fit for a dictionary when it jumped the track to be used in situations having nothing to do with railroads. The earliest evidence for the figurative application is found in a 1908 quotation from McGaffry's *Show Girl,* where a character asks an inattentive waiter in a restaurant, "Waiter, are you asleep at the switch?"

Other examples of the phrase having this generalized meaning, "unobservant, preoccupied, or neglectful," followed in short order. We have, for example, from 1915, "The net player was asleep at the switch and never saw the return." More recently, from 1975, we have "The rest of the class, asleep at the switch, is impressed by Caz's work." Even with automated switches in everything from railroad yards to computers, there is still plenty of opportunity to be asleep at the switch.

1909 pork barrel

As an actual container for storing pig meat in brine, the pork barrel has been with us since the early days of the Republic. It seems to have been a measure of present and future prosperity. A farmer's almanac of 1801 urges readers to "mind our pork and cider barrels." A midcentury author states, "I hold a family to be in a desperate way, when the mother can see the bottom of the pork barrel." "I know our crops will be short next season," declares another almanac, "for the brine has all leaked out of the pork barrel!"

In the twentieth century, modern refrigeration made the actual pork barrel obsolete. But it took on new life in referring to political bills that bring home the bacon to a legislator's district and constituents. *Pork* had been used at least since the 1870s as a label for politically motivated federal funding for local projects like post offices. We read in the *Congressional Record* in regard to an 1888 rivers and harbors appropriation, "Has the pork been so cunningly divided amongst the members of the House in this bill that its final passage is assured?"

By 1909, *pork barrel* itself was making the rounds of Congress. An article that year explains that the Democratic Party "has periodically inveighed against the extravagance of the administration, but its representatives in the Legislature have exercised no critical surveillance over the appropriations. They have preferred to take for their own constituencies whatever could be got out of the congressional 'pork barrel.'" Similarly, an article in 1916 opposing a "trend towards national defense on the basis of the State militia" argues that it is "a triumph for the pork-barrel."

Even without ever having seen an actual pork barrel, we continue to use the term today for its vivid negative implications. A pork barrel suggests fat and grease, not only in its contents but also in those who reach for it.

1910 barbershop

Once a staple of America's main streets, the barbershop (1832) has generally given way to the hair salon. Like as not, it's in a

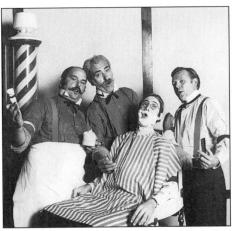

mall (1958) or mini-mall. But barbershop quartet music lives on under the aegis of S.P.E.B.S.Q.S.A., or the Society for the Preservation and Encouragement of Barber Shop Quartet Singing in America, Inc., founded in 1938. It is also exemplified in the Broadway musical *The Music Man.*

In the original production, the Buffalo Bills barbershop quartet sang such well-known pieces as "Ida Rose" and "Sweet Adeline." Women officially took up the practice of barbershop music in the 1940s with the establishment of Sweet Adelines, Inc., their counter to S.P.E.B.S.Q.S.A.

This distinctly American form of unaccompanied singing derives its name from the place where its practitioners supposedly performed, the barbershop. We find the musical use of that word as early as 1910 in a song by William Tracey titled "Play That Barber Shop Chord."

Barbershop is characteristically performed by four singers, each with a distinct lyric. In the male version, the melody is accompanied by bass and baritone voices at a lower pitch and a tenor higher than the melody, thus creating a close harmony. Baritones sometimes sing above as well as below the lead to make the chords so often associated with barbershopping. No notes are sung unaccompanied. However, the harmony may be intentionally shifted while a single note is sung. The songs are usually sentimental to the point of being corny.

A possible origin of barbershop singing is barber's music, noted in 1660 in the diary of the Englishman Samuel Pepys. It is defined by the *Oxford English Dictionary* as "harsh and discordant singing by those waiting to be served."

1911 blues

America has long had the blues, but not until African Americans set the blues to music did we know what to do with them. Actually, the first blues in America were blue devils, which were low spirits brought over from England. An American proverb of 1770 says, "Gamble has been long indisposed with the Blues." Washington Irving in 1807 wrote of a man "under the influence of a whole legion of the blues," and a young U. S. Grant wrote in 1846, "I came back to my tent and to drive away, what you call the Blues, I took up some of your old letters."

African Americans had better reasons than most to feel the blues. So perhaps it is not surprising that they were the ones to make the most of the blues by setting them to music. This kind of blues came into being a few years ahead of JAZZ (1913), to which it is related, thanks to W. C. Handy (1873–1958). We will locate the beginning of what he called the *blues* in 1911; its fame was spread by his "Memphis Blues," published in 1912, followed in 1914 by the even more famous "St. Louis Blues." Following his lead, Americans of all colors have been hearing and singing the blues ever since.

1912 movies

A funny thing happened on the way to the movies. The term is attested as a title in a New York publication of 1912, " 'Movies' and the Law." But movies hadn't started out with such a slangy name. Instead, at their birth in 1889, celluloid images of motion were dignified with compound words derived from classical Greek elements by their inventor, Thomas Edison. He called his camera a *kinetograph,* from the Greek words for "motion" and "write," and his projector a *kinetoscope,* from the words for "motion" and "view." A decade later a competitor patented a similar device with the name *biograph,* from the Greek for "life" and "write," as in *biography.*

That should have been that. Edison and his successors were following the usual practice of nineteenth-century inventors who had given us the telegraph (1805), photograph (1839), telephone (1876), and phonograph (1877), not to mention kinetics (1864), kinesiology (1894), and the lithograph (1825), seismograph (1858), kaleidoscope (1817), and periscope (1879). But unlike these others, the movies escaped from the Greek. First they were known by the plain descriptive terms *motion pictures* or *moving pictures.* Then somebody began saying *movies,* and soon everybody was.

Well, not everybody. The producers and exhibitors of motion pictures, anxious to elevate their art, resisted the designation *movies,* though to little avail. They added sound to their pictures and were rewarded with the name *talkies,* which disappeared only when all films had sound and were called *movies* once again. In the 1920s, they established the Academy of Motion Picture Arts and Sciences—only to have their annual awards nicknamed with the trademark *Oscars.*

The cinema has indeed become an art form in the twentieth century. But it is as a mass medium rather than as an elite art that American movies have permeated the whole world with our culture, or at least with glamorous stereotypes of the American way of life.

The jazziest American contribution to the vocabulary of English is *jazz* itself. From obscure origins among African Americans in New Orleans a century ago, the music and the word we use for it have become familiar the world over. Jazz has been called "the most significant form of musical expression of American black culture and America's outstanding contribution to the art of music," blending elements of African music, work songs, hymns, dances, marches, and Creole music, and developing through the blues and ragtime into a new syncopated improvisational style. Jazz flourished in New Orleans before World War I, in Chicago in the 1920s, and in New York and throughout the country after that. White performers learned it from African Americans and added to the variety of jazz styles.

The music hardly needs an introduction. But what about the word? Unfortunately, its beginnings are especially obscure. It may have come from an African word, or from a performer's name, among other possibilities. But nobody would have dared include *jazz* in a respectable book or article a century ago because it was decidedly obscene, referring to sexual activity. Gradually, though, *jazz* came to mean any vigorous, enthusiastic activity, and eventually it became reputable enough to mention.

Curiously, the earliest evidence of *jazz* so far discovered is in a San Francisco newspaper of 1913, referring to a baseball team back from spring training "full of the old 'jazz.'" As the story goes, the name was next used to advertise a local dance band as "the jazziest tune tooters in all the Valley of the Moon." It appears that bandleader Bert Kelly then brought the word to Chicago in 1914. Meanwhile, the music that we now know as *jazz* had long been developing in New Orleans. It was known as *ragtime* (1897) until *jazz* arrived and took over in 1917. From then on, jazz has jazzed up our lives.

1914 backpack

While our relations across the Atlantic were marching off to war in 1914, Americans were backing off into the woods. No longer living in the wilderness, we felt nostalgic for it. We were reading *Outing* magazine, whose name meant something bucolic and unpolitical back then. In June, instructions in that magazine for folding a blanket into a convenient "back-pack" generated great excitement. Two years later, while the war in Europe continued to rage, Horace Kephart's book *Camping and Woodcraft* enthused, "Back-packing is the cheapest possible way to spend one's vacation in the wilderness."

The civilized American's enjoyment of the outdoors continued unabated in the peacetime Roaring Twenties, as evidenced again in the pages of *Outing,* this time in March 1921: "How about that little back-pack tent you are going to have for your trip next summer or fall?" We have backpacked for pleasure ever since.

Not content with conquering the wilderness, in the 1990s the backpack became the urban carrier of choice as well, supplanting the duffel bag (1917) for travelers, the book bag in schools, and, for some, even the briefcase (1917) and shopping bag (1886) on city streets. The smaller fanny pack (1967), worn lower down and in front by city dwellers, carries valuables next to a more intimate region of the body.

1915 flapper

In the late nineteenth century, the DUDE (1877) was the emblem of outrageously elegant youth. In the early twentieth century, it was the young woman's turn. Behold the flapper, first attested in 1915 by the great curmudgeon H. L. Mencken. "The Flapper of 1915," he wrote, "has forgotten how to simper; she seldom blushes; and it is impossible to shock her."

Where the flapper came from in 1915 is not a mystery. For several previous decades, *flapper* had been a well-known slang term designating a young girl. In 1905, for example, there is a reference to "a red-faced flapper, with a lot of freckles and a pigtail." The flapper of the Roaring Twenties affected a girlish look and insouciance, so she acquired the name as well.

Just as there were self-conscious handbooks for YUPPIES (1984) later in the century, so there was a *Flapper's Dictionary: As Compiled by One of Them,* published in 1922. Therein she was defined as "the ultra-modern, young girl, full of pep and life, beautiful (naturally or artificially), blasé, imitative, and intelligent to a degree who is about to bloom into the period of womanhood and believes that her sex has been and will continue to be, emancipated to a level higher than most mortals have been able to attain."

After the 1929 flap in the stock market, and with the Great Depression of the 1930s leaving her flat, the flapper was a flop in the 1930s and is now as outdated as the speakeasy (1889). We still speak of her, but only in the context of a time long gone by.

1916 IQ

Think about it! In 1916, Americans in general first learned about general intelligence thanks to a book by Lewis M. Terman, professor of psychology at Stanford University. The book was *The Measurement of Intelligence: An Explanation of and a Complete Guide for the Use of the Stanford Revision and Extension of the Binet-Simon Intelligence Scale.* Published by Houghton Mifflin Company in Boston, New York, Chicago, Dallas, Atlanta, and San Francisco, this book changed the way we think of intelligence by giving it a scientific, mathematical name and number.

The name and number were the *IQ.* Terman explained: "The intelligence quotient (often designated as *I Q*) is the ratio of mental age to chronological age." And the mental age was determined by his tests of higher mental abilities, six tasks for each year of mental age from three to fourteen plus two sets of six tasks for adults. The three-year-old was asked to point to nose, eyes, mouth, and hair. The "Superior Adult" was asked to paraphrase an abstract statement, repeat seven digits reversed, and figure out how to get exactly 7 pints of water using containers of 3 pints and 5 pints.

Testing thousands of children and adults to create his scales, Terman reached conclusions that surprised contemporary Americans. IQ, he discovered, was gradually distributed from one end of the scale to the other, meaning that neither the "genius" nor the "feeble-minded" had a separate type of mind. Teachers and parents usually underestimated the intelligence of "feeble-minded" children and overestimated that of "superior" children. And gender made no difference in average IQ. Woman were as smart as men!

But Terman also found lower average IQ among criminals, members of lower social classes, Indians, Mexicans, and blacks, thus providing "scientific" support for race prejudice. Not until much later in the twentieth century were cultural biases of IQ tests called into question.

Later in the century, too, other kinds of intelligence were observed and tested for, including creative ability and emotional intelligence, or *EQ* (1995). Perhaps not coincidentally, *e* and *q* are the first two letters of *equal,* calling *equal opportunity* to mind.

1917 GI

For much of the twentieth century, *GI* has been the common designation for the American fighting man—or woman. However, the GI was born early in the century not as a soldier but as a trash can.

Originally the initials *GI* formed an abbreviation that stood for the material from which a trash can was made, galvanized *i*ron, and its source, *g*overnment *i*ssue. During World War I, when the term first came to attention in the American Expeditionary Force, *GI can* was the doughboys' trash talk for a German artillery shell. "After dark that night," went one account, "Fritz came over and started dropping those famous G.I. cans." And another: "We crossed the river on a span of a sunken bridge that was struck by a G.I.C." German shells were also just plain *GI*s, as in this 1918 poem: "There's about two million fellows, and there's some of them who lie/ Where eighty-eights and G.I.'s gently drop."

Shortly before the start of World War II, the GI (for *gov*ernment *i*ssue, or *general i*ssue) became human. There had been GI soap, GI shoes, and GI clothes; now there was the GI soldier, soon shortened to plain *GI*. By the time World War II began, *doughboy* (1865) had been completely displaced by the more versatile *GI,* the term that remains in use today. And whatever the effects of GI food, the military *GI* has nothing to do with the gastrointestinal *GI* of the medical profession.

1918 D-Day

The Yanks were coming! In April 1917, after three years of the Great War that was consuming Europe, we abandoned our neutrality and declared war on Germany, the country we saw as the aggressor. By June of that year, the first units of the American Expeditionary Force reached the battlefields of France. The A.E.F. provided much assistance to the French and British, and victory was achieved and an armistice declared the next year, on the eleventh day of the eleventh month of 1918.

Because we were last on the battlefield, most of the military vocabulary added to our language during World War I

came from the British, like the name of the new military vehicle the *tank*. But apparently it was the Americans who contributed a technical term that would become famous a quarter of a century later, during World War II. Field Order No. 8 from the First Army of the A.E.F., of September 7, 1918, begins, "the First Army will attack at H-Hour on D-Day with the object of forcing the evacuation of the St. Mihiel salient."

The British used *zero hour* in discussion of an operation whose time was not yet determined or to be kept secret, but Americans preferred *H-Hour* and *D-Day*. In the next World War, with American general Dwight Eisenhower in supreme command, the term for the first day of the Allied invasion of France, June 6, 1944, was the American *D-Day*. That D-Day was and is so famous that it successfully invaded our general vocabulary to become a term that can refer to any day of action or decision. Other letters were combined with *Day* to give similar emphasis to a particular day, such as *V-E Day* and *V-J Day* for the 1945 endings of the war in Europe and Japan, respectively, and *E Day* for "Education Day" (also attested as early as 1945).

1919 T-shirt

The walking advertisement of late twentieth-century American culture got its start as a humble item of men's underwear and got its name because when spread flat it formed a stubby letter *T*. Its little sleeves and round collar distinguished the T-shirt from the standard sleeveless undershirt of the day. The sleeves may also have helped bring the T-shirt out of hiding in the 1930s and 1940s, since they offered a gesture toward modesty as well as a cache for a pack of cigarettes.

Once they were on view, T-shirts became canvases for images and messages. In addition to basic white, they soon came in all shades; and equally important, they displayed first the emblems of schools and teams, and then every design or slogan imaginable. Today a public event is hardly complete without its accompanying T-shirt. Cold weather doesn't slow us down; we just cover the T-shirt with a sweatshirt, a 1925 American invention.

Though it must have been around at least a year earlier (hence our 1919 date), we first read of the T-shirt in F. Scott Fitzgerald's 1920 *This Side of Paradise.* In the novel, a wealthy, self-absorbed 15-year-old boy from Lake Geneva, Wisconsin, heads off to prep school in Connecticut with a wardrobe including "six suits summer underwear, six suits winter underwear, one sweater or T shirt, one jersey. . . ." Exciting words of the Roaring Twenties—FLAPPER (1915), *sheik, cat's pajamas*—have faded into history, but the two informal garments we began to wear in those times, the T-shirt and the sweatshirt, hang in our vocabulary more prominently than ever.

1920 normalcy

It won the presidential election for Warren G. Harding in 1920: *normalcy*, a word that he rescued from obscurity. After the disruption of the World War, Harding said on the campaign trail, it was time to get back to normal: "America's present need is not heroics but healing; not nostrums but normalcy; not revolution but restoration." He repeated the word in his inaugural address the next year: "Our supreme task is the resumption of our onward, normal way. . . . We must strive to normalcy to reach stability."

Normalcy was popular with the voters. But since it was a newly prominent word uttered by a politician, reactions to *normalcy* were mixed. Language purists sneered that Harding's word was a mistake for *normality*. They explained that *–ity* is the usual suffix for words like *normal,* while *–cy* is only attached to words that end in *t,* as in *democracy* from *democrat*. However, there were language purists among Harding's supporters too, and they found *normalcy* lurking in dictionaries and articles as far back as 1857, attracting no criticism (or attention of any sort) before Harding used it.

The *normalcy* debate of the 1920s is now long gone, and *normalcy* is now more normal than *normality* to describe the way things usually are or the way we think they ought to be. After Harding, however, politicians have been less eager to use the word in their slogans, perhaps because Harding's normalcy led to the Teapot Dome scandal, perhaps because normalcy is hard to determine in our MULTICULTURAL (1941) world.

1921 media

Until the Roaring Twenties, a medium was a person, not a publication, and media—well, there wasn't such a thing. The medium would set bells ringing and tables hopping in a darkened room by conjuring connections with departed spirits. And *media* was just an obscure Latin plural of *medium.*

Then came modern advertising and a sense of *media* that had nothing to do with the sphere of the spiritual. Suddenly in the advertising world it was smart to speak of placing ads in different *media,* or in one particular *media,* the word being used as a singular as well as a plural. This new *media* has been traced as far back as a 1921 play by two smart members of New York City's Algonquin Round Table, George S. Kaufman and Marc Connelly. In advertising, the new plural *medias* also was coined. Advertising professionals were reported in 1927 as stating, "It was finally decided to allot a definite media to each member," and touting "one of the best advertising medias in the middle west."

The original means of mass communication were print: magazines, journals, and newspapers. A collective name for them was already available: *publications.* Then radio and television were added to the mix, and *publications* would not stretch to fit. Needing a term to encompass them all, we borrowed *media* from the advertising people and have used it ever since, ready to accommodate newer media like the Internet. We have also used the term to refer to journalists as a group or the communications industry as a whole. How else could we put it nowadays than to say that the media have a profound influence on our lives?

1922 cold turkey

By 1922, cold turkey was not always a leftover from Thanksgiving dinner. For an addict, it was quite the opposite. "This method of sudden withdrawal," explained a writer that year, "is described in the jargon of the jail as 'the cold turkey' treatment." It meant "to immediately and completely give up a substance, such as narcotics or alcohol, to which one was addicted."

The shock to the system was such that few addicts voluntarily chose it. "Mention of the 'cold turkey treatment' gives a chill of horror to a drug addict," said *Newsweek* in 1933. "It means being thrown in jail with his drug supply completely cut off." And Mickey Spillane wrote in *I, the Jury* (1947), "I doubt if you can comprehend what it means to one addicted to narcotics to go 'cold turkey' as they call it."

This use of *cold turkey* is an outgrowth of a previous sense, attested as early as 1910, meaning "extreme plainness and directness," going back to *talk turkey,* attested in 1830. Carl Sandburg used the term this way in a 1922 letter: "I'm going to talk cold turkey with the booksellers about the hot gravy in the stories."

Nowadays going cold turkey is not restricted to narcotics and alcohol addiction. We speak of it as an extreme means of quitting any attachment or habit that we find hazardous to our health: cigarettes, chocolate, a television show, sex—perhaps even a sports team.

1923 hijack

In the early years of Prohibition, the word *hijack* was suddenly hijacked into American English. "I would have had $50,000," says a character in a story in the 1923 *Literary Digest,* "if I hadn't been hijacked." To this day nobody knows where *hijack* came from, so we can enjoy speculating about its origin without fear of contradiction. One plausible explanation is that it came from a holdup man saying something like, "Stick 'em up high, Jack," which then became "High, Jack" when he was in a hurry. Another possibility is that it came from the slang word *jack,* meaning "to rob with a weapon." In any case, *hijack* certainly had to do with holdups. To hijack in the 1920s was to seize a truck, or perhaps a boat, carrying illegal liquor, and make off with it. It was an action of one criminal gang against another, an illegal appropriation of an illegal cargo.

The end of Prohibition in 1933 did not end the usefulness of *hijack.* Rather, the meaning of the term broadened to include any illegal takeover of a vehicle, even one with a legitimate cargo. A hijacker was a kidnapper of a vehicle. And if the vehicle was a public conveyance that held passengers rather than goods, a hijacker was a kidnapper indeed.

Hijacking took off in the 1960s when for the first time it happened in the sky. In 1961 hijackers commandeered American planes and made them fly to communist Cuba. Hijackers in communist countries, on the other hand, forced pilots to get them out. And soon there were those who did it just for money. This aerial piracy was immediately termed *skyjacking* by reporters and headline writers. But *hijack* remained the usual word, even for airplanes. And by the mid-1970s, airport security had been tightened enough to make skyjacking rare again.

Back on earth, however, the summer of 1991 introduced a new kind of hijacking peril: taking a car from its driver by force. It was apparently in Detroit where the problem began and where the new crime of "Robbery Armed, Unlawful Driving Away an Auto" got the name *carjacking.* This has maintained its own meaning distinct from *hijacking* because the robber's interest is not in the contents or passengers but in the vehicle itself.

1924 brainstorm

Originally a brainstorm was a momentary malfunction of the mind, a "cerebral disturbance," in the words of an 1894 investigator. A bright idea was not yet called a *brainstorm* but a *brain wave,* as far back as *Harper's* magazine of 1890: "Lucilla, with what she was fond of terming a brain wave, comprehended the situation." But by the 1920s *brain wave* was subsiding, while *brainstorm* took over the meaning of "a sudden surge of ingenuity."

The first instance of this transferred sense, "He had a brainstorm," is recorded in the magazine *College Humor* in early 1925. Many brainstorms took place after that, such as this one from 1941: "Then I had the brainstorm of getting an English star like Howard to play the part," and another from 1993: "Then one of the guys working here had a brainstorm."

But if one brainstorm could produce fertile ideas, how about a whole monsoon? Alex Osborn of the noted advertising agency Batten, Barton, Durstine and Osborn had a brainstorm of his own in 1938: the brainstorm session, or group brainstorming. In the 1950s Osborn's style of brainstorming took the business world by storm. An article in *Business Week* in 1955 explains that it involved "free-wheeling sessions that encourage wild ideas but prohibit any evaluation or discussion until the session is over." Both the method and the word have spread to other countries and languages. It even shows up in Russian as a word pronounced very much like *brainstorming.*

1925 motel

The announcement came in *Hotel Monthly* for March 1925: "The Milestone Interstate Corporation . . . proposes to build and operate a chain of motor hotels between San Diego and Seattle, the hotels to have the name 'Motel.'"

It was only the dawn of the motel age, but Interstate was seeing far into the future. At the time, roads for automobiles were still primitive, and so were most lodgings for travelers by car. The first such places were simply campgrounds with parking spaces nearby, though they were often furnished with tents or cabins. Reflecting their character, they took names like *auto camp* (1922), *tourist camp* (1923), *motor camp* (1925), *rest cabins* (1934), and *tourist park* (1936). To suggest a more comfortable kind of accommodation, proprietors sometimes used the word *court*, as in *motor court* (1936), *cottage court* (1936), *tourist court* (1937), and *auto court* (1940).

But there were more and more car travelers who preferred the comforts and conveniences of a hotel, so *motel*—which contains four-fifths of *hotel*—gradually evicted all other names, including the short-lived *autotel* and *autel* (both 1936). Indeed, *motel* has even rendered its parent phrase *motor hotel* obsolete.

Meanwhile, on the model of *motel,* we have the *boatel* (1957) at dockside, for those who drive on water, and the *zootel* for pets. There is even a *snotel*, a site where snow surveys are conducted during the winter at Rocky Mountain National Park.

1926 Bible Belt

As transportation improved and the United States became more specialized by region in the later nineteenth century, we began to belt the country, labeling the different parts according to their products. There is a reference to a wheat belt (in northern Ohio) as early as 1863. The first oil belt, running from New York to Kentucky, was mentioned in 1865. We also spoke of the great cotton belt of the South in 1871, the fruit belt of the Michigan peninsula in 1874, a gold belt in northern Georgia in 1879, the Midwestern corn belt and the California redwood belt in 1882, the "grain-belt of the Pacific slope" in 1886, the orange belt of Florida in 1889, the "Chautauqua grape-belt . . . about two or three miles wide lying upon Lake Erie" in 1897, and an iron belt in Alabama in 1902.

Following this pattern, when railroads standardized time across the continent, what we now call *time zones* were referred to as *time belts* (1894). And imaginative Americans remarked on other kinds of belts: the fever belt of the Southern states (1893), and the grim lynching belt of the South, where lynchings of African Americans were all too common around the turn of the century (1900). But the *belt* that hit hardest in the American consciousness was the *Bible Belt*, a term invented in the 1920s by H. L. Mencken. He wrote in the *American Mercury* for February 1926 of a Jackson, Mississippi, newspaper "in the heart of the Bible and Lynching Belt." The Baltimore satirist was not intending kindness when he applied this label to the middle and southern parts of the country that took the Bible literally and seriously. Later uses of the term have been more or less positive, depending on the writer's attitude toward fundamentalist Christianity.

New *belts* have emerged with Americans' changing perceptions of themselves. The name *sunbelt*, used for the southern states from coast to coast, along with their growing populations, was a 1967 invention of political writer Kevin Phillips. Before long, a name was coined for its opposite, the older states of the East and upper Midwest where heavy industry, especially steel, was in decline: *rust belt* (1985).

1927 macho

Meanwhile, south of the border, there was that other North American country from which we had freely taken words throughout the nineteenth century—words like RANCH (1831), RODEO (1844), CAFETERIA (1853), VIGILANTE (1860), *buckaroo* (1827), *bonanza* (1844), *placer* (1848), *hoosegow* (1909), and *ten-gallon hat* (1927, from *galón*, "braids"). Oh, and *gringo* (1849), referring to citizens of the United States. Not content with all these borrowings, we took much of the northern part of their country of origin as well during the mid-nineteenth century.

Our fascination with Mexico endured in the twentieth century. A particular fascination for the gringo male was the notion of extreme masculinity embodied in *macho*. Spanish *macho* seemed to offer opportunities for manliness and toughness unavailable in English. *Macho* was apparently known in the West by 1927; it made its way back to the New York weekly *The Nation* early in 1928, when a correspondent wrote, "Here I was in their midst, a Macho Yankee Gringo, yet treated with consideration." More recently, author Norman Mailer was one who took *machismo* seriously. In his 1961 *Advertisements for Myself* he wrote, "Every American writer who takes himself to be both major and *macho* must sooner or later give a *faena* [a ritual performance like a bullfighter's] which borrows from the self-love of a Hemingway style."

In our era of increasing egalitarianism, macho movie heroes remain the rage, literally and figuratively. And in 1992, astronomers gave the ultimate tribute to a newly discovered (or at least imagined) celestial body, like a planet but larger, by naming it *Massive Astrophysical Compact Halo Object,* *MACHO* for short.

1928 athlete's foot

Otherwise known as *tinea pedis,* at least among doctors, it can be the scourge of the locker-room showers. *Athlete's foot* spread into the American English vocabulary in a 1928 issue of *Literary Digest:* "Athlete's foot . . . is a popular name for ringworm of the foot, from which more than ten million persons in the United states are now suffering."

The association of athletes and this variety of ringworm had to wait until the twentieth century, when Americans, including athletes, finally began to take a serious interest in hygiene. Occasional baths had been the limits of American cleanliness in previous centuries. Now, not only did athletes have running water in their *locker rooms* (itself a term of the first decade of the twentieth century), they had communal showers. Floors in the locker-room environment are usually wet, making ideal conditions for lurking fungi.

In fact, medical authorities say, the association with athletes is unfounded. Most people already carry the fungi; one recent estimate is that 70 percent of the population may be afflicted to one degree or another. The little organism thrives in moist and airless environments, like that created by wet feet in shoes. If the skin between the toes is kept healthy and dry, we rarely have problems with athlete's foot.

1929 jalopy

We find a definition in print in 1929: "Jaloppi—A cheap make of automobile; an automobile fit only for junking." The definition has stayed the same, but it took a while for the spelling to stop bouncing around. Among the variants have been *jallopy, jaloppy, jollopy, jaloopy, jalupie, julappi, jalapa,* and *jaloppie.*

John Steinbeck spelled it *gillopy* in *In Dubious Battle* (1936): "Sam trotted off toward the bunk houses, and London followed more slowly. Mac and Jim circled the building and went to the ancient Ford touring car. 'Get in, Jim. You drive the gillopy.' A roar of voices came from the other side of the bunk house. Jim turned the key and retarded the spark lever. The coils buzzed like little rattlesnakes."

Jalopy seems to have replaced *flivver* (1910), which in the early decades of the twentieth century also simply meant "a failure." Other early terms for a wreck of a car included *heap, tin lizzie* (1915), and *crate* (1927). But where *jalopy* came from, nobody knows.

1930 bulldozer

The bulldozer as we know it, "a large caterpillar tractor with a plow on the front end for moving earth," pushed its way into our vocabulary by 1930. It was noted in the magazine *Water Works and Sewerage* for June of that year: "The bulldozer is built for heavy duty." The name suggests a machine with the strength of a bull.

However, the first bulldozers back in the 1870s were not machines at all, nor bulls. They were people who could be said to give others a dose of maltreatment fit for a bull. In Louisiana during Reconstruction, *bulldozers* were racist bullies. According to an account in a New York newspaper of 1877, they were "an organization of armed white men, whose ostensible business it is to keep the Negroes from stealing the cotton crop. On election day, however, the 'Bulldozers' go gunning for

Negroes who manifest a disposition to vote the Republican ticket." That year the *Congressional Record* reported, "A band of bull-dozers came into Saint Francisville [Louisiana], and by their yelling and hallooing . . . put the entire inhabitants in a mortal terror."

But bulldozing was not confined to the South, nor to racist attacks. In 1892, for example, the Louisville *Courier-Journal* wrote, "The people of Louisville . . . will never surrender their rights to Johnny Davenport's proposed gang of ballot-box stuffers and bulldozers." And politicians declared that they should not, or would not, be bulldozed.

Bulldozer so effectively describes the force of the modern machine, able to overpower the resistance of the earth in a way that pick and shovel could never do, that it is no wonder that the term was appropriated for the earthmoving engine. To *bulldoze* still means "to intimidate, to push through regardless of opposition." But because someone chose to give the name *bulldozer* to a machine, we no longer associate the word with mean-spirited humans.

1931 skid row

A 1931 dictionary of *American Tramp and Underworld Slang* gives the earliest evidence for *skid row,* which is defined as "the district where workers congregate when in town or away from their job." From that it is easy to derive the modern meaning of "a squalid district inhabited chiefly by derelicts and vagrants," in the words of *The American Heritage Dictionary of the English Language, Third Edition.* But there was a long road leading up to it.

Originally, in fact, it was a road, not a row. The first skid road was exactly what it says: "a road made of logs known as *skids*." Such roads were built in the Pacific Northwest in the late nineteenth century to bring timber to market. The skids were laid across the road every five or six feet so that timber could be hauled by horses to a river or other shipping point without getting stuck in the mud. To reduce friction as the timber was hauled, workers would grease the skids. Someone whose life was slipping downhill was said to be *on the skids*.

Before long, therefore, *skid road* also became a designation for the parts of towns where lumbermen congregated, streets known not for their elegance but for their cheapness and rough life. And since these lumbermen were mostly single and nomadic, and often enough out of work, their skid road was the place for all sorts of down-and-outs. The earliest so-called *skid road* was apparently Yesler Way in Seattle.

At the turn of the twentieth century, *skid road* was still localized in the Northwest. But as the century progressed, tramps (1664) and HOBOES (1847) took it throughout the country. Removed from any association with lumbering, the *road* of *skid road* was reinterpreted as *row,* the usual designation for a stretch of residences and businesses. Thus the derelict sections of cities like Chicago and New York became known as *skid row*s. Through an attempt to make better sense of the phrase, it had become a road to nowhere.

1932 hopefully

In the depths of the Great Depression, the supreme expression of American optimism, *hopefully* in the sense "it is hoped," made its appearance in the pages of the *New York Times Book Review.* "He would create an expert commission," said the 1932 review, "to consist of ex-Presidents and a selected list of ex-Governors, hopefully not including Pa and Ma Ferguson." But the 1930s were not particularly hopeful times, and *hopefully* was used only marginally for many years after. It was finally in the prosperous 1950s and early 1960s that *hopefully* hopped into our everyday conversation, where it has thrived ever since.

Not that the word *hopefully* itself is new or American. Using *hopefully* to indicate that a person is full of hope has been practiced in the English language for more than three centuries. The old meaning occurs in expressions like "He went to work hopefully." This means the subject was optimistic when he went to work. The modern "Hopefully, he went to work" has nothing to do with the subject's attitude but instead expresses the judgment of an outside observer.

Hopefully as we use it nowadays declares that the situation is full of hope, that a goal has hope of being fulfilled. We like it because it implies analysis of the situation rather than just a wish. To say "*I hope* the plan will succeed" is merely to utter a personal desire; "*Hopefully,* the plan will succeed" expresses the cautious optimism of an objective observer. We also like it because, while exuding optimism, it leaves us a way out. It's as optimistic as *certainly* or *surely,* but it makes no guarantees. No wonder politicians like it.

And for just this reason, no wonder some critics have been sharply critical of *hopefully.* In the 1970s, one said it "makes me physically ill"; another denounced it as "the most horrible usage of our time." They give various explanations, but they were probably most bothered by the way *hopefully* absolves a person or organization from responsibility while lending an air of optimism. The modern *hopefully* operates just like *certainly, thankfully,* and *mercifully* in expressing a general attitude, however, so there is no valid grammatical objection to it. Hopefully, its critics will find better uses for their time.

1933 supermarket

This has been a supercentury for America, not just in technology and world affairs but also in language. And *super–* has been a superproductive prefix for us in the twentieth century, so much so that we could choose a *super* word for almost every entry. To allow room for others, however, we will confine the *super*s to this one year.

The main stimulus for our *super* vocabulary has been superscience. On the example of a few older words like *supersaturate* (1788) and *supercharge* (1876), the twentieth century blossomed with *superconductor* (1913), *supersonic* (1919), *superalloy* (1948), *supercomputer* (1968), the computer *superchip* (1978), the weather *supercell* (1985), *supergreenhouse effect*

(1986), and *superquake* (1989), to name just a few. Most of the recent examples listed above are American inventions.

Another *super* source was the 1903 translation of Friedrich Nietzsche's German *Übermensch* as *superman*. In America in 1938, his philosophical creation donned a cape and was transformed into a man of action, the Superman of the comics.

Our super-duper (1940) *super*s have included *superhighway* (1925), *superglue* (1946), the *supermom* (1976) who raises *superkids* (1977), and the *Super Bowl* (1969), the ultimate football game and the most watched event in America. There was also a *super* that made a profound change in American shopping habits: the supermarket.

Until the 1930s, we shopped at small neighborhood grocers, butchers, and bakers. But the new chain stores, enjoying the advantage of large-scale buying, found advantages in large-scale selling as well. *Chain Store Age* magazine wrote in 1933, "The 'One-stop-drive-in super market' provides free parking, and every kind of food under one roof." Gradually smaller grocery stores disappeared, unable to match the low prices of supermarkets. At the end of the twentieth century the supermarkets had triumphed so thoroughly that *super*– was superfluous, and the term *market* was again used by itself, now to refer to one of super size.

1934 whistlestop

Now that passenger trains hardly stop anywhere in America, the idea of a whistlestop seems romantic, conjuring up a little place where a train would stop if signaled by a whistle. That is indeed what *whistlestop* means. A 1934 dictionary of American slang gives it a neutral definition: "*Whistle Stop,* a small town." In the heyday of railroad travel, however, it was not a compliment. It meant a place hardly worth a toot.

The term was so insulting that it played a role in the Presidential election campaign of 1948. The underdog, Democratic President Harry Truman, campaigned across the nation by

train. Mocking Truman's efforts, Republican Senator Robert Taft declared that the President was "black-guarding Congress at whistlestops all across the country." The Democrats were delighted at Taft's inadvertent insult to the towns in Truman's itinerary, and they managed to turn *whistlestop* into something of an honorific. "That phrase was invented by Senator Taft on October 8, 1948," Truman later said. "The Republicans were trying to make fun of my efforts to take the issues in that campaign directly to the people all over the country."

Truman's success inspired whistlestop campaigns in later years. President Bill Clinton, for example, made his way by train to the Democratic Convention for his renomination in 1996. As train travel became less commonplace, trains and whistlestops gained in nostalgia. A candidate on a whistlestop tour nowadays appeals to our sense of the safe, friendly, down-to-earth way of life we imagine Americans once had. Whistle-stopping brings the candidate back to the people passed over by airplanes and bypassed by interstate highways. And maybe it will even bring Harry Truman's luck.

1935 boondoggle

A boondoggle was just a little recreation for Boy Scouts and cowboys until the government took over. Some say it began as a craft project to keep Scouts busy and quiet, braiding the ends of a lanyard or leather strap to be worn around the neck for decoration or to hold something like a key. Similarly, at home on the range on an idle day, cowboys would make boondoggles by weaving together odd scraps of leather as decorations for their saddles or other equipment. In the mid-1930s, at the height of the Great Depression, someone who was skeptical about newly created government jobs gave them the contemptuous name of *boondoggles.*

We can see the transformation of boondoggle from private pastime to public waste in a *New York Times* article of April 4, 1935, with the headlines "$3,187,000 Relief is Spent to Teach Jobless to Play . . . 'Boon Doggles' Made . . . Aldermen Find These Are Gadgets." An instructor in boondoggling explained to the city aldermen, "They may be making belts in leather, or maybe belts by weaving ropes, or it might be belts by working with canvas, maybe a tent or a sleeping bag. In other words, it is a chamber of horrors where boys perform crafts that are not designed for finesse and fine work, but simply a utility purpose."

Ever since, *boondoggle* has been the standard and indispensable epithet for purposeless and wasteful projects in government and business. Where the odd-sounding word came from no one knows, but it resembles extravagant inventions of the early nineteenth century like SOCKDOLAGER (1827). Perhaps only *boondoggle* is sufficiently outrageous for proper censure of an outrageous waste of time.

1936 streamline

In 1936, we were in the midst of streamlining not just our transportation but our furniture, our fashions, our bodies, our work—seemingly every aspect of our lives. The *Baltimore Sun* offered this advice in November 1936: "Those who watch financial fashion observe a tendency to streamline capital setups for tax purposes." The previous year saw publication of a book, *Streamline for Health;* the next year the *Denver Post* suggested, "*Streamline* your dance frock." We streamlined our radios and our toasters to match the new streamlined trains. We even built buildings in the streamlined style later called *art deco* (1966).

Where did all this streamlining come from? For many years *streamline* had been a technical term used by scientists and engineers. In this century of high speed, they had been working to streamline vehicles, particularly the new airplanes, to reduce wind resistance. And as trains and cars became faster, they too seemed to need streamlining.

In May 1934, on the opening day of the *Century of Progress* world's fair in Chicago, the world's attention was drawn to a Burlington Railroad passenger train, the *Zephyr*, which arrived from Denver in 13 hours 5 minutes, less than half the time of the previous record. What was its secret? Light weight and streamlining. Soon the *Zephyr*'s smooth horizontal lines were imitated on typewriters and desks, dining tables and bed frames, houses and sheds—objects that were not to likely to be hurled at high speed through the air. Formerly boxy automobiles too were redesigned to look as if they were racing along even when they were parked. By the time designers of this era got through with streamlining, it had little to do with air flow and much to do with appearance.

Towards the end of the century, when cars were redesigned to reduce wind resistance and increase fuel efficiency, *streamline* could not be used; the word implied a style (and an old-fashioned one at that) instead of a technical process. The term we use nowadays for reducing drag and going with the flow is *aerodynamic*.

1937 groovy

The first to be in the groove were African-American jazz musicians, early in the 1930s. They are no longer around to tell us where this *groove* came from, but scholars have speculated. Maybe it began with that relatively new invention, the phonograph, whose sound came out right when the needle was in the groove; maybe the musicians—virtually all of them men— were creating yet another metaphor for sex. No matter. What matters is the COOL (1949) sound when a player is really in the groove, not forcing the music but letting it flow. "The jazz musicians gave no grandstand performances," wrote an admiring reviewer in 1933, "they simply got a great burn from playing in the groove."

It could be summed up with the word *groovy,* defined in 1937 as a "state of mind which is conducive to good playing." Before long, there were groovy audiences as well as groovy performers, and by the 1940s things in general could be groovy. Love was groovy, skating was groovy, even pitching a no-hit baseball game was groovy. (By the way, since the early 1900s, the center of the strike zone in baseball has been known as the *groove,* and a pitcher who throws a fastball there is said to be *grooving.*)

Groovy was in the air everywhere in the hip, laid-back counterculture of the 1960s, when *feeling groovy* was the ultimate ambition and praise, as well as the title of a hit song. To *groove* was "to have fun." "Life as it is really grooves," declares a fictional letter from a group of groovy young dropouts in a 1969 short story by John Updike. Later generations have not always felt so groovy, but they know how to use the word when they want to speak so their elders can understand.

1938 teenager

In the first part of the twentieth century, we made a startling discovery. There were teenagers among us! Until then, we had thought of people in just two stages: children and adults. And while childhood might have its tender moments, the goal of the child was to grow up as promptly as possible in order to enjoy the opportunities and shoulder the responsibilities of an adult. The girl became the woman, the boy became the man. It was as simple and significant as that.

Or was it? The reforms of the early twentieth century, preventing child labor and mandating education through high school, lengthened the pre-adult years. In earlier times, a person reaching adult size at age thirteen or fourteen was ready to do adult work. Now adult size was achieved as soon as ever, but preparation for adult responsibilities lasted until age eighteen or later. Thus the years ending in –*teen* became something new and distinctive. Depending on your point of view, these years were either to be savored as the best of times, combining childhood freedom with adult physical maturity, or endured as years of hazard, combining childish irresponsibility with adult urges.

To match our gradual recognition of this new phenomenon, we adopted new terminology. First, in the 1920s, we began to use *teenage* to speak of clothes and activities, girls and boys, in the latter cases recognizing the teen years but still assigning them to childhood. About two decades later, against the backdrop of depression and war, *teenager* was born. The exact date has yet to be determined; the word makes a matter-of-fact appearance in a 1941 issue of *Reader's Digest,* but being derived from long-established *teenage,* it must have been around at least a few years earlier.

The teenager remade our world. The concept is profoundly democratic by right of chronology: every child, regardless of wealth or merit, can look forward to an age of vigor and independence. And it is subversive: why should any teenager enjoying freedom submit to the authority of adults? With the discovery of this new age, ours has been the century of the teenager ever since.

1939 jukebox

Music and entertainment are two ways in which African Americans have made major contributions to American culture. Put African-American music together with a national itch for technological invention, and you have the jukebox, a device in which the patrons of an eating or drinking establishment place coins in return for entertainment with recorded music.

Juke itself is an African word. In the Wolof language of West Africa, *juke* means "to make mischief" or "to lead a wicked, disreputable life." In America, in the Old South, the word managed to survive slavery and emancipation well into the twentieth century. A juke, juke house, or juke joint was a place to make mischief in the company of other like-minded revelers. Sometimes it was a tavern, sometimes a dance hall, sometimes a brothel.

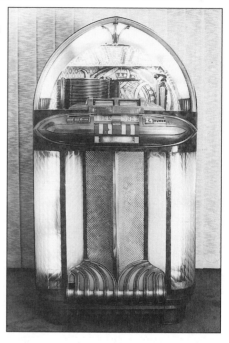

"Back yonder," recalled a writer in 1937, "a 'juke' was a place, usually a shack somewhere off the road, where a field negro could go for a snort of moonshine."

By the time the coin-operated record player was invented, the juke thus had a reputation as an exotic place for having a good time. Borrowing the supposed excitement of the juke along with its name, the jukebox spread throughout the country in the late 1930s. *Time* magazine noted in 1939, "Glenn Miller attributes his crescendo to the 'juke-box,' which retails recorded music at 5 cents a shot in bars, restaurants and small roadside dance joints."

Playing it costs more than a nickel nowadays, but the jukebox has survived the transition from records to CDs, becoming a sophisticated, high-tech musical accompaniment to good times in bars and eating places even today.

1940 jeep

Jeep was a term that carried humor before it carried soldiers. It also carried a wide variety of other military meanings before it became the designation for the "half-ton four-by-four command-reconnaissance car" first manufactured for the U.S. Army in September 1940.

Both the design and the name had their beginnings in the 1930s, years before they came together in the first production models. The design of the as yet unnamed vehicle apparently originated with a tank captain in 1932, and its development involved three different manufacturers over the rest of the decade. Meanwhile, the term *jeep* was undergoing its own development. In the military, *jeep* could mean "a recruit," "a poorly-fitting coat," or the Link Trainer for pilots. In civilian life, Eugene the Jeep was introduced March 16, 1936, as a new character in the Popeye comic strip. Eugene was a small but mighty creature whose cry was "jeep, jeep."

The combination of connotations, military and civilian, little and yet powerful, inspired somebody to call the new military vehicle a *jeep* and thereby fix the word's meaning for future generations. In World War II American soldiers brought the modern meaning of *jeep* with them to all corners of the globe. After the war the jeep gained a civilian dimension; the sturdy box with four-wheel drive, open to nature and the elements, became popular for civilian recreation and scientific adventures; the word was even capitalized and trademarked by one manufacturer. The vehicle remains popular today, more than half a century after it first appeared.

1941 multicultural

During the deadliest war of the deadly twentieth century, the term *multicultural* emerged as an antidote to an *–ism* that had brought much suffering. The *–ism* was *nationalism* (1844), the insistence that one nation was superior to all others and should impose its culture on the rest of the world. The antidote was named in a book review in the *New York Herald-Tribune* for July 1941 applauding "a fervent sermon against nationalism, national prejudice and behavior in favor of a 'multicultural' way of life." *Multiculturalism* (1965) meant "respect for the ways of all nations and peoples," not just one's own.

After the war, the idea of being multicultural raised doubts not only about nationalism but also about imperialism and colonialism. After the brutal midcentury experience of those *–isms*, it was no longer easy to assume that any single culture was so superior that it justified the domination of others. The word *multicultural* advocated coexistence. To our north, for example, Canadians used *multicultural* to describe their attempt to accommodate both English and French culture and language in their commonwealth.

In the United States, multicultural led a quiet life until it became a key word in the "culture wars" of the 1980s and 1990s. Liberals began voicing their dream of the United States as a multicultural country, one with diverse peoples and cultures drawn from all over the world, sharing a common belief in freedom and democracy. Instead of seeing the country as a MELTING POT (1907) cooking up a single American way of life, they celebrated diversity.

They also began to expand the definition of culture beyond ethnicity, race, and religion to include gender and lifestyle, so that *multicultural* could mean "respect for different ages, sexes, physical or mental capabilities, and sexual orientations." At an extreme, respect might even be demanded for the distinct "cultures" of vegetarians, animal rights activists, millenarians, and transvestites. For some conservatives, this was too much. They saw multiculturalism as undermining respect for our unique American ideals and way of life, for the Western Civilization from which these ideals sprang, and for "family values." The debate continued inconclusively as the century drew to an end.

1942 gizmo

How did we win the war? Well, we had the right gizmo when we needed it. The term is an honorable American invention, like *doodad* (1877) and *doohickey* (1914), the latter a Navy word that helped us win World War I. A couple of decades later, when we had to make the world safe for democracy all over again, we added to our arsenal both *whatchamacallit* (1942) and the modern *gizmo*.

Nobody knows where *gizmo* came from, but we think the Marines told it to us. The evidence is from two articles, both published in November 1942. *Leatherneck* magazine explained, "When you need a word for something in a hurry and can't think of one, it's a *gizmo*." And *Yank* that month agreed: "Leathernecks . . . even have a name for a whatsis. They call it a 'gizmo.'" *Gizmo* survived the transition to civilian life and has become an indispensable verbal tool of modern technological civilization.

1943 acronym

As wartime production of names using initials reached an all-time high, it was high time to give a name to the growing arsenal of alphabetic abbreviations. That need was met in a note in the February 1943 issue of *American Notes and Queries:* "Your correspondent who asks about words made up of the initial letters or syllables of other words may be interested in knowing that I have seen such words called by the name *acronym,* which is useful, and clear to anyone who knows a little Greek."

Greek? Yes, *acronym* follows the model of other designations for types of words, like *synonym, antonym,* and *homonym.* The *–nym* means "a kind of word"; *acro–* means "top, peak, or initial," as in *acrobat* or *acrophobia.* Sometimes scholars distinguish between initialisms, which are simply a series of letters pronounced one after the other, like *USA* (1795 as "*U*nited *S*tates of *A*merica," 1848 as "*U.S. A*rmy"), *GOP* (*G*rand *O*ld *P*arty, 1883), IQ (1916), and GI (1917), and hard-core acronyms, which are initials pronounced as a separate word, like *WAC* (a member of the *W*omen's *A*rmy *C*orps, 1943), SNAFU (1944), and *radar* (*ra*dio *d*etection *a*nd *r*anging, 1941). In general use, however, these are all called *acronyms.*

And what were the acronyms so busily produced during World War II? Initialisms ranged from *PX* (*p*ost *ex*change, 1941) to *V.D.* (*v*enereal *d*isease, 1942) and included the names of numerous agencies such as *OPA* (*O*ffice of *P*rice

Administration), *OSS* (*O*ffice of *S*trategic *S*ervices, predecessor of the present *CIA* or *C*entral *I*ntelligence *A*gency), and *WPB* (*W*ar *P*roduction *B*oard). Acronyms pronounced as words included *CARE* (*C*ooperative for *A*merican *R*elief in *E*urope, 1945) at war's end, and after the war *NATO* (*N*orth *A*tlantic *T*reaty *O*rganization, 1949). Soon after the establishment of the U.N. (*U*nited *N*ations fighting the Axis, 1942) a plethora of acronyms, some of them quite long, blossomed. Two of the longer ones are *UNESCO* (*U*nited *N*ations *E*ducational, *S*cientific, and *C*ultural *O*rganization, 1945) and *UNRRA* (*U*nited *N*ations *R*elief and *R*ehabilitation *A*dministration, 1943).

1944 snafu

We could easily have given *snafu* pride of place in 1941, because it is already attested then in the journal *American Notes and Queries* with the polite definition "*Snafu,* situation normal." But we have saved this military creation for 1944, the year of greatest mobilization on all sides in World War II, when there were opportunities for snafus as never before.

In addition to the numerous official ACRONYMS (1943) of wartime, the sometimes frustrating experience of military life in the Second World War stimulated the improvisation of unofficial acronyms as well. Most of them involved the pair of letters *f.u.*, which was translated politely as standing for "fouled up" in dictionaries intended for family use. Among themselves, members of the armed forces most often used a stronger *f*-word. Use your own preference in considering the examples that follow.

These words generally were written in lowercase letters, perhaps because they were unofficial, or perhaps to avoid suggesting impropriety by camouflaging them as ordinary words. They included *fubar,* meaning "*f*---ed *u*p *b*eyond *a*ll *r*ecognition," and the similar *fubb,* for "*f*---ed *u*p *b*eyond *b*elief," as well as *tarfu,* for "*t*hings *a*re *r*eally *f*---ed *u*p." There was *janfu,* meaning "*j*oint *A*rmy and *N*avy . . . ," and *GFU,* referring to an individual who *G*enerally *F*ailed to *U*nderstand the situation— or something like that. But like the humorous abbreviations surrounding the birth of *OK* in 1839, most of the World War II coinages were short-lived. The exception was *snafu,* explained as "situation *n*ormal: *a*ll *f*---ed *u*p."

Maybe the success of *snafu* resulted from the distinctive way it was used. A snafu was not an attitude but an event: "a mistake, a foulup, a glaring error." There was a need for an emphatic designation like this in civilian life too, so *snafu*s have been plentiful ever since.

NEARING

THE

MILLENNIUM:

1945-1998

$\mathcal{E}$ xactly what the latest era means to the idea of America and which of our recent words will stand the test of time will be hard to tell until the twenty-first century lends us perspective. We can only guess which expressions later generations will admire or ridicule, use or forget. But we have ample evidence to help us answer a more immediate question: If we were already modern by 1944, what was left after that to propel us Americans toward the millenium? The answer, in a word, seems to be *showbiz* (1945), the *cold war* (1946), and *geeks* (1978). In the postwar balance between war and peace, the guitar proved to be mightier than the sword. At the start of the current era, the *iron curtain* (1946) set the stage for more than forty years of cold war. But the military might of Soviet Communism was no match for America's more open society, captialism, and popular culture. *Rock and roll* (1951), played by *DJs* (1950) on the radio, and television, with its captivating images and *sound bites* (1973), helped keep Western notions of individual liberty alive in Eastern Europe. Beginning with *cybernetics* (1948), ever more powerful computers running ever more impressive *software* (1959) allowed Western nations to push the *envelope* (1988) of technology and demonstrate the material importance of the free flow of information. These developments finally coalesced into the rock that smashed the iron curtain without a shot being fired.

So it was that cold warriors were transformed into *couch potatoes* (1976) who required *aerobics* (1968) to work off the *fast food* (1954) they consumed.

Meanwhile we discovered *swing voters* (1964), *role models* (1956), *yuppies* (1984), and *soccer moms* (1996).

Southern *sit-ins* (1960) helped reverse laws enforcing racial discrimination. Soon there was *affirmative action* (1965) providing opportunities for minorities and women. We combatted *ageism* (1969), sexism and other *–ism*s to the point of being *PC* (1990). We protected the environment by making materials *biodegradable* (1961) and *carpooling* (1962).

But we also paid attention to the *bottom line* (1970), shopping for bargains and avoiding *ripoffs* (1967). The pace of life was too much for some of us, who *went postal* (1994), while others just said *Not!* (1992).

As the century neared its end, we found something new to worry about in the *millenium bug* (1998). Somehow, though, we will probably manage to keep our *cool* (1949).

1945 showbiz

It was a spectacular year for world history—and for the American language. We won the war in Europe and Asia, establishing new national boundaries which even now remain mostly in place. We added the atomic bomb to our arsenal and our language—and began to learn to live with it. But our word of the year is even more powerful than that. We turned to peace with pent-up energy for entertainment, a dominating element of the Americanized world today. The end of the war was, in short, a time for showbiz.

And *Variety,* the slangy entertainment newspaper, had it ready for us even before V-J Day ended the war in the Pacific.

A headline on May 30 announced "Cantor's Showbiz Tribute." In its June 13 issue, the paper commented, "Big-league baseball already had rearranged its team travel schedules to a minimum. However, show biz has done nothing about this yet."

Showbiz was an abbreviation of *show business,* an old and honorable American term that had been around since at least 1850. So the clipped *showbiz* could have remained part of just one publication's style. But it caught on elsewhere because its breezy informality suited the increasing brashness and informality of its subject.

In the years since 1945, atomic weapons thankfully have never been used in war, but American showbiz became such a powerful cultural weapon that today the remotest corners of the globe know about Hollywood, MTV, and Madonna.

1946 iron curtain *and* cold war

The curtain came down and the temperature dropped. That was the political climate of 1946. In the first full year after the end of World War II, the long-sought peace had become another kind of war. It was the climate in which, a few years later, George Orwell published *1984* with its famous slogan, "War is Peace."

Though it had been fabricated in Europe, and had earlier been used even by Hitler's propaganda minister Joseph Goebbels, *iron curtain* was first put prominently on display on March 5, 1946, at Westminster College in Fulton, Missouri. There it was the focus of a speech by Winston Churchill, the prime minister who had led Britain to victory in World War II. He warned his audience of what looked like aggressive preparation by the Soviet Union for yet another war: "From Stettin in the Baltic to Trieste in the Adriatic, an iron curtain has descended across the continent. Behind that line lie all the capitals of the ancient states of central and eastern Europe. Warsaw, Berlin, Prague, Vienna, Budapest, Belgrade, Bucharest, and Sofia, all these famous cities and the populations around them lie in the Soviet sphere and all are subject in one form or another, not only to Soviet influence but to a very high and increasing measure of control from Moscow." This, Churchill said, "is certainly not the liberated Europe we fought to build up. Nor is it one which contains the essentials of permanent peace."

At about the time Churchill was pointing out the curtain, journalist Herbert Bayard Swope used the phrase *cold war* in a speech he wrote for financier and political adviser Bernard Baruch. Baruch decided not to use the phrase publicly, however, until a year later, when in Columbia, South Carolina, he declared, "Let us not be deceived: today we are in the midst of a cold war."

1947 baby-sit

Baby-sitting is such a universal practice in America today that it is hard to imagine that the verb to *baby-sit* came into being only around 1947. It developed from the term *baby sitter,* first used about ten years earlier. Before then, when parents left the house, did they leave their children "home alone" (another very recent phrase, from the 1990 movie of that name)? Or did they always take their children with them when they went out? Neither alternative seems likely, but the advent of the baby sitter still marks a new social phenomenon.

Until the mid-twentieth century, most parents who could afford a night out could also afford servants. Those who could not afford servants would be likely to have relatives, perhaps in the same household, or neighbors who could be trusted to care for the children when the parents had to be gone. It was the postwar development of suburbia, made up of separate residences for middle-class families without servants or extended family, that changed the nature of temporary childcare from a family or neighborly exchange into a commercial practice, most often involving the enterprise of teenage girls who charged a modest hourly rate.

Baby sitters nowadays are adults as well as teenagers, relatives as well as relative strangers, and unpaid volunteers as well as paid workers. You can also baby sit someone or something other than a baby or child; the object can be an adult who needs care or even an item entrusted to someone's temporary safekeeping.

1948 cybernetics

We who spend so much time in the cyberworld owe it all, or at least the *cyber–*, to the American scientist Norbert Wiener. For his 1948 book *Cybernetics* he derived the prefix from classical Greek *kubernētēs*, meaning "one who steers," and added the suffix *–ics* to indicate that it was a science like physics or mathematics. Wiener, a mathematician, proposed *cybernetics* as the study of systems of control and communication, in particular those of the human mind and the computer. The analogy between mind and machine introduced by cybernetics made possible the development of primitive computers into machines that imitate human modes of thinking.

As computers gradually extended their influence, so did *cyber–*, as a prefix having to do with computers and electronic communication. There was the cyborg of the 1960s, an imagined "cybernetic organism" that was part human and part computer. There was cyberphobia, "fear of computers," in the 1980s. And in the 1990s practically anything could have *cyber–* in its name if it involved computers or the Internet. For the New Words Committee of the American Dialect Society, John and Adele Algeo in 1994 and 1995 collected well over one hundred *cyber* words from *cyberbabe* to *Cyberzine*—including *cyberboor, cyberchat, cyber-community, cybercop* (government monitor of Internet communications), *cybercrime, cybernaut* (adventurer on the Internet), *cybernut, cyberporn, cybrarian* (librarian who uses computers), and *cyberscam*.

With his proposal to put computers within the reach of every schoolchild, President Clinton could be said to be building a cyberbridge to the twenty-first century.

1949 cool

Isn't it cool to wait so long to bring up this word? After all, when we're cool, we're not in a hurry.

Referring to a comfortable temperature on the other side of hot, *cool* has been around as long as the English language. But in certain slang uses, *cool* is a much newer phenomenon. It was after World War II, in 1947, that the Charlie Parker Quartet recorded a number called "Cool Blues." In 1948, *Life* magazine introduced *cool* to a general audience in the title "Bebop: New Jazz School is Led by Trumpeter Who is Hot, Cool and Gone." For the benefit of general readers, *The New Yorker* in July 1948 explained, "The bebop people have a language of their own. . . . Their expressions of approval include 'cool'!"

All this was leading, perhaps in 1949, to the sense of *cool* meaning "composure or self-control." We find written evidence of this use first among African Americans, as in the dialogue of a 1953 novel: "Dig yourself, creep, don't lose your cool." By the 1960s, everyone seemed to have cool to lose or to keep.

Over the years, many different meanings of *cool* have accumulated, all available to cool Americans in recent times. *Cool* has meant "daring" (1839), "clever" (1924), "exciting" (1933), "stylish" (1946), "cautious" or "under control" (1952), and "satisfactory" or "OK" (1953). To *cool it* has meant "to stop" (1952), "to die" (1960), and "to relax" (1986). In the 1990s, among young people, *cool* in the sense "approval or appreciation" has even taken on a distinctive pronunciation closer to that of *cull.* That's cool.

1950 DJ

Perhaps it was a headline writer for the show-business journal *Variety* who thought up the term *disc jockey* to signify "someone who plays discs (phonograph records) for an audience, on the radio or at a social gathering." The issue of August 6, 1941, has an article on New York City record jockeys, compressing *record* to *disc* for the headline. The August 13 issue picks up *disc* throughout: "Gilbert is a disc-jockey who sings with his records," and "Art Green disc-jockeys from Manhattan Beach" (in California).

After *disc jockey,* numerous other humorous *jockey*s were coined: *bus jockey* (driver), *typewriter jockey* (typist), and *slide-rule jockey* (airplane navigator), for example. But it was the abbreviation *DJ,* also appearing as *d.j.* and *deejay,* that marked the growing importance of the disk jockey and of recorded popular music in the 1950s. The DJ had become an arbiter of popular taste.

Discotheques, or discos, introduced in the 1950s and 1960s, allowed reinterpretation of *DJ* as "disco jockey." In the 1970s, the term *talk jockey* was invented, meaning "host of a radio talk show," later shortened to the rhyming *talk jock* and instigating the coinage of *shock jock* for the host of a "shock" talk show of the 1990s. In the early 1980s, the new technology of music videos inspired the term *video jockey,* shortened to *VJ.*

Amid these spinoffs, the original *DJ* lives vigorously on. "The d.j. can still hope to help people transform their daily selves through music," solemnly wrote a New York nightclub DJ in a 1996 *New Yorker* article.

1951 rock and roll

A great advance in American civil liberties, as well as a revolution in music, took place as a result of the introduction of rock and roll in 1951. The introducer was Alan Freed, a disc jockey in Cleveland, who used the term to undermine the segregation of popular music into black and white. African-American popular music of the day, known as *rhythm and blues,* was increasingly influential, but radio stations and the record industry insisted on having white performers for white audiences. The only way a song composed and performed by blacks could reach a wider audience was for it to be remade by a white group.

Freed was able to get around the prohibition against African-American music on his radio station by coining a catchy name that was new and therefore all-encompassing. He wouldn't fight to play the forbidden rhythm and blues; instead, he would treat his audiences to what he called *rock and roll.* And while that term did not end music segregation overnight, it eventually made segregation impossible, as both black and white performers took up the phrase and together developed the new rock and roll. From the beginning it was also known informally as *rock 'n' roll.* By the mid-1960s the triumph of rock and roll was so complete that the name of the genre, now performed by musicians of all races all over the world, shrank to *rock*. No longer needed for music, the full phrase *rock and roll* recently has been used to mean "get going, move along," as in "Let's rock and roll."

Freed, who went on to greater fame and misfortune, is appropriately memorialized in Cleveland's Rock 'n' Roll Museum. But he did not actually invent *rock and roll;* he just gave

it a new definition. Freed probably picked up *rock and roll* from the lyrics of a 1948 rhythm-and-blues hit called "Good Rockin' Tonight." Before that, both *rock* and *roll* had sexual meanings in jazz and blues, as in "My Man Rocks Me with One Steady Roll," recorded by Trixie Smith in 1922, which inspired Bill Haley's famous "Rock Around the Clock" in 1954.

1952 Ms.

Women finally got the vote in America in 1920, but that hardly marked the end of their battle for equal status and respect. There was the matter of title, for example. Men were addressed simply as *Mr.,* but women were addressed as either *Mrs.* or *Miss,* depending on marital status.

Reforming everyday language to eliminate sexism is not easy, but the case of *Mrs.* and *Miss* was helped by practical business considerations. Neither *Mrs.* nor *Miss* is neutral; either can be insulting if it is wrongly applied. To get it right means making the effort to determine personal information usually irrelevant to the matter at hand.

No wonder, then, that a suggestion to neutralize the distinction by using simply *Ms.* was well-received by businesses. In 1952 the National Office Management Association in a booklet titled *The Simplified Letter* recommended to its members, "Use the abbreviation Ms. for *all women* addressees. This modern style solves an age-old problem."

But the problem was not quite so promptly solved. Many women preferred the age-old designations, so a revised edition of *The Simplified Letter* a few months later simply recommended, "Use the abbreviation Ms. if not sure whether to use Mrs. or Miss."

The new designation and its association with feminism were furthered by the founding of *Ms.* magazine in 1971. The form of address *Ms.* had both simplified matters of address by providing a neutral, practical title for women, equivalent to *Mr.* for men, and increased women's options: now a woman can use *Mrs., Miss,* or *Ms.* according to her own preference.

1953 UFO

It is no coincidence that the first reported sightings of unidentified flying objects came after the revelations of the secret military projects of World War II. America has always been a land of invention, from the cotton gin to the telephone, from the airplane to the MOTEL (1925). But wartime inventions raised the status of our technology from awe-inspiring to mythic. Working in total secrecy while spending billions of dollars building whole cities and manufacturing plants, the Manhattan Project succeeded in extracting the energy of the atom and building a doomsday weapon. What could not be accomplished by the American military working in secret? What else was being accomplished?

This was the background for sightings of peculiar objects in the skies, beginning in June 1947, in the Southwestern desert area which had so many secret military installations. The objects could be some new super-secret aircraft developed by the U.S. military. Or could they have been developed by some other technologically advanced beings, perhaps from beyond the Earth or the solar system? After all, we now knew that the technology to permit space travel was possible. And these elusive objects traveled far faster and maneuvered far more adroitly than even a jet airplane.

There were many skeptics, however, who considered the objects pie in the sky—or more exactly "flying saucers" (1947), since excited observers had described the objects as saucer-shaped. The name *flying saucers* caught on, making serious research difficult. As a 1953 book *Flying Saucers Have Landed* complained, "ever since the cliché 'flying saucer' was coined, the greatest and most exciting mystery of our age has been automatically reduced to the level of a music hall joke."

The believers preferred the solemn government designation *unidentified flying object*, first used in 1950. But that was a little weighty for everyday use, so in 1953 the acronym *UFO* was coined to replace it. It has dignified the pursuit of the elusive objects ever since. Those who study them have been known at least since 1959 as *ufologists,* and their field of study has been *ufology.* But most people still couldn't find the alien spaceship in the tail of the Hale-Bopp comet of 1997, and the saucers—oops, UFOs—still haven't landed on the White House lawn.

1954 fast food

The pace of modern life is fast, and nowhere is it faster than in America. We want fast transportation, fast communication, fast computers, fast photos, fast music, fast repairs, and fast service from the businesses we patronize. It is from the last of these that we got *fast food.*

At first, it was a matter of fast service. *Fountain and Fast Food Service* was the title of a trade magazine, which published statements like this from 1951: "The partners have become old hands at spotting the type of conventioneer that will patronize their fast food service." Gradually *service* disappeared, and in 1954 we find *fast food* by itself in the title "Fountain and Fast Food." Incidentally, the trade magazine renamed itself *Fast Food* by 1960. In February of that year, the magazine noted, "Delicate scallops are *really* fast food . . . because they come ready to cook." And in July it remarked, "Fast food type restaurants do the lion's share of business for breakfast and noon meals eaten out."

The fast food revolution was a quick success throughout the land, and two decades later it was conquering the world. "The U.S. outcry against infiltration from the south is matched in vehemence by our neighbors' outcry against fast-food imperialism and the gradual Americanization of their own societies," noted the *Christian Science Monitor* in 1982.

Thanks to fast food, families that formerly ate home cooking now eat out or bring back take-home fast food in record numbers. Its virtue is speed, not quality. Its less than ideal nutritional value may have influenced the coining of another term twenty years later, one that also puts a four-letter epithet in front of *food: junk food* (1973).

1955 hotline

In these days of sophisticated electronics and instant global satellite communication, it is hard to remember that a *hotline* was originally just an actual telephone line directly linking two parties so that it would be available round the clock for instant communication. The first such designated hotlines defended us against a Soviet air attack. A *New York Times Magazine* article in August 1955 explained that the Continental Air Defense Command included "twelve air divisions, tied in by 'hot line' communications with one another and with the Army, Navy and Civil Defense Administration. They are like a giant nerve system where a distant pinprick brings an instant reaction throughout the whole organism." In those early days, when most phones were black, the hotline would often be marked by a red telephone.

In 1963, one particular hotline became hot news. In the aftermath of the previous year's Cuban missile crisis, when miscommunication between the United States and the Soviet Union nearly led to war, the two sides established a telephone and teletype "hot line" between the White House and the Kremlin so the leaders of the two nations could talk at a moment's notice. That line was opened August 30, 1963. Before the year was over, business picked up on the idea; the British Overseas Airways Corporation announced a reservations hot line linking London and New York.

Nowadays *hotline* (usually spelled as one word) most often refers not to the telephone line itself but to a service available instantly by telephone. There are hotlines for problems like drug abuse and loneliness, as well as for advice on grammar and cooking turkeys. Many of these nowadays are called *help lines* (1980) or go by names describing the type of service, such as *Kids' Line* (1983), *Parentline* (1990), and *High Society Sexline* (1986).

1956 brinkmanship

How do you fight a war without going to war? After ten years of COLD WAR (1946) with the Soviet Union, that was a paradox we were still trying to resolve. But President Eisenhower's secretary of state, John Foster Dulles, had no doubts about it. "The ability to get to the verge without getting into the war is the necessary art," Dulles said in an interview early in 1956. "If you cannot master it, you inevitably get into war. If you try to run away from it, if you are scared to go to the brink, you are lost."

There was good reason to be scared. Both the United States and the Union of Soviet Socialist Republics were armed and dangerous. The United States had tested its first hydrogen bomb in 1952, the U.S.S.R. in 1953. Both sides had long-range aircraft to deliver the bombs. Neither side was deterred by the fear of "nuclear winter" (1983), an idea whose time would not come for thirty more years. In classrooms, the best we could do for our schoolchildren was to hold "duck and cover" drills so they could practice shielding themselves from the flash and blast of a distant atomic bomb.

Not every American favored going to the brink. Former governor Adlai Stevenson of Illinois, twice nominated as the Democratic candidate to run against Eisenhower, criticized Dulles in a speech in February 1956: "No, we hear the Secretary of State boasting of his brinkmanship—the art of bringing us to the edge of the nuclear abyss."

That word *brinkmanship* was modeled on the "gamesmanship" of Stephen Potter's 1947 book, *The Theory and Practice of Gamesmanship or the Art of Winning Games Without Really Cheating.* The sporting and humorous connotations of the suffix *–manship* applied to such a serious subject imply that the practitioner of brinkmanship is playing with catastrophe. Though the cold war is over, high-risk politics are not, and *brinkmanship* remains a vivid word to describe them.

1957 role model

Sometimes we learn by imitation. We look around for somebody who is doing what we want to do in a way that we admire or at least accept. And then we take that person as an example to follow.

It doesn't take a ROCKET SCIENTIST (1985) to notice that people imitate each other. But it does take a social scientist to come up with a name for the person who is imitated: the *role model.*

We say *role model* easily now, but inventing that term took years of hard work on the part of American sociologists. They began by talking about reference groups, the "groups whose behavior serves as a model for others." Then the first big breakthrough: There are also reference individuals, "particular people that we imitate." Then a false start: How about calling these people *reference idols*? After all, we talk about idols and heroes often enough. But somehow *reference idols* didn't catch on.

Meanwhile, in the 1950s, the sociologist Robert K. Merton was making a distinction between reference individuals, who serve as patterns for living, and role models, whom we imitate in specific roles like chasing tornadoes, playing basketball, or parenting. We find the latter in a collection of articles about the "student-physician" in 1957: "By the time students enter law or medical school, those whose decisions were made earliest are most likely to have a role model."

Today, Merton's careful distinction is long forgotten by everyone, except perhaps sociologists. Nowadays role models can model whole lives as well as particular skills. We seek good role models to follow and criticize those who are bad role models. And we know that when we grow up, for better or worse, we can expect to be role models too.

1958 Murphy's Law

In 1958, an article in *The Nation* explained, "There is an old military maxim known as Murphy's Law which asserts that wherever there is a bolt to be turned, someday there will be someone to turn it the wrong way." The article was a sign that *Murphy's Law* was beginning to flourish in the civilian world as well as the military.

The basic statement of Murphy's Law is "If anything can go wrogn, it will." It has enough variations to fill at least one book. "Murphy's Law states that if it is possible to connect two things together the wrong way round, then someone will do it that way," explained the *New Scientist* in 1967. Or there is "Murphy's first law of biology," revealed in *Scientific American* in 1970: "Under any given set of environmental conditions an experimental animal behaves as it damn well pleases." One other variant is from the Gulf War: "Anything you do can get you shot, including doing nothing."

Where did this name come from? " 'Murphy' was a fictional character who appeared in a series of educational cartoons put out by the U.S. Navy," explained astronaut (later Senator) John Glenn in his 1962 book *Into Orbit*. "Murphy was a careless, all-thumbs mechanic who was prone to make such mistakes as installing a propeller backwards."

According to another story, there was a Captain Edward A. Murphy, Jr., who worked on the effects of acceleration on humans who were riding rocket sleds at Wright Field Aircraft Laboratory shortly after World War II. Setting up the sensors for measuring physical effects, he managed to connect them all backwards. That supposedly inspired Major John Paul Stapp, one of the people riding the sleds, to name the phenomenon *Murphy's Law*.

1959 software

The early computers were massive aggregations of hardware, a term first used for them in 1947. That was not a new word, just an application of the long-established word *hardware,* meaning "metal components and tools." But the hardware shell of the computer protected a soft heart.

At first this interior was made up of programs (1946) written in a code (1946) of *1*s and *0*s that instructed the computer in its own binary language. Then it included operating systems (1961) and countless more programs, ever more user-friendly (1979). All these were like thoughts in the human brain—dependent on the hardware yet not part of it. In contrast and analogy to *hardware,* therefore, everything you could not touch or see, the intangible instructions that made the computer work, took the name *software* in the late 1950s. The new term is attested in a 1960 article in *Communications of the Association for Computing Machinery:* "Nearly every manufacturer is claiming compatibility with all other equipment via such software as COBOL."

In recent times, the creation of *software* has inspired numerous other computer words with the suffix *–ware.* Among them are *freeware* and *shareware,* meaning "software available free to all or for free trial on the honor system," *vaporware,* "software promised but not yet in existence," and *wetware,* "the human brain."

1960 sit-in

The sit-in was a strike tactic used by American labor unions as long ago as 1937. But *sit-in* did not attract much attention until, two decades later, the civil rights movement gave new meaning to that term as well as to race relations in our country. Early in 1960, the movement tried a new kind of nonviolent action. To protest segregation laws in the South that prohibited blacks and whites from using the same facilities, a group of blacks would take seats at a whites-only lunch counter. Refusing to go away when they were refused service, the blacks remained at the counter, politely renewing their requests, until they got food or got arrested. They called what they were doing a *sit-in.*

Soon the ideas behind the sit-in spread to other means of protesting against racial segregation, and during the 1960s other *in* terms were invented to describe them. Sympathetic whites joined blacks at swim-ins and wade-ins to end the color

barrier in public pools and beaches. There were march-ins
and lie-ins, stand-ins for tickets at segregated movie theaters,
walk-ins at art galleries, study-ins at schools, play-ins at parks,
kneel-ins at churches, rest-ins at segregated rest rooms. Even
the term *drive-in* (1941) was borrowed (from the outdoor
movie theater) to refer to integrating whites and blacks at motels and roadside stands.

Returning from civil rights protests in the South, college
and university students began using sit-in tactics for other
kinds of protests, including some directed against administra-
tors and policies on their own campuses. As the Vietnam War
intensified, faculty and students organized marathon teach-ins
and read-ins to learn about the war and protest American
involvement.

In the counterculture of the 1960s, the *–in*s spread to describe events like a smoke-in for legalized marijuana, a hang-in
at an art gallery for artists to display their paintings, a love-in
to celebrate love, and the ultimate participatory performance,
the be-in. Eventually there were so many kinds of *–in*s that
one contemporary writer said the 1960s would be remembered
as "the 'in' decade."

1961 biodegradable

It took the inventiveness of modern science to create a need for words like *recycle* (1926) and *biodegradable*. Until this century, those concepts were so familiar that they needed no name. Things were too valuable to not to be recycled, and when they finally wore out, they were almost always biodegradable. Containers were built to be used again and again. They were made of metal that could be refabricated, or glass, clay, or wood that would eventually return to earth. Houses were built to last, vehicles and clothes to last till they wore out. (According to Oliver Wendell Holmes's popular poem, the deacon's wonderful one-hoss shay lasted a century before collapsing.) People made a living by collecting old rags and scrap metal.

But the twentieth century brought new materials and manufacturing techniques, lowering the cost of things while making them impervious to decay. Ours was the century of the throwaway (1903), and what we threw away stayed around to haunt us. Aluminum would not rust; plastics would not crumble; artificial fibers would not rot. Litter became a persistent problem on beaches, parks, and roads. Landfills overflowed. Detergents caused rivers and ponds to foam. We had to ask whether the materials of modern life could vanish inconspicuously into nature when we finished with them.

It took a new word to express this new concern: *biodegradable*. It was borrowed from the scientists and first attested in 1961 in a book on industrial microbiology: "Compounds with strictly linear side chains and those containing one or two methyl branches on the carbon atom attached to the benzene ring are readily biodegradable." By 1962, *Chemical and Engineering News* was bringing *biodegradable* down to earth in discussing "feedstock . . . suitable for the production of a completely biodegradable detergent." And we developed new ethics and passed new laws to give preference to the biodegradable so that we would not be buried in our indestructible junk.

1962 carpool

The original car pool was an invention of World War II. On the home front, gasoline, along with many other scarce items, was being rationed. An automobile was a luxury, to say the least. Driving to and from work alone was frowned upon. But you could serve the war effort if you joined a car pool and shared rides and driving with others. *Reader's Digest* used the term in 1942: "I don't believe I care for anything, thank you. I'm just in their car pool." *McCall's* the next year remarked, "On a master map of the city car pools are plotted."

After the war, attitudes about driving relaxed, and for a while there was little more to say about car pools. But along with increasing concern for the environment, *carpool* became a verb, first attested in the *National Review* for May 22, 1962: "You have to proceed to the consideration of the relative values of carpooling with large or small families."

And in the oil crisis of the 1970s, everyone was concerned about carpooling. In 1973, the Environmental Protection Agency urged "much greater use of car pooling and mass transportation just about everywhere." In 1974, the *New York Times* joked, "The Government should encourage bundling as a night-time fuel-saving equivalent to car pooling." There was also the new name *carpooler* (1972) for someone who would "carpool it" (1973) to work or play.

Nowadays, to expedite travel for carpoolers, some highways use express lanes and diamond lanes (1976). The latter are traffic lanes marked with large diamonds to signify that they are prohibited to those driving alone. To ease the way into joining a car pool signs along highways encourage people to call services which match riders and drivers.

1963 duh

In 1963, the *New York Times Magazine* explained the usefulness of this little word: "A favorite expression is 'duh.'... This is the standard retort used when someone makes a conversational contribution bordering on the banal. For example, the first child says, 'The Russians were first in space.' Unimpressed, the second child replies (or rather grunts), 'Duh.'"

Well, duh. It's a no-brainer. It began as an outward expression of a slow-witted cartoon character's mental processes, as in a 1943 *Merrie Melodies* movie: "Duh. . . . Well, he can't outsmart me, 'cause I'm a moron." Later in the twentieth century it blossomed into every man, woman, and child's condescending exclamation upon hearing a self-evident and thereby unnecessary remark. It is so simple that it is one of the first verbal weapons learned by children, so effective that it stays in their linguistic arsenal as they grow to adulthood. For maximum effect, *duh* can be extended long and loud, with an extra twist in the pitch of the voice.

Because it stoops to the presumed mental level of the remark on which it comments, *duh* can backfire, implying that the perpetrator rather than the recipient is dimwitted. But since most of us are not ROCKET SCIENTISTS (1985), who cares? We've made our point, regardless. Duh!

1964 swing voter

In the eighteenth century, at election time, political parties began asking us to vote for their TICKET (1756). In the nineteenth century, some of us were inclined to look across party lines and vote a "split ticket" (1836), though others stayed faithful to the "straight ticket" (1856). In the twentieth century, fickleness in the electorate grew to a point where we needed a new term: *swing voter*.

The term seems to have been first recorded during the 1964 presidential campaign pitting Lyndon Johnson, the incumbent and a liberal Democrat, against his conservative Republican challenger, Barry Goldwater. "Extremism in the defense of liberty is no vice," Goldwater told the Republican convention in his acceptance speech. "Moderation in the pursuit of justice is no virtue." Large numbers of voters with moderate political views disagreed, and many Republicans became swing voters, helping Johnson to an overwhelming victory.

The use of *swing voter* in 1964 may have been influenced by another new meaning of *swing* that was first attested that year. To *swing* was "to swap sexual partners," and *swingers* were those who did it. "As Gilbert Bartell discovered, getting started in swinging is easy," explained *Time* magazine a few years later. "All that is required is a copy of *Kindred Spirits, Ecstasy, Swingers' Life,* or any one of 50 scruffy magazines filled with ads and advice on 'The Etiquette of Swinging' and 'How to Organize an Enjoyable Swinging Party.'" Perhaps there was a hint of sexiness in being a swing voter, even if not a swinging one.

Nowadays, political strategists carefully calculate the critical constituencies upon whom to concentrate. Swing voters, those who are sitting on the fence waiting to be persuaded, are particularly promising targets. Presidential candidates also concentrate on uncommitted swing states ready to swing to either side.

1965 affirmative action

"The contractor will not discriminate against any employee or applicant for employment because of race, creed, color, or national origin," declared Executive Order 11246 of September 24, 1965. "The contractor will take affirmative action to ensure that applicants are employed, and that employees are treated during employment, without regard to their race, creed, color, or national origin. [A few years later a fifth category was added: sex.] Such action shall include, but not be limited to the following: employment, upgrading, demotion, or transfer; recruitment or recruitment advertising; layoff or termination; rates of pay or other forms of compensation; and selection for training, including apprenticeship. The contractor agrees to post in conspicuous places, available to employees and applicants for employment, notices to be provided by the contracting officer setting forth the provisions of this nondiscrimination clause."

That was the beginning of affirmative action as we know it today. The term had been used in legal contexts to refer to action taken to uphold a corporate policy of fair labor practice as early as 1935, and statements similar to Executive Order 11246 had been issued since the early 1960s, but it was this declaration from President Lyndon Johnson that made affirmative action a national policy. It was different from mere nondiscrimination, as the director of the U.S. Office of Civil Rights explained in 1973: "The premise of the Affirmative Action concept . . . is that systematic discrimination in employment has existed, and unless positive action is taken, a benign neutrality today will only preserve yesterday's conditions and project them into the future."

Thirty years later, the policy of affirmative action in government and business was still in effect, with evident results in greater employment of minorities and women. It has been repeatedly tested in the courts, with varying outcomes. Exactly what measures affirmative action requires, and whether it should continue as a policy, are as much a matter of debate now as ever before.

1966 credibility gap

In war, truth is the first casualty. That maxim seemed evident as the United States mired itself deeper and deeper in the Vietnam War and protests at home became correspondingly more strident. As President Lyndon Johnson attempted to finesse the failures of the war by escalating our involvement and putting on a face of increasingly unfounded optimism, he fell into what would be called a *credibility gap*.

The term was used in the headline "Dilemma in 'Credibility Gap'" in 1965, but it became widely understood and discussed in 1966, after a December 1965 *Washington Post* story referred to "growing doubt and cynicism concerning Administration pronouncements. . . . The problem could be called a credibility gap." Soon pundits of various shades, as well as political opponents, were gaping at the gap.

Unpopular in part because of the credibility gap, Johnson, who had won so handily in 1964, did not even try for reelection in 1968. But though Johnson retired, *credibility gap* did not. It was used in 1970, for example, by an African-American leader declaring that President Nixon's administration "faces a credibility gap of enormous proportions" with blacks.

Other gaps have also been discovered in twentieth-century America. There was the missile gap, a Democratic complaint against the Republican administration in the late 1950s that the United States had not kept up with the Soviet Union in production of intercontinental ballistic missiles. We have also spoken of a generation gap (1967), "differences in values, goals, and attitudes between younger and older generations," and the gender gap (1977), "differences in values, goals, and attitudes between men and women."

1967 rip off

To the rebellious, politically radical youth of the late 1960s, *steal* was too bourgeois a word. It implied criticism of the act of "liberating" wrongfully acquired property that had been stolen from "the people" by "capitalist pigs." So they *ripped off* that verb from urban African-American slang, as in a 1967 article in *Trans-Action:* "The hustler burns people for money, but he also 'rips off' goods for money; he thieves, and petty thieving is always a family hustle."

Rip off appears in a 1970 *New Yorker* article in words shouted by a young woman: "We're sitting here, and Chemical Bank is gloating about how they're going to rip us off! Well, we're going to go into the streets and rip you off! "

By 1970, *rip-off* was a noun too, in the service of the radicals' "class struggle." A publication of that year defined *rip-off* as "capitalist exploitation."

As the *New Yorker* article indicates, *rip off* also was useful in expressing outrage on the part of innocent victims. So in a 1971 issue of the magazine *Frendz,* we find, "The young people are well aware that they are being ripped off by these parasites, and, quite naturally, think that the visiting musicians are on the side of the promoters." Not long thereafter *rip off* is also found in the sense of "plagiarize."

The radicals of the '60s and '70s have yielded to the conservative YUPPIES (1984) and apolitical Generation X (1991), but *ripped off* remains a forceful term to use to protest against maltreatment.

1968 aerobics

During the twentieth century, Americans devised so many labor-saving devices for travel, work, housekeeping, and entertainment that we needed to invent means of exercising our bodies. One invention was aerobics, a scientific-sounding word for an exercise program first designed to keep American astronauts in condition. But because inventions like cars, power lawnmowers, dishwashers, and electric can openers meant that fewer and fewer Americans were earning their living or caring for their homes by the sweat of their brows, it soon became apparent that Middle America needed aerobics even more than the astronauts did.

Major Kenneth Cooper of the U.S. Air Force, who invented the astronauts' aerobics and published a best-selling book on it in 1968, expected the exercises to be carefully monitored for pulse rate and oxygen consumption. But on the popular front, thanks especially to actor and entrepreneur Jane Fonda, who made a popular aerobics videotape, *aerobics* became the name for a kind of exercise routine accompanied by upbeat music and led by an aerobics instructor. You could drive to a health club (1961) for aerobics classes or work out to a videotape in the privacy of your own home. The more relaxed 1990s developed a kinder, gentler form of aerobics known as *low impact,* in which one foot is always in contact with the ground.

1969 sexism *and* ageism

If we have learned one lesson this century, it is that ideology can do harm. Two of the leading twentieth century ideologies, fascism and communism, caused untold misery for untold millions in the middle of the century. By the end of the century, we were beginning to recognize that other *–ism*s could also cause more harm than good. We no longer felt comfortable with our prejudices.

Racism was the most prominent of these. In the early 1900s, *racialism* (1907) and then *racism* (1936) were used in a neutral or even positive sense to describe widely held beliefs that certain races were superior to others. Conveniently, the proponents of racism always found that the race to which they belonged was the superior one. Racism justified maltreatment of other races, as with the JIM CROW (1829) laws of the South. The horrors that were produced by racism both at home and as carried to its logical extreme by Nazi Germany finally led to its disfavor.

As we considered policies of AFFIRMATIVE ACTION (1965) to counter the effects of racism, we began to take official action against other prejudicial beliefs, calling them *–ism*s too. By 1969 both *sexism* and *ageism* were well-known terms. We have attestations for both in the previous year, including this declaration: "The parallels between *sexism* and *racism* are sharp and clear. Each embodies false assumption in a myth." And from an article in the 1970s: "A few years ago the great intellectual enemy of the movement was called gerontophobia—fear of aging, loathing of the aged. Today … the target has shifted from *gerontophobia* to *ageism*—a new word for a new thought. The term probably appeared in print in 1968, when Carl Bernstein wrote a piece in *The Washington Post* on a housing controversy where the word was used by Dr. Robert Butler."

Since then, other more debatable *–ism*s have been coined by those who are sometimes labeled *PC* (1990): *heightism* (1971, favoring tall people), *speciesism* (1975, favoring humans over other species), and *lookism* (favoring good-looking people), for example.

1970 bottom line

The bottom line is, it's hard to tell when Americans truly began to focus on the term *bottom line*. We find an isolated early instance in 1967 from the *San Francisco Examiner:* "George Murphy and Ronald Reagan certainly qualified because they have gotten elected. I think that's the bottom line." In 1970 comes a financial attestation, in a book called *Up the Organization:* "All overheads should be brought down to the bottom line for bonus purposes on principles agreed to in advance." After that, *bottom line* became an established way of saying we were all business. "IBM has always been heavy on corporate paternalism," noted *Newsweek* in 1971. "Learson may well be willing to sacrifice some of that for those results on the bottom line." And in *Harper's Bazaar* that year: "His only interest is in the bottom line. He doesn't know or care about books or art or music or even his own wife—only about the bottom line."

The revolutionary, anti-authoritarian 1960s were over, and we were getting back to business. Today the *bottom line* is "the main theme, the final result, the end rather than the means." It can have any subject, even cigars, as in this 1973 question and answer: "Do you miss our Havana cigars?" "Well, in answer to that, and to get to the bottom line, I don't smoke."

We remain committed to *bottom line* in all sorts of contexts. In the Web pages of Heaven's Gate, whose members departed this world by poisoning themselves at Easter 1997 as the Hale-Bopp comet passed by, we find the heading "Do's Intro: Purpose—Belief: What Our Purpose Is—The Simple 'Bottom Line.'"

1971 workaholic

Alcoholic, the parent of all addictive words, has been with us for over a century. It is first attested in 1891. But its numerous dysfunctional (1959) offspring, like *workaholic,* are more recent. It poses the question whether Americans became addicted in more ways during the twentieth century, or whether we just finally recognized that we were so variously addicted.

The founding of Alcoholics Anonymous in 1935 focused attention on alcohol addiction, as well as AA's 12-step program and "support group" (1969) meetings for dealing with addiction. In the 1960s, someone had the idea of taking *–holic* as a suffix meaning "addict," and a whole new category of addictions followed. One of the first and most important is *workaholic*. It was announced in the 1968 article "On Being a 'Workaholic' (A Serious Jest)" in the journal *Pastoral Psychology:* "I have dubbed this addiction of myself and my fellow ministers as 'workaholism,'" wrote Wayne Oates, a professor of psychology of religion at Southern Baptist Theological Seminary. However, it was the appearance of Oates's book *Confessions of a Workaholic* in 1971 that propelled that term and prompted many writers to start using the suffixes *–aholic, –holic,* or *–oholic* to describe "all-consuming obsessions," not all of them so serious.

In the 1970s, if not obsessed with work, we could be addicted to play, as in *golfaholic, footballaholic, basketball-oholic, bingoholic,* or just plain *leisureholic;* to foods, as in *beefaholic, peanuntholic,* and *ice creamaholic;* and to SUBSTANCES (1975), as in *hashaholic* (for hashish) or *mariholic* (for marijuana), as well as *tobaccoholic.* An American could be a book-oholic, catalogueoholic, eclipsoholic, gambler-oholic, game show-oholic, note-oholic, or phone-oholic. Other obsessions for which authors coined terms with *–aholic* in the 1970s include worry, news, credit, punning, shopping, and junk.

Many of these words have a short life span, but they are easily reinvented. The most predictable term in this whole family is the one which always seems to reappear just before Valentine's Day: *chocoholic,* another invention of the *workaholic* era.

1972 Watergate

Like Buncombe County, North Carolina (see BUNKUM 1819), Watergate was a little-known place that became significant in the American language thanks to politicians in Washington, D.C. During the 1972 presidential campaign, it happened

that the Democratic National Committee had its headquarters in a Washington residential and office building that was known as "The Watergate" for its location at former site of docks on the Potomac River. On June 17, 1972, several men were caught breaking in to the DNC office at The Watergate. What looked at first to be a minor burglary eventually was discovered to have direct links to President Richard Nixon's re-election campaign and to the president himself. During two years of investigative reporting, judicial proceedings, and Congressional hearings leading to Nixon's resignation, the growing scandal of "dirty tricks" involving the Committee to Re-elect the President kept the name *Watergate,* even though most of the tricks took place in the courts, in Congress, and in the White House itself.

The flood of commentary on *Watergate* spilled over into many *Water–* terms, including *Watergater, Watergatish, Watergatology, Watergimmick,* and *Watergoof.* But those quickly faded. The long-lasting linguistic contribution of *Watergate* was a new suffix, *–gate,* to indicate any political scandal involving a coverup. At first it may have been just a joke; a 1973 issue of the humor magazine *National Lampoon* wrote of a fictional Volgagate in Russia. But soon there was a Winegate in France, Cattlegate in Michigan, Motorgate in Cleveland, and many others. Two decades later, President Bill Clinton's administration had to deal with Travelgate, the politically motivated firing of the White House travel staff. And the questionable involvement of the president and his wife in the Whitewater real estate dealings in Arkansas was inevitably called *Whitewatergate*.

1973 sound bite

How long is a sound bite, "a brief broadcast appearance in which an expert or politician or citizen comments on an issue of the day"? In a paid political advertisement, it could be as long as thirty seconds, as in a 1987 *Newsweek* comment on presidential candidate Gary Hart: "Hart's refusal to reduce himself to a 30-second sound bite is an admirable—and difficult—stance in an age of media politics." But in TV news, fifteen seconds is more like it, as in a newspaper article from September 1988: "During the debate, the candidates want to accomplish at least two major goals—avoid major mistakes and provide some quotable comments, particularly those that can be used for a 15-second sound bite for television news shows." Even that is longer than ordinary citizens ordinarily get. *Time* magazine commented in 1985, "TV's formula these days is perhaps 100 words from the reporter, and a 'sound bite' of 15 or 20 words from the speaker."

In comparison, the fifteen minutes of fame that artist Andy Warhol said comes to everyone seems an eternity. We would say more but—our time is up, so on to the next word.

1974 streak

In the spring of 1974, the Vietnam War was finally winding to an end, President Nixon was nearing impeachment for WATER-GATE (1972), and across the country American college students were streaking. That is, they were making brief rapid appearances in public without their briefs or any other apparel—except, sometimes, their shoes, the better to make a quick streak.

Both the activity and the name for it began in the 1960s. In 1965 streaking was such a fad at the University of Colorado that some students tried it on vacation in Mazatlan, Mexico, only to be shot at and jailed for two days without their clothes. A 1967 column by San Francisco writer Herb Caen explained, "If you're in Sausalito one of these nights, and some guy with no clothes on runs past, fast as hell, you're seeing a 'streaker.' It's a contest, called 'Streaking,' that started a few years ago on the campuses, and seems to be reviving. The idea is to be seen naked by as many people as possible without getting caught."

It was in 1974, though, that streaking became a nationwide fad. There were streakers in student cafeterias, on public streets, at performances of plays. A fine spring night even saw a "streak-off" between two colleges in one small Midwestern town, with a large crowd of student spectators cheering the contestants as they unexpectedly erupted one by one from the shadows for their flash of fame. Nothing quite like it has happened since.

1975 substance

There is such a substantial difference among the different kinds of addictive drugs and drinks that it's hard to think of a name that would characterize them all. They come in the form of pills and powders, solids and liquids; they are swallowed, smoked, injected, applied to the skin. They have different effects on mind and body. Is there a word to distinguish them from harmless food and drink? There wasn't. But experts in the treatment of addiction needed a label for what they were treating, and so did politicians, educators, and the public. In the 1970s, therefore, some deep thinker noticed that all the mind-altering agents had one thing in common: they were substances. So *substance abuse* became the name for "the overdoing of anything that one could ingest." The term was in use by 1975, when an article in *U.S. News and World Report* mentioned "the office of substance abuse services in the Michigan Department of Public Health."

Substance itself goes back a long time in English and even longer in Latin. *Sub* means "under" and *stance* means "stand," so originally *substance* was that which "stands under" (or underlies, as we would say) its outward appearance. In the science and philosophy of the Middle Ages, subtle distinctions were drawn between this *substance*, the essential nature of something, and *accident*, the superficial features.

It is doubtful, however, that the coiners of *substance abuse* were thinking of medieval philosophy. More likely, they were borrowing the ordinary modern meaning of *substance:* "any kind of matter or material." The only problem was to distinguish their particular new use of *substance* from the more general. This they did by putting it in specific phrases. *Substance abuse* was the first of these. More recently, at colleges and universities, certain student residences have been specifically designated *substance-free,* that is, places where alcohol, tobacco, marijuana, and other addictive substances will not be allowed.

1976 couch potato

Very few words have a birthday so precise, and so precisely known, as *couch potato*. It was on July 15, 1976, we are told, that *couch potato* came into being, uttered by Tom Iacino of Pasadena, California, during a telephone conversation. He was a member of a Southern California group humorously opposing the fads of exercise and healthy diet in favor of vegetating before the TV and eating junk food (1973). Because their lives centered on television—the boob tube (1966)—they called themselves *boob tubers.* Iacino apparently took the brilliant next step and substituted *potato* as a synonym for *tuber.* Thinking of where that potato sits to watch the tube, he came up with *couch potato.*

Or so the story goes, as told in the subsequent registration of *Couch Potato* as a trademark. In any case, when the new phrase reached the ears of Robert Armstrong, another member of the boob tubers, he drew a cartoon of a potato on a couch, formed a club called the Couch Potatoes, registered the trademark and began merchandising Couch Potato paraphernalia, from T shirts to dolls. He published a newsletter called *The Tuber's Voice: The Couch Potato Newsletter* and a book, *Dr. Spudd's Etiquette for the Couch Potato.*

If the story ended there, *couch potato* would have been as passing a fad as the "pet rock" (1975) of the same vintage. But since the 1970s the tube has grown more alluring and the couch potato culture more compelling, especially with the 1980s invention of the zapper (1985), or remote control. No longer a cartoon character, the couch potato is now one of us.

1977 loony tunes

Meaning "absurd, crazy; foolish," this slang expression derives from the Warner Brothers' cartoon series *Looney Tunes and Merrie Melodies,* a trademark of Warner Brothers, Inc. Thanks to those *Loony Tunes,* since at least 1975 (for the noun) and 1977 (for the adjective) it has been possible to write about "today's looney-tunes salary structure" in baseball (*Seattle Times,* 1990), or to say "My husband is loony tunes" (*USA Today,* 1991). A book reviewer for *Newsday* in 1991 considers a Paul Theroux character "a dislikable looney-toon of a man who crunches down health food, arranges kinky dates with his own wife . . . and places personal ads in dubious publications."

The inspiration for the first word of *loony tunes* comes ultimately from the moon and a bird. As far back as the thirteenth century in England, the moon was said to influence the mind, and a sufficiently influenced person was called a *lunatic.* Then, centuries later, in the new colonies of New England a bird with a weird haunting call was named the *loon* (1634). The sound made by this bird seemed lunatic enough to suggest the epithets *drunk as a loon* (1830), *crazy as a loon* (1845), *wild as a loon* (1858), and *mad as a loon* (1877). Moon and bird came together in *loony,* another Americanism first attested in Bret Hart's 1872 *Heiress of Red Dog:* "You're that looney sort of chap that lives over yonder, ain't ye?"

The *tunes* of *loony tunes* are simply *cartoons* abbreviated and respelled to match the *Merrie Melodies,* because Warner Brothers cartoons always used sound and music. Their first was "Sinkin' In the Bath," released in 1930, and gradually the zany characters we know today joined the cast.

1978 geek

For centuries, a *geck* or *geek* was nothing but "a loser, a fool, a simpleton." The word in its various pronunciations was established in the English language as long ago as 1515, attested by the line "He is a foole, a sotte, and a geke also." But in the late twentieth century, Americans made something else of *geek*.

Early in the century, we started to use *geek* to mean "a performer in a carnival sideshow, a supposed savage or wild man." Researcher David W. Maurer wrote in 1931, "The word is reputed to have originated with a man named Wagner of Charleston, W. Va., whose hideous snake-eating act made him famous."

The stage was thus set for the next American evolution of *geek* as another kind of person, one whose talents were concealed behind an awkward exterior. The exact date is hard to pin down, but in student slang of the 1970s and later, a *geek* was someone who partied too little and studied too much. And when these geeks migrated to Silicon Valley and began building computers and writing software programs that made them millionaires, they gained respect.

In the 1990s, *alpha geek* was a term of humorous respect for the person in a workplace who knows the most about computers. And the richest man in America was the alpha alpha geek, billionaire Bill Gates of Microsoft.

1979 stealth

"Key technologies that have been identified are the following," said the magazine *Aviation Week* in 1979, "Stealth technology. Engines and fuels. Avionics."

After the invention of radar (1941), successfully used for nearly half a century, the next advance in weaponry was the invention of an airplane that would resist radar detection. The first airplane designed to do so, the B2 Stealth bomber, was a U.S. Air Force project so stealthy that even the name (with a capital letter) did not become visible until the late 1970s. The successful Stealth combination of materials and angles which

absorb and deflect radar signals was developed for that airplane during the 1980s. During that decade, the Navy began to consider its own Stealth technology for submarines under water.

But the story of *stealth* does not stop there. It appears, or rather disappears, on Mars, where "much of the large black feature near the equator . . . has been informally dubbed 'Stealth,' since it shows no radar return whatever," according to *Science News* in 1989.

And on Earth, *stealth* has slipped into political jargon. A *stealth candidate* is one who avoids the traditional public forums, or who avoids taking a stand on the issues, or whose support does not show in the polls, thus remaining undetected as a serious threat. A 1992 article explained that *stealth campaign* is "a term coined from an interview made after the 1990 elections by the Virginia-based Christian coalition's Ralph Reed. . . . 'It's like guerrilla warfare,' Reed was quoted as saying. . . . 'If you reveal your location, all it does is allow your opponent to improve his artillery bearings. It's better to move quietly, with stealth, under cover of night.'"

1980 gridlock

Thanks to traffic engineers, we are no longer stuck for a word about getting stuck. It's *gridlock*, where the flow of traffic through the grid of intersecting streets is locked into immobility. In a city, this happens when cars cannot clear an intersection after the lights have changed. On highways, too many cars trying to enter an already full road may have the same effect. The *New York Times Magazine* introduced the word to nonspecialists in 1980: " 'gridlock' is to highway engineers what 'meltdown' is to nuclear engineers—a panic inside a nightmare inside a worst case. Instead of going with the traffic flow, everything stops and every frenzied driver leans on his horn."

It was too good a word to leave to the engineers. By the early 1980s, any kind of complete stoppage or jam could be called *gridlock,* and the resulting terms ranged from *telephone gridlock* (1984), used when overcrowded telephone lines give everyone a busy signal, and *corporate gridlock* (1985), when a corporation is stuck in its traditional ways, to *vocal gridlock* (1983), the condition of being too frightened to speak, rare in our talkative world. Politicians have made the most of *gridlock,* including *legislative gridlock* (1982), when a divided legislature is unable to act, and *government gridlock* (1995), when the president and Congress shut down the federal government because they are at odds.

1981 wannabe

We live in an age not of heroes but of wannabes. Or so it seemed in the early 1980s, when *wannabe* evolved from slang question to mocking answer.

Wannabe came from the polite "What do you want to be?" reduced to a quick spoken "Whaddaya wannabe?" And the answer, as early as 1981, was "a wannabe." At least it seemed that way to a less-than-thrilled older generation of achievers. *Wannabe* was used not by the wannabes themselves but by those who watched and found them lacking.

Surfers were among the first to be stung by the wannabes. In 1981, *Newsweek* reported, "Before long the beaches were jammed with hordes of novices known as wannabees (as in, 'I wanna be a surfer')." A 1987 article in the *Illustrated London News* explained, "What bothers surfers is that only a quarter of that money is being spent on surfboards. The rest is spent by people surfers call 'wanna bes.' They don't surf but they want to, so they dress the part, as have non-participating fans of tennis and skiing."

Other writers mentioned a witch-burner wannabe, a Bedouin wanna-be, a Christian wannabe, and Roman wannabees, to take examples just from 1989.

Another kind of wannabe imitated a personality rather than an activity. Depending on age, gender, and proclivity, a young person might wannabe, for example, a Madonna wannabe, a Rambo wannabe, an Arnold (Schwarzenegger) wannabe, an Annie (from the musical of that name) wannabe, a Johnny (Carson) wannabe, or an Elvis wannabe. (Last names generally aren't needed.) In an age of celebrities rather than heroes, wannabes need only make themselves into look-alikes (1947). It is enough to copy the clothes, hairstyles, and mannerisms of their ROLE MODELS (1957).

There are also people who really want the job: would-be gang members and governors, parents and commodities traders. As long as they remain candidates, observers can smile at them as wannabes.

1982 like

You may be like, "Something's wrong here. Surely *like* was in the American vocabulary before 1982?" Of course. *Like* is an old friend, going back as far as the English language itself. In the Middle Ages, centuries before America was dreamed of, *like* had developed most of its present versatility. Originally a verb ("I like this"), long ago it also became an adjective ("under like circumstances"), a noun ("the like of it"), a preposition ("like a winner"), and a conjunction ("like a winner is"—a usage still deplored by purists, despite its age).

As if this were not enough, however, Americans invented two new uses for *like* in the twentieth century. One was the hip interjection used to mark any pause in speaking, or to emphasize what follows: "I'm, like, so hungry that, like, I'm, like, going to the store, like, right now." In the 1950s, if not before, jazz musicians were employing this *like,* and by the 1960s it had spread to the awareness of any TEENAGER (1938) who wanted to appear COOL (1949).

Far more radical, however, was the innovation of *like* that emerged in the 1980s. It was first reported by linguist Ronald Butters in 1982: "Many speakers who use narrative *go* also have a narrative use of *to be* (usually followed by *like*) where what is being quoted is an unuttered thought, as in *And he was like 'Let me say something.'*" Perhaps this began as an accidental spin-off of the *like* interjection which, as it floated around in the sentence, combined with the verb *be,* used to introduce a speaker's thoughts. "So I'm, This is amazing!" punctuated with *like* became "So I'm, like, This is amazing!"

That was, like, a way cool way of saying "I'm thinking." And since thoughts often turn into spoken words, it was also a way of saying "I said," or "she said," or "he said," with feeling. It began as a teenage fad, but in the 1990s it spread across the country and across age barriers so that even middle-aged Americans were like, "What's so strange about that?" This new use of *like* in place of *thought* or *said* had become a familiar, and hardly even noticed, part of the American vocabulary.

1983 greenmail

It was a good year for greed as well as green—green, that is, in the sense of money, deriving ultimately from the GREENBACK of United States currency invented in 1862. The year 1983 saw another American monetary invention: greenmail. This is a shade more lucrative than the ancient and dishonorable word, *blackmail,* from which its name derives. Blackmail began in the lawless territory between England and Scotland in the 1500s, when predatory bands of men demanded an unjustified rent, or *black mail,* from those who lived on the land. Such practices were not confined to those borderlands, so *blackmail* later was applied to any extortion of money under threat.

In America in the early 1980s, the fattest and easiest targets for blackmail were not individuals but corporations. And the pressure to make them pay could be applied openly and legally. All it required was a supply of cash to buy lots of stock in the company. A threat to take it over would be made, then the company would be allowed to buy back those shares at an inflated price, making a big profit for the "blackmailer" that could be used to attack another company. Because this practice operated in the financial markets (*green*), and because it was not hidden or illegal (*black*), someone called it *greenmail,* and the name stuck. "Corporations are scurrying to combat a perceived threat from those professional investors who practice 'greenmail'—putting pressure on a company to get a buyout for cash," reported the *National Law Journal* in March 1983.

The idea of creating an off-color variant of *blackmail* may have come from *graymail* (1973), a name for a criminal defendant's threat to expose government secrets if prosecuted for betraying them. The CIA is said to have originated the word *graymail,* preferring that to the more ominous *blackmail* in such cases.

Green, meanwhile, also took on another new meaning, starting in the late 1960s. While corporate raiders were practicing greenmail, environmentalists were advocating green labeling and green taxes as part of a "green revolution" (1969) to protect the natural world from being ruined by humans.

1984 yuppie

Thanks to a book by two of their kind, yuppies burst on the American scene early in 1984. In an article that year titled "Here Come the Yuppies!" *Time* inquired, "Who are all those upwardly mobile folk with designer water, running shoes, picked parquet floors and $450,000 condos in semislum buildings? Yuppies, of course, for Young Urban [or Upwardly-Mobile] Professionals, and the one true guide to their carefully hectic life-style is *The Yuppie Handbook.* . . . Tongue firmly in chic, Authors Marissa Piesman and Marilee Hartley tirelessly chronicle the ways of the Yuppie, along with its less-known subspecies the Guppie (Gay Urban Professional) and Puppie (Pregnant Urban Professional)."

George Orwell had predicted the ruthless dictatorship of Big Brother in his novel *1984*, but the figure of satire in America that year was someone entirely different. The yuppie was a person in young adulthood, living in or near a city, ambitious, successful, materialistic, and self-indulgent. Reducing ponderous terminology to its initials and adding a diminutive suffix, the authors of *The Yuppie Handbook* not only named the target of their satire but also identified that target as a whole new demographic group for advertisers and politicians to pursue.

With the suffix *–ie, yuppie* followed the pattern of other two-syllable words describing types of young people: *preppie, hippie,* and *yippie. Preppie* (1962) was a half-derisive, half-affectionate term for someone who attended a private college-preparatory school or who dressed and acted like the stereotypically rich and success-bound prep-school student. *Hippie* (1965) identified a whole counterculture. *Yippie* (1968) came from the name of an irreverent, politically radical group of hippies, the Youth International Party.

Once *yuppie* was coined, other initialisms followed: *buppie* (1986) identified a black yuppie, *suppie* (1987) a Southern one, *yuca* (1988) a Cuban-American (with a play on the name of the yucca plant). There was even *skippie* (1987), a school kid with income and purchasing power. And there was the yuppie disease (1986), a.k.a. *chronic fatigue syndrome* (1981).

1985 rocket scientist

Of the technological feats of the twentieth century, those of the scientists who designed rockets were among the most spectacular, truly out of this world. They reached their apogee in the years after World War II, when expatriate German rocket scientists helped us reach new heights on Earth and in space.

Developing rockets that could break the bonds of gravity and achieve Earth orbit required complex engineering design and mathematical calculations. The world of the rocket scientist (1952) was, and still is, perceived as one in which complex thinking rests on an understanding of mathematics, aerodynamics, materials, and chemistry beyond the grasp of the rest of the human race. Their opinion was respected: "Take it from the rocket scientists who expect to fly to Mars some day," said the Baltimore *Sun* in 1952. "Flying saucers are not space ships from another planet."

But in the mid-1980s, as near as lexicographers can determine, *rocket scientist* underwent a subtle change in meaning. Rocket scientists were no longer so often in the news. When they were mentioned, it was in the phrase "You don't have to be a rocket scientist," as in this example from the *Atlanta Journal and Constitution* in 1992: "Mr. Coons says Grand Slam—like McDonalds's—is 'constantly looking for new ways to increase the frequency of people coming in.' You don't have to be a rocket scientist, he adds, to know that only happy customers will come back."

Why *rocket scientist* instead of, say, *computer scientist* for this phrase? Perhaps because computer scientists were all-too-familiar GEEKS (1978), while *rocket scientist* called up the old image of a German-accented professor, something of an Albert Einstein in a white coat. So we continue to use *rocket scientist,* as in this comment from the Republican national convention of 1992, reported in the *New York Times:* "You don't have to be a rocket scientist to figure out that whatever went on in Houston, fair or unfair, 'family values' took on a connotation that was a gigantic negative."

1986 dis

Since English was first spoken in North America, *dis* has covered a lot of distance. Our discussions since those times have included many disagreements, disputes, disappointments, and disasters. There was much disillusion, discouragement, and distress. We have often had discontented dissidents promoting disorder and disunion. On the whole, *dis* has been a dismal prefix.

But none of these words earned the distinction of being recognized just by its first syllable until the most respectful of all came along, the *dis* of *disrespect.* In the 1980s, African-

American performers gradually brought this *dis* to everyone's attention in a new style of music they called *rap* (1976), featuring rapid rhyming talk. Along with break dancing (1983), rap music was part of the hip-hop (1983) urban culture these entertainers introduced, which was well-publicized by 1986. A well-known rap by the group Public Enemy in 1987 declared, "A magazine or two is dissin' me and dissin' you."

Thanks to the First Amendment to the Constitution, open disrespect has been a permanent feature of American political discussion, so the simple insulting syllable *dis* was quickly picked up by politicians and commentators of all sorts. "Are you dissing me?" is a way for a recipient of disrespect to respond in the same dissing style as the disser, avoiding the unsuitably formal "Are you showing disrespect for me?" With such disparate usefulness, *dis* has remained a vigorous element of our discourse.

1987 codependency

In the 1980s, even if we did not wake up with a hangover, we learned that waking up next to a significant other (1953) with a hangover is a hangup in itself. The hangup of the non-addicted is addiction to the addicted. Get it?

If that's confusing, maybe we needed a new word. So we put it this way: In such a situation, we suffer from a condition known as *codependency* or *codependence*. That is what we learned from the 1987 publication of Melody Beattie's book *Codependent No More,* along with countless articles on the subject. We discovered that we had grown up in *dysfunctional families* (1981), where one of the adults was addicted to a substance like alcohol or drugs or to a behavior like gambling, sex, watching television, or even exercise, and the other adult was addicted to the addict. By helping the addicted one get through the day, the non-addicted family members were being codependent.

Since so many people can be said to exhibit some sort of addictive behavior, we discovered how normal it is to come from a dysfunctional family and be codependent. The co-dependency spreads because it makes children dysfunctional, leading them to enter into dysfunctional relationships as adults, either as addicts or as their codependents.

Fortunately, the 1980s also gave us the tools to combat codependency. We went to counselors, clinics, and support groups (1969) to share our feelings as "adult children" (1983). At the end of the decade, self-help reached its epitome when we learned to get in touch with our "inner child" (1990).

1988 envelope

Long before 1988, in the early years after World War II, *push the envelope* was on the cutting edge (1951) of aviation. It referred to the *envelope,* or limit of performance for an aircraft, and test pilots like Chuck Yeager who had "the right stuff" (in the phrase popularized by Tom Wolfe's best-selling 1979 book) were always on the edge of danger, pushing the envelope.

But it was only in about 1988 that we pushed the envelope of *pushing the envelope* beyond the fields of aviation and space so that it stretched to fit any enterprise. We began to speak of such matters as "pushing the envelope of taste," to take a 1991 example from the *Wall Street Journal.* Astronomers with the Hubble telescope, criminals with alibis, movie directors with scenes of violence or absurdity, con artists, and corporate raiders can now be said to be pushing the envelope in their various fields of endeavor.

We have many ways of saying it. Sometimes it is the edge of the envelope that we expand or stretch as well as push, whether in aircraft speed, computer power, campaign finance, or lifestyle. So in 1992, for example, Marilyn Quayle, wife of Vice President Dan Quayle, explained that she went rollerblading in neon tights because "I like anything that stretches the edge of the envelope a little bit."

1989 virtual reality

In the late 1980s, inhabitants of cyberspace (see CYBERNETICS 1948) were virtually certain they were inventing a new reality. It would be far better than the reality sought by philosophers, poets, and scientists in earlier ages because *virtual reality* could be custom-made. Medieval philosophers had found reality sometimes in things, sometimes in ideas, sometimes in the mind of God. More recent thinkers had looked to nature, society, or the workings of the human mind. But in the late 1980s, computer geeks were busy constructing their own world of virtual reality, bounded only by the limitations of electronic inner space.

This virtual reality had its modest beginnings thirty years earlier in the invention of virtual memory (1959), a method of overcoming the physical limits of a computer by making it think it had more random-access memory (RAM) than it actually did. The computer would use space on a storage drive as if it were its own RAM. That led to the use of *virtual* for anything involving a computer that was other than it seemed. The proper software could give a computer virtual storage (1966) and other virtual hardware.

In the late 1980s, *virtual* was applied to users of computers too. A community of people who did not meet face to face but only by computer became known as a *virtual community*. To bring members of a virtual community literally in touch with one another was one of the purposes of virtual reality. It involved haptics, "the use of computer-actuated gloves or body wraps to stimulate the sense of touch." Virtual reality would even enable them to engage in *virtual sex*.

As the end of the century neared, virtual reality remained a programmer's dream, but it was coming closer and closer to reality. With continuing improvement in computer technology, it is virtually assured of success.

1990 PC

In the 1980s, it was a personal computer. In the 1990s, it became a powerful controversy.

The innocent initials *PC,* which at various times have signified *p*er *c*ent, *p*ost *c*ard, and *p*ropositional *c*alculus, have been widely used for *p*ersonal *c*omputer (1977) ever since IBM introduced the IBM PC early in the 1980s. The abbreviation *PC* (1978) has largely displaced *personal computer* as the standard term, and both have made the former name *microcomputer* (1971) nearly obsolete.

Meanwhile, however, in the long-running policy clash in politics and culture between left and right, liberal and conservative, *PC* has become a booby-trapped label for *p*olitically *c*orrect attitudes that liberals advocate as sensitive and conservatives condemn as overly euphemistic. Should we be sensitive to every possible instance of *–ism*s like *racism* (1936), SEXISM (1969), and *heightism* (prejudice against short people), for example? Should our schools be MULTICULTURAL (1941)? Should we use the term *chair* instead of *chairman,* and *first-year student* instead of *freshman*? Are healthy people just *temporarily abled*? The extremes get silly, but the questions have serious implications for the body politic and our own lives.

In previous decades *politically correct* belonged to the left wing, whether communists insisting on strict adherence to the party line or liberals urging enlightened views, as in Tony Cade's *The Black Woman* (1970): "And a man cannot be politically correct and a chauvinist too." But in the 1990s conservatives appropriated the term and applied it to what they saw as excesses. It could even be applied anachronistically for a touch of humor, as in a 1990 article in the *Washington Post:* "Massachusetts patriots protesting the tax on the beverage imposed by the British government on the Colonials not only overturned cargoes to make a giant teapot out of the Boston Bay, but took to serving coffee in their own homes to be PC."

It was in about 1991 that familiar old *about* took on a new connection. It had long been used to relate the subject matter of something written, said or thought: a book about Noah Webster, a question about silk stockings, or an idea about dinner. Anything that told a story could be *about:* a mural about the hardships of the poor, or a movie about Robin Hood.

But could cities, clothes, sports, religion, a rock group, parts of the body, and life itself contain messages too? In the early 1990s, Americans began to say so. "St. Louis is about families," said one writer. "Jeans are about sex," declared Calvin Klein. "Wrestling is about pushing your mind and body to their limits," wrote an athletic supporter in Ithaca, New York. "Our Jewishness is about attending services," said a woman in West Virginia. "The Grateful Dead are about celebration and freedom," said their spokesman. "Hair is about power; hair is about rebellion," wrote a newspaper columnist. "Perhaps breasts were always about power," mused a woman in *Esquire*. "Fun was for the Eighties. The Nineties are about survival," announced *Playboy*.

All these were new ways of using *about*. They came from the *what it's all about* so often said in the 1960s and 1970s. Now, more often than not, *what* and *all* are left behind. "Around here the holiday spirit means more than picking out a great gift at the mall. It's about giving of ourselves," wrote a reader to *Seventeen* magazine in 1991. "Food is not just about a party. It's about a quality of life," said the chef of the year in 1992. "This campaign is not about the outside world. It's about the U.S. of A.," said presidential candidate Pat Buchanan that year. And how do you develop your sense of humor? "It's not about telling jokes," lecturer Julie Kurnitz explained in 1994. "It's about seeing the absurdity of life."

1992 Not!

It was a brand-new expression in 1992. *Not!*

No, this use of the one-syllable negative, tacked on after a split-second pause for emphasis to emphatically deny what has been confidently stated before, was not invented in 1992. In fact, as slang researchers Jesse Sheidlower and Jonathan Lighter discovered, *Not!* was humorously around at the very start of the twentieth century. George Ade wrote in 1900, "Probably they preferred to go back to the Front Room and hear some more about Woman's destiny not." (Ade was perfect at punctuation. Not!) A cartoon of 1908 depicts a husband waking up from a nightmare and telling his wife, "That confounded rarebit I ate last night is making me sleep lovely. NOT!!!"

Nevertheless, *Not!* did not make much of a noise in American English after the 1920s. Its revival apparently began in 1978, when comedians Steve Martin and Gilda Radner used it in portraying "The Nerds" on the television comedy program *Saturday Night Live.* But it was not until 1992, when *Not!* reached the big screen in the movie *Wayne's World,* that it burst into general American conversation. Even Vice President Dan Quayle used it that year, in saying he liked the television show *Murphy Brown*—Not! And *Business Week* could publish a serious article about sexual discrimination beginning "Progress? Not!"

After 1992, *Not!* did not sustain such prominence, but it lingers in the vocabulary of adults and children alike, ready for use on especially sarcastic occasions. It's such a subtle expression. Not!

1993 newbie

It was the year of the newbies, upsetting the cozy cyber-community (1994) on the Internet (1988). Remember? *Time* wrote in December 1993, "Instead of feeling surrounded by information, first-timers ('newbies' in the jargon of the Net) are likely to find themselves adrift in a borderless sea." The next year *InfoWorld* complained, "Because so many newbees are logging in every day, it is getting harder and harder to get connected to those information sources that are popular."

Newbie is especially popular in, and seems to have been popularized through, the informal communications which abound on the Internet listservers—those electronic bulletin boards where subscribers are supposed to stick to the topic, but frequently digress, especially if they are newbies. Such digressions can prompt flame wars (1992) from the regulars.

Before they burgeoned on the Internet, newbees played football. Here is a report on the San Diego Chargers from the *Los Angeles Times* of August 1985: "It had to do with newbees. I could be wrong on the spelling, but newbees are the rookies among the Blue Angels. Three of these newbees happened to be having a peaceful lunch when suddenly they were called upon to sing. This is what happens to rookies—or newbees—at the Charger training camps." References to newbies in the military, the mafia, and politics also predate the explosive popularity of *newbie* among Internet users.

Newbie probably owes some connection in its construction to WANNABE (1981) and *freebie* (1942) and even the much older *used-to-be* (1853) and *wouldbe* (1605). The spelling still varies between *newbie* and *newbee,* though the pronunciation is the same in either case.

1994 go postal

An unforeseen phenomenon of the 1990s was rage in the post office. It was expressed not by impatient customers but by occasional postal employees frustrated with their jobs or their lives. In a few shocking instances, employees fired weapons in post offices and sorting facilities, causing dozens of casualties. By 1994, *going postal* or *going postal worker* was being applied to crazy or violent outbursts at any workplace.

Perhaps the term reached full strength in the aftermath of a well-publicized Washington conference on workplace violence sponsored by the U.S. Postal Service in January 1994. There it was reported that over the past decade, thirty-four postal workers had been killed and another twenty-six wounded by fellow employees. These statistics were monstrous or minuscule, depending on how you looked at them. But though they seemed to indicate that the Postal Service was a fairly safe place to work, to the public they affirmed its association with workplace violence.

The association of *go* with *postal* to indicate violence comes from similar crazy phrases: *go berserk* (1908), *go crazy* (1930), and *go ballistic* (1971). The latter developed both because ballistic missiles reached great heights and because they were prone to loss of control early in flight.

An example of *go postal* in full flight is in a 1995 article by "the Grammar Doctor" in the *Tampa Tribune:* "The next time Jerry Rice goes four quarters without a touchdown, some NFL cornerback is sure to explain that he 'defensed him pretty good.' It's enough to make a grammar purist go postal."

1995 Newt

On a rare occasion a person's name becomes a word, like GARDENIA (1760), LYNCH (1780), or BLOOMERS (1851). But in 1995, Republican Congressman Newt Gingrich not only became a word, he became a whole vocabulary.

Leading his new conservative majority into battle against established liberal programs, Gingrich was the talk of Washington. As he made plans to fulfill the 1994 election "Contract with America" by cutting government agencies and entitlements right and left (especially left), political pundits, perhaps better called *punned-its*, came up with words to describe his every mood and attitude.

There was *Newt* the verb, as in this report from the *Philadelphia Tribune* of January 1995: "But U.S. Reps. Tom Foglietta, Bob Borski and Chaka Fattah have issued a report: 'Newting Philadelphia: The Effect of the Republican Contract on Philadelphia,' which says the city will lose more than $15 billion in federal aid over the next seven years."

Gingrich has been a verb, as well, as in this example in the *Boston Globe* from April 1995: "Anne Taubes Warner, the chairwoman of the Belmont selectmen who was defeated in recent town elections, blamed her loss on the national swing to the right. 'We got Gingriched,' she said."

The *new* in *Newt* resulted in coinages like *Newt Dealer, Newt World Order, Newtspeak* (after George Orwell's *newspeak* in *1984*), *Newt kids on the block, Newt age fashion* ("conservative chic"), and *What's Newt.* Other puns included *Newtonian, Newtron bomb, Newtritional,* and *Newtopia.* His followers were called *Newtoids* and *Newties* and practiced *Newtworking.* Gingrich himself was given the nicknames *Newtster* and *Newty Boy.*

Not every word of the moment lasts more than a moment. As Gingrich's fortunes sank in 1996, so did most of this enthusiastic vocabulary. Unless Newt's opponents are newtered, these words will be just a flash in the pun.

1996 soccer mom

In the presidential election of 1996, the political strategists for Bill Clinton and Bob Dole discovered a newly significant voter to whom they hastened to pay their respects. They called her the *soccer mom*. They and the American electorate were informed about the hard-working upscale young woman of the 1980s who had married, started a family, and transformed herself into a hard-working upscale mother of the 1990s with a political agenda of her own.

The soccer mom was portrayed as someone who managed her children's development as energetically as she had managed her yuppie career. She championed soccer as a sport for her children, not only for the fresh air and vigorous exercise but also for providing, in its American youth version, equal opportunity for both genders, all ages, and all athletic abilities, free of the MACHO (1927) posturing of American professional sports. So she piled her kids, and her neighbors' kids, in her minivan and drove them to weekday soccer practice and weekend games.

Though the soccer mom was affluent, she was said to have a liberal attitude toward government support of education and welfare, and to favor the charismatic and residually liberal Candidate Clinton. With her help, he won handily over traditional conservative Dole.

1997 Ebonics

Thanks to a resolution passed by the Oakland, California, school board on December 18, 1996, Americans in 1997 not only focused on *Ebonics,* or "African-American English," but also invented a new suffix to describe any dialect or way of speaking.

The name *Ebonics* had been invented more than twenty years earlier, on exactly January 26, 1973, by Robert R. Williams, an African American and professor of psychology at Washington University in Saint Louis. Its first published appearance was in a 1975 book edited by Williams, *Ebonics: The True Language Of Black Folks.* Williams fashioned the term *Ebonics* by combining *ebony* (for "black") and *phonics* (for "the scientific study of speech sounds"), and he used *Ebonics* to identify the variety of English spoken by many black Americans as a language or at least a dialect of its own rather than merely "bad English." Aside from some Afrocentrists, however, everyone else continued to call it *Black English* or, in a more scholarly vein, *African-American Vernacular English*, for the next two decades.

Then the Oakland school board, concerned that its black students (some 53 percent of the total) were not learning as well as they should, passed a resolution recognizing that most of these students spoke Ebonics and calling for improved instruction in Standard English. Overlooking the board's emphasis on the standard, the predominant reaction was one of shock at the respect and recognition for African-American Vernacular English implied by the word *Ebonics*.

As the shock subsided, the often sarcastic notion grew of making *–onics* or *–bonics* a suffix designating any dialect or distinctive way of talking. Among the countless inventions were *Chicagonics* for Chicago talk, *Hebonics* for Jewish speech styles, *TVbonics* for the language of television game shows, and *Greasebonics* or *Mechanics English* for the language of automobile repairpersons.

1998 millennium bug

Will the millennium end in war, pestilence, famine, earthquakes, volcanoes, floods; with the sinking of California to join Atlantis under the sea, the coming of the Antichrist, the rapture of the faithful into heaven, or maybe even campaign finance reform and a balanced federal budget? Perhaps none of the above, despite many predictions. But there is one certain peril that humanity faces as the century hurtles to its end: the millennium bug.

Until recently, the millions of computer programs that account for our lives paid no attention to the next century. When they needed to enter a year, they used just the last two digits: *60* for 1960, *97* for 1997. That is fine through 99, but computers will understand *00* as a return to 1900. A person who works from 1970 through 2000 will have accumulated minus 70 years toward retirement; in 2000 there will be 90 years of negative interest on money deposited in 1990.

In other words, as *Time* explained in 1997, "The snafu— a.k.a. the Millennium Bug—arises because corporate and government computers recognize years by their last two digits, and thus will be unable to tell the year 2000 from 1900. Fixing the problem," *Time* adds, "could cost $600 billion."

Another name for it is the *Year 2000 Problem,* abbreviated *Y2K,* as in *The Wall Street Journal* from January 1997: "Cyberapocalypse is less than three years away, if you believe the hype about the Year 2000 Problem. Known in geek-speak as 'Y2K,' this is the bug that affects mostly older computers...." *Year 2000 Problem* is the earlier term, noted in 1991, but the 1995 *millennium bug* seems to be gaining ground.

So the Year 2000 is coming early. Before that deadline, thousands of computer programmers will spend millions of hours and billions of dollars to keep the most important corporate and government programs from catastrophe. Two years ahead of the millennium, the *millennium bug* will be the linguistic preoccupation of 1998.

INDEXES

Word Index

This index lists in alphabetical order all words that appear as headwords or are discussed as words in the text. Headwords are indicated by small capital letters. Elements of headwords that are idioms, such as *mustard* in *cut the mustard,* are also listed in this index.

debunk, 120
deejay, 247
DIME, 89
DIS, 280
disc jockey, 246
DIXIE, 156
Dixieland, 156
DJ, 246
d.j., 247
dog, 192
doohickey, 237
doughboy, 215
DOWNTOWN, 135
drive-in, 257
drop a dime, 90
drug, 111
DRUGSTORE, 111
drugstore cowboy, 84
DUDE, 174
dude, 203
DUH, 259

E

E Day, 216
E pluribus unum, 92
EBONICS, 290
EDITORIAL, 130
emigrant, 93
employer, 26
English corn, 8
English wigwam, 20
ENVELOPE, 282
envelope, 113
EQ, 214

F

false step, 100
FAN, 182
fan, 89
fanzine, 183
farm, 28, 131
FAST FOOD, 251
FILIBUSTER, 150
fire into the wrong flock, 132

firefly, 83
First Nations, 6
FISHING POLE, 94
fishing rod, 94
FLAPPER, 212
flivver, 225
FLUNK, 123
flunk out, 123
flunky, 124
flying saucer, 250
forbid, 148
foreman, 26
forty-niner, 147
frankfurter, 181, 192
fraternity, 123
freeware, 256
French fries, 175
fried cake, 119
FRONTIER, 35

G

gamesmanship, 253
gang, 193
GANGSTER, 193
GARDENIA, 67
geck, 273
GEEK, 273
gender gap, 263
generation gap, 263
GERRYMANDER, 113
get off the dime, 90
GI, 214
GI can, 214
Gingrich, 288
GIZMO, 237
GO POSTAL, 287
goatee, 184
goer, 41
GOO, 200
goo-goo, 200
GOOBER, 134
gooey, 200
googly, 200
goop, 201
GOP, 238

jazz, 55, 209
jean, 154
JEEP, 235
JELLYBEAN, 202
JIM CROW, 128
JIMSONWEED, 38
JOHNNYCAKE, 54
jonakin, 54
Jonakin, 34
journeycake, 54
juke, 234, 235
JUKEBOX, 234
jumping in the bandwagon, 178
junk food, 251

K

KATYDID, 63
KEEP THE BALL ROLLING, 139
KENO, 115
kinetograph, 210
KNOW-HOW, 137

L

lady, 25
land loafer, 135
land loper, 135
LAND OFFICE, 36
land office, 27
land-office business, 37
Latino, 186
legislative gridlock, 275
LENGTHY, 40
LEVEE, 72
level teaspoon, 111
LIGHTNING BUG, 83
LIKE, 276
LIPSTICK, 176
LOAF, 134
loafer, 135
locker room, 224
LOG CABIN, 76
log cabin, 121
log house, 76
LOGGER, 50

loggerhead, 51
LOGROLLING, 95
lookalike, 276
LOONY TUNES, 272
low impact, 264
lowbrow, 201
lunatic, 272
lute, 54
LYNCH LAW, 84
lynch law, 157
lynching, 84, 85

M

MACHO, 223
MAMMOTH, 104
MANHATTAN, 10
Manhattan clam chowder, 11
Manhattan cocktail, 11
market, 229
mash, 34
master, 26
MAVERICK, 165
measuring cup, 111
MEDIA, 218
media, 130
MELTING POT, 205
microcomputer, 284
MIDWAY, 190
MILEAGE, 64
MILLENNIUM BUG, 291
MINUTEMAN, 79
Miss, 249
MISSTEP, 100
MOOSE, 10
MOTEL, 221
MOTHER COUNTRY, 12
motion picture, 210
MOVIES, 210
moving picture, 210
MOXIE, 173
Mr., 249
Mrs., 249
Ms., 249
MUCKRAKER, 204
MULTICULTURAL, 236

multiculturalism, 236
multiversity, 123
MURPHY'S LAW, 254
MUSH, 34
mustard *see* CUT THE MUSTARD

N

nationalism, 236
Native American, 6, 138, 186
needy, 194
Negro, 187
nep, 47
NEW ENGLAND, 11
New England, 6
new frontier, 36
NEWBIE, 286
NEWT, 288
NIFTY, 164
Niger, 187
nonsense, 120
NORMALCY, 217
normality, 217
NOT!, 286

O

O.F.M., 138
OK, 138
ON PICKET, 80
on the skids, 227
on the warpath, 65
op-ed, 130
OPOSSUM, 9
ordinary, 117
orneriness, 117
ORNERY, 117

P

PALEFACE, 122
parched, 16
PARCHED CORN, 16
PASSENGER PIGEON, 87
passing the buck, 58
PATENT, 21

patent line, 22
patentee, 22
pay dirt, 147
PC, 284
PC, 265
P.D.Q., 172
PEACE PIPE, 68
peanut, 134
personal computer, 284
peter, 152
PETER OUT, 152
pharmacy, 111
Philadelphia ice cream, 56
PHONY, 196
piece of eight, 50
PIKER, 15
PILGRIM, 30
pilgrim, 31
PIONEER, 117
placer, 147
PLANTATION, 28
plantation, 13
PLANTER, 13
planter, 41, 44
planter's punch, 14
PODUNK, 145
POISON IVY, 88
poker, 32
pompion, 30
pork, 207
PORK BARREL, 207
PORTAGE, 43
postal *see* GO POSTAL
POTATO CHIP, 175
potato crisp, 175
POTHOLE, 126
POWWOW, 17
PRAIRIE, 78
prairie schooner, 49, 58, 79
preppie, 279
President's House, 112
private, 26
PROGRESS, 97
prohibit, 148
PROHIBITION, 148
promoter, 169

Turkey Day, 7
Turkish delight, 202
twister, 107
two-bit politician, 50
two-bit saloon, 50
TWO BITS, 50

U

UFO, 250
ufologist, 250
ufology, 251
UNDERGROUND RAILROAD, 141
UNDERPRIVILEGED, 193
unidentified flying object, 250
UNION, 64
uptown, 135
USA, 238

V

vagrant, 146
VALEDICTORIAN, 67
vaporware, 256
V.D., 238
V-E Day, 216
VENUS'S FLYTRAP, 77
Venus's pride, 77
VETERAN, 99
VIGILANTE, 157
VIRTUAL REALITY, 283
VJ, 247
V-J Day, 216
vocal gridlock, 275

W

WAC, 238

wampum, 19
WAMPUMPEAG, 18
WANNABE, 275
wannabe, 287
WARPATH, 65
WATERGATE, 267
waycar, 158
wiener, 192
wetware, 256
WHISTLESTOP, 229
WHITE HOUSE, 112
Whitewatergate, 269
WHOLE HOG, 128
wife, 25
WIGWAM, 19
woman, 25
woodchuck, 55
WORKAHOLIC, 266

Y

YANKEE, 71
Year 2000 Problem, 291
yellow journal, 195
YELLOW JOURNALISM, 194
yippie, 279
Y2K, 291
you, 124
YOU-ALL, 124
you guys, 124
you-uns, 124
youse, 124
yuca, 279
YUPPIE, 278

Z

zero hour, 216

Chronological

Index

1711	jackknife	1779	cowboy
1712	catnip	1780	lynch law
1713	classmate	1781	blue laws
1716	schooner	1782	belittle
1721	store	1783	passenger pigeon
1730	two bits	1784	poison ivy
1732	logger	1785	bug
1733	barbecue	1786	dime
1736	awakening	1787	abolition
1738	ten-foot pole	1788	squatter
1739	johnnycake	1789	immigrant
1740	banjo	1790	reservation
1742	groundhog	1791	fishing pole
1744	ice cream	1792	logrolling
1745	covered wagon	1793	Anglophobia
1748	buck	1794	cavort
1750	bluegrass	1795	progress
1751	chowder	1796	stenographer
1752	katydid	1797	bogus
1753	mileage	1798	veteran
1754	Union	1799	revival
1755	warpath	1800	misstep
1756	ticket	1801	spook
1757	breechclout	1802	mammoth
1758	Indian file	1803	stud
1759	valedictorian	1804	tornado
1760	gardenia	1805	artery
1761	peace pipe	1806	cocktail
1762	armonica	1807	slave driver
1763	caucus	1808	rowdy
1764	bust	1809	cookbook
1765	Yankee	1810	drugstore
1766	levee	1811	White House
1767	bayou	1812	gerrymander
1768	bee	1813	airline
1769	tar and feather	1814	keno
1770	log cabin	1815	cuss
1771	Venus's flytrap	1816	ornery
1772	totem	1817	pioneer
1773	prairie	1818	cruller
1774	minuteman	1819	bunkum
1775	on picket	1820	shanty
1776	American	1821	cure-all
1777	Indian summer	1822	paleface
1778	lightning bug	1823	flunk

1824	you-all	1869	showboat
1825	blizzard	1870	bathtub
1826	pothole	1871	boom
1827	sockdolager	1872	jambalaya
1828	whole hog	1873	Chautauqua
1829	Jim Crow	1874	canning
1830	editorial	1875	P.D.Q.
1831	ranch	1876	moxie
1832	bark up the wrong tree	1877	dude
1833	Hoosier	1878	potato chip
1834	goober	1879	jackpot
1835	loaf	1880	lipstick
1836	downtown	1881	bandwagon
1837	Christmas tree	1882	graham cracker
1838	know-how	1883	skyscraper
1839	OK	1884	hamburger
1840	keep the ball rolling	1885	hello
1841	deadhead	1886	fan
1842	underground railroad	1887	sideburns
1843	suffrage	1888	credit card
1844	rodeo	1889	Hispanic
1845	tintinnabulation	1890	Afro-American
1846	Podunk	1891	country club
1847	hobo	1892	sweatshop
1848	grapevine	1893	midway
1849	tenderfoot	1894	cold feet
1850	prohibition	1895	hot dog
1851	bloomers	1896	gangster
1852	filibuster	1897	underprivileged
1853	cafeteria	1898	yellow journalism
1854	peter out	1899	cereal
1855	bluejeans	1900	phony
1856	high muckamuck	1901	grass roots
1857	shindig	1902	goo
1858	piker	1903	highbrow
1859	Dixie	1904	cut the mustard
1860	vigilante	1905	jellybean
1861	caboose	1906	teddy bear
1862	greenback	1906	muckraker
1863	AWOL	1907	melting pot
1864	deadline	1908	asleep at the switch
1865	commuter	1909	pork barrel
1866	nifty	1910	barbershop
1867	maverick	1911	blues
1868	carpetbagger	1912	movies

1913	jazz	1956	brinkmanship
1914	backpack	1957	role model
1915	flapper	1958	Murphy's Law
1916	IQ	1959	software
1917	GI	1960	sit-in
1918	D-Day	1961	biodegradable
1919	T-shirt	1962	carpool
1920	normalcy	1963	duh
1921	media	1964	swing voter
1922	cold turkey	1965	affirmative action
1923	hijack	1966	credibility gap
1924	brainstorm	1967	rip off
1925	motel	1968	aerobics
1926	Bible Belt	1969	sexism and ageism
1927	macho	1970	bottom line
1928	athlete's foot	1971	workaholic
1929	jalopy	1972	Watergate
1930	bulldozer	1973	sound bite
1931	skid row	1974	streak
1932	hopefully	1975	substance
1933	supermarket	1976	couch potato
1934	whistlestop	1977	loony tunes
1935	boondoggle	1978	geek
1936	streamline	1979	stealth
1937	groovy	1980	gridlock
1938	teenager	1981	wannabe
1939	jukebox	1982	like
1940	jeep	1983	greenmail
1941	multicultural	1984	yuppie
1942	gizmo	1985	rocket scientist
1943	acronym	1986	dis
1944	snafu	1987	codependency
1945	showbiz	1988	envelope, push the
1946	iron curtain, cold war	1989	virtual reality
1947	baby-sit	1990	PC
1948	cybernetics	1991	about
1949	cool	1992	Not!
1950	DJ	1993	newbie
1951	rock and roll	1994	go postal
1952	Ms.	1995	Newt
1953	UFO	1996	soccer mom
1954	fast food	1997	Ebonics
1955	hotline	1998	millennium bug